A House of Prayer for All People

A House of Prayer for All People

Contesting Citizenship in a Queer Church

David K. Seitz

University of Minnesota Press
Minneapolis • London

Portions of the Introduction and chapter 1 were published as "Why Do You Go There? Struggle, Faith, and Love at the Metropolitan Community Church of Toronto," in *Any Other Way: How Toronto Got Queer*, edited by John Lorinc, Jane Farrow, Stephanie Chambers, Maureen FitzGerald, Tim McCaskell, Rebecka Sheffield, Tatum Taylor, Rahim Thawer, and Ed Jackson (Toronto: Coach House Books), 305–7; reprinted with permission. Portions of chapter 4 were published as "'Is This Enough Proof?' Queer 'Limbo Life' in Canada's Waiting Room," *Mask Magazine*, The Multiple Words Issue, no. 11 (December 2014), and as "Limbo Life in Canada's Waiting Room: Asylum-Seeker as Queer Subject," *Environment and Planning D: Society and Space*, first published August 31, 2016, doi:10.1177/0263775816667074.

Published by the University of Minnesota Press
111 Third Avenue South, Suite 290
Minneapolis, MN 55401-2520
http://www.upress.umn.edu

ISBN 978-1-5179-0213-1 (hc)
ISBN 978-1-5179-0214-8 (pb)

A Cataloging-in-Publication record for this book is available from the Library of Congress.

The University of Minnesota is an equal-opportunity educator and employer.

For Elfrieda, who always could listen

. . . these I will bring to my holy mountain,
    and make them joyful in my house of prayer;
their burnt offerings and their sacrifices
    will be accepted on my altar;
for my house shall be called a house of prayer
    for all peoples.
Thus says the Lord God,
    who gathers the outcasts of Israel,
I will gather others to them
    besides those already gathered.

ISAIAH 56:7–8 (NEW REVISED STANDARD VERSION)

Contents

Repairing Bad Objects

Improper Citizenship in Queer Church

> *I do not have the aim of moving beyond x but the aim of setting there awhile, dedramatizing the performance of critical and political judgment so as to slow down the encounter with the objects of knowledge that are really scenes we can barely get our eyes around.*
>
> —Lauren Berlant, "Starved"

The Sign That Martine Loved

Martine and I were drinking our second glasses of wine at my kitchen table when she told me about a moment at our church that had profoundly irked her. One Sunday, my friend and interview subject discovered that church leaders had moved a prominent, beloved sign mounted behind the altar to the back of the worship hall, replacing the original front sign with another.

The sign that had been displaced to the back of the church bore a variant of Isaiah 56:7: "My house shall be a house of prayer for all people." The new text that framed the altar and now greeted congregants, friends, and visitors as they entered the worship hall read simply "Welcome home."

As Martine's knowledge of the church and her time there vastly outpaced my own, I inquired, somewhat puzzled, "So what's the difference?"

Martine replied that while she remained attached to our church—a large, predominantly lesbian, gay, bisexual, transgender, and queer (LGBTQ) congregation in Toronto, Canada—she didn't necessarily feel "at home" there as a black bisexual woman. A gifted musician and organizer, Martine had encountered persistent barriers to her leadership at the church, barriers she linked to the congregation's often limited willingness to grapple openly or adequately with questions of race and gender.

1

Reflecting on her experiences and those of others, Martine disputed the "Welcome home" sign's confident, settled presumption that others would or should find the space homelike.

Martine told me that the old, displaced sign, by contrast, had located the possibility of meaningful inclusivity in the future, suggesting that welcome for "all people" would remain a perpetually unfinished project, constantly striven toward but never settled or axiomatically accomplished. Both signs referred to a promise of some kind—a promise of substantive belonging. But the new sign treated that promise as already fulfilled, whereas its predecessor made a more proleptic gesture: a promise from God, Isaiah, and church founders of a "house of prayer for all people" that *could be*. "My house shall be a house of prayer for all people" also addressed formal and everyday practices of religious authority within and beyond the church, seeming to proffer better modes of relationality, not only between God and humans but also among humans themselves. Martine said she preferred such a promise to a confident declaration of welcome because she felt the temporal structure of the former authorized her to contest injustices within and beyond the church.

Martine's insights about this configuration of institutional and spiritual narratives in church space—her critique of the gap between the promise of a "house of prayer for all" and the dissatisfying conceit of that welcoming "home" as a fait accompli—intimate that this dispute about religious ornamentation, which secular liberalism would code as "private" or "internal" to a faith community, is also a scene of *citizenship*. Promises like those Martine identifies—and tensions between hollow assurances of enfranchisement and the radical potential of bold proleptic claims—also figure prominently in queer theorist Lauren Berlant's (1997) pathbreaking work on citizenship. For Berlant, citizenship comprises a "promise which, because it was a promise, was held out paradoxically: falsely, as a democratic reality, and legitimately, as a promise, the promise that the democratic citizenship form makes to people caught in history" (19). In Berlant's view, discourses of citizenship are both ruses, deeply hypocritical from the vantage of minoritized subjects "caught in history," and sites of potentiality, contestation, and the prospect of downward redistribution. While Berlant's primary object is U.S. citizenship, her work deftly models how citizenship can be conceptualized broadly and diffusely, as a "cluster of promises" around solidarity, rights, redistribution, sympathy, and belonging (2011a, 23). And although citizenship is viciously policed by nation-states through a proliferation of juridical, discursive, and material violences, thinking citizenship on Berlant's loosened terms suggests it is hardly the exclusive purview of nation-states or state actors alone. As Berlant (2007), Engin Isin (2002), and others (Ong 2006; Painter and Philo 1995; Holston and Appadurai 1996; Grundy and Smith 2005; Painter 2006) have argued, citizenship encompasses sociocultural, affective, and economic domains alongside and intertwined with the juridical register, and proves geographically wily, diffuse, and multiscalar. Framing Martine's quarrel with our church as a scene of citizenship, then, links it to dramas of Canadian nationhood concerning race, gender, diaspora, class, and sexuality—but not only that. Formal and ordinary political contestations, often affectively fraught, around unfulfilled promises of solidarity and belonging also make the city of Toronto, local and global LGBTQ institutions, and the church itself vital spaces of citizenship.

This book investigates one queer congregation, the Metropolitan Community Church of Toronto (MCCT), and the urban, transnational, and national spaces and collectivities it transects, as a key material and metaphorical space where people feel their way through citizenship. The book seeks to apprehend both the limits and potential of the promise on that displaced sign that Martine loved—"My house shall be a house of prayer for all people"—and the ways people negotiate their relationships to such promises through desire, solidarity, attachment, and contestation. Simultaneously, the project tracks the relationships between the affective process of queer rapprochement with church—repairing and recasting what for many comprises a "bad" religious object—and transformative approaches to citizenship. It takes up the resonances and fissures between promises of capacious politics emerging from LGBTQ religious activism and the theoretical project of queer "subjectless" critique, which aims to push queer theory and politics beyond the fetish of identity in liberal identity politics (Eng, Halberstam, and Muñoz 2005). By considering moments when queer faith-based organizing proves capable of undoing its own identitarian terms of reference, the book contributes to the ongoing critical reevaluation of both citizenship and religion as "bad objects" for queer theory.

Indeed, as Isaac West (2014) notes, citizenship in queer studies is somewhat habitually reduced to nation-state violence and written off as beyond repair. Yet subjectless queer critique—queer theory "without proper object"—harbors a multitude of political implications that a reformulated, geographically diffuse concept of citizenship can powerfully illuminate (Eng, Halberstam, and Muñoz 2005; Butler 1994). What promises like "a house of prayer for all people" offer, and at times deliver, is an *improper queer citizenship*—citizenship that takes neither LGBTQ identity nor the nation-states as exclusive or even primary referents, even when it ambivalently traffics in the idioms of both. Likewise, where Western law and discourses of secularism tend to figure organized religion and sexual freedom as constitutively opposed (Jakobsen and Pellegrini 2003; Scott 2011)—ossifying religion as a "bad object" for feminist and queer struggles—this study points to people's capacity to repair a religious institution, to fashion of it a "good-enough" object, not only in the service of the liberal affirmation of LGBTQ identities but in the service of far more capacious spiritual and political itineraries.

Whether this queer church or any institution can make good on the promise of a house for all people is another matter. But, as Martine suggests, the truth-value of the promise of improper queer citizenship is hardly knowable in advance—leaving room for attention to its performativity, what the promise *does*, how it enables people to feel and act politically (Sedgwick [1997] 2003). Thus, I set out to map everyday political and affective dynamics of improper queer citizenship in the space of the church and the more diffuse spaces of affinity and collectivity that the church helps engender. The chapters of the book situate the church and the intimacies it fosters as spaces of vexed *attachment*, where people work through messy alliances and contradictory aspects of the church's history, norms, and ministry in order to sustain a relation to an impure but "good-enough" church (Winnicott 1953); as spaces of *contestation*, where the "proper objects" of urban LGBTQ struggle are debated and recast; as spaces of *desire*, where people articulate and enact a wide, ideologically incoherent proliferation of religiously inflected fantasies about "global" queer solidarity and community; and, finally, as spaces of *solidarity*, where people both cite and flout Canadian (homo)nationalist discourse in order to support LGBTQ asylum seekers on a theological rather than identitarian basis. Throughout, I argue that the promise of an improper queer citizenship depends not simply on people's trenchant or savvy political analysis but also on people's capacity for what Eve Sedgwick ([1997] 2003), building on Melanie Klein (1975), calls affective *reparation*. Thinking through my experiences in church and the relationships I formed there compels me to insist upon an understanding of citizenship and religion as objects of a complex reparative yet unredemptive love—love that integrates good and bad fragments of its object but remains sober about its object's limits and can thus continue to work for transformation.

Queer church, I contend, proves an especially rich, if perhaps incongruous, case study for investigating the affective dynamics of improper queer citizenship, because of its profound affective density, its prolific multiscalarity, and its inhabitation as a site of ongoing contestation as well as welcome. The church promises to extend sympathy, solidarity, rights, and recognition within the space of the congregation to "all people" gathered there, and likewise vows to fight for the extension of that promise of substantive belonging at a range of geographical scales. People come to MCCT precisely because of its religious and ostensibly identitarian character, in their nonsovereignty, queer damage, and vulnerability, with fantasies of being made whole (Berlant and Edelman 2013). Yet reinvigorated political desires also speak and work through the church, a space where people grapple with the psychic effects of repudiated desire (Georgis 2006), undoing coherent identity politics and proffering a more capacious citizenship. It is through the affective work of repairing religion and religious space—decidedly "bad objects" for many queers—that people at MCCT simultaneously work to repair and recast citizenship on more expansive terms.

Improper Queer Citizenship?

Twenty-five years have passed since the publication of the texts often considered inaugural to queer theory—texts that, informed by a rich and sometimes messy tangle of Foucauldian and psychoanalytic insights, rethink sexuality not as an identity but as a diffuse domain of power and subject formation, deeply imbricated with others (Sedgwick 1990; Butler 1990). In that time, queer theorists have repeatedly and productively insisted on the dexterity and broad salience of queer thought, on the utter nonnecessity of an LGBTQ-identified referent, object, or subject for queer theory or politics. In her pivotal essay "Against Proper Objects" (1994), Judith Butler builds on her work in *Gender Trouble* (1990), which famously demonstrates the deep enmeshment of discourses of binary gender in the "heterosexual matrix." Insisting on the profound linkages between feminist and queer inquiry and stakes, Butler calls for a refusal in feminist and queer studies of so-called proper objects, challenging disciplinary moves that limit queer theory to visibly LGBTQ referents and that cleave women's and gender studies from gay and lesbian studies:

Perhaps the time has arrived to encourage the kinds of conversations that resist the urge to stake territorial claims through the reduction or caricature of the positions from which they are differentiated. The "grounds" of autonomy are precisely these sites of differentiation, which are not grounds in any conventional sense. These are rifted grounds, a series of constituting differentiations which at once contest the claim to autonomy and offer in its place a more expansive, mobile mapping of power. There is more to learn from upsetting such grounds, reversing the exclusions by which they are instated, and resisting the institutional domestication of queer thinking. For normalizing the queer would be, after all, its sad finish. (21)

Butler trades in explicitly geographical metaphors, condemning provincial disciplinary "territorial claims" and highlighting the political utility of "rifted grounds" and queer analysis that proffers "a more expansive, mobile mapping of power." Crucially, at stake for Butler in contesting the disciplinary normalization of queer theory is the prospect of capacious critical social and cultural analysis. By advocating queer theory without "proper object," Butler aims not to vacate queer studies but to nurture the production of scholarship that continuously scrambles to keep the production of gender, sexuality, race, class, and still more vectors of difference and power in view.

In one particularly dexterous, pathbreaking queer mapping of power, black feminist Cathy J. Cohen (1997) lays out the stakes and prospects for a capacious queer studies and politics even more explicitly. Approaching queerness as an estranged relation to processes of normalization rather than a bounded identity, Cohen marshals a long history of racist sexual pathologization in the United States, from marriage policy to the Moynihan report to welfare policy debates, demonstrating that black people in the United States have been discursively rendered sexually abnormal, consigned to the outskirts of heteronormativity regardless of their sexual identifications. What would it mean, Cohen asks, to think of racialized figures with a range of sexual identifications and object-choices—punks, bulldaggers, and welfare queens alike—as parts of a queer coalition demanding answerability and solidarity? Such a "reconceptualization of the politics of marginal groups," Cohen contends, "allows us . . . to search for those interconnected sites of resistance from which we can wage broader political struggles. Only by recognizing the link between the ideological, social, political and economic marginalization of punks, bulldaggers, and welfare queens can we begin to develop political analyses and political strategies effective in confronting the *linked yet varied sites of power* in this country" (462 [emphasis added]).

Such calls for capacious analysis and politics of sexuality have generated profound excitement. Yet queer scholars have had to continue to insist on sexuality's diffuse, wily character and its imbrication with a wide range of vectors of subject formation and social ordering. More than a decade after "Against Proper Objects," David Eng, Judith Halberstam, and José Esteban Muñoz (2005) lamented that, despite the insights of Butler, Cohen, and others, "much of queer theory nowadays sounds like a metanarrative about the domestic affairs of white homosexuals" (12). Eng, Halberstam, and Muñoz propose "what might be called the 'subjectless' critique of queer studies" (3) to challenge the production and reproduction of queer studies' "own canonical set of proper subjects and objects" (12). Gathering a provocative collection of essays that confront questions of religion, temporality, imperialism, capitalist crisis, diaspora, law, and race, the three insist on a queer studies that "disallows any positing of a proper subject *of* or object *for* the field by insisting that queer has no fixed political referent" (3 [emphasis original]). Such work refuses to take sexuality as a bounded object or marked identity, instead following Foucault ([1976] 1978) in approaching it as an "especially dense transfer point" for a range of relations of difference and power (103).

It proves vital to aver here that calls to embrace a subjectless critique of queer identity have received an ambivalent reception, including among queer of color critics. In an influential rejoinder to and reformulation of queer critiques of identity, E. Patrick Johnson (2001) uses the southern U.S. black idiom "quare" as an alternative rallying point for a capacious intersectional politics, one responsive to the sustained (not the same as essential) salience of blackness as a ground of both oppression and collective subject formation. Johnson rightly calls for understanding recourse to identitarian politics, particularly for racialized queers, as strategic and contingent, rather than necessarily uncritical or earnest. I read Johnson's insight as helpful in situating subjectless queer critique's contextual and provisional utility. Subjectless queer critique proves *most* generative insofar as it interrupts the tendency to certify and coronate the most privileged LGBTQ subjects (in the United States and Canada, this often means white, cisgender upper- and middle-class men) and their political concerns as the "proper objects" that synecdochically stand in for and dominate LGBTQ politics and scholarship. Subjectless queer critique can also dislodge the elevation of LGBTQ identity over the wider range of uses of sexuality to scapegoat marginalized subjects. At the same time, not all identitarian formations are created equal or make recourse to identity politics in the same fashion. Recourse to the romance of identity and the fantasy of sovereign subjectivity can prove psychically and politically dangerous for all subjects, and particularly so for multiply marginalized subjects, because it forecloses access to vulnerability and repudiated desire, and courts co-optation by the state and the market. But that potential danger makes all the more important a context-specific understanding of the conditions under which (and affective sophistication with which) differently situated actors invoke identity (see King 2015). Thus, by deliteralizing the relationship between identity and politics, subjectless queer critique can also help to open up an understanding of the nonidentitarian affects, sensibilities, and practices that proliferate even and especially in the midst of ostensibly identitarian political formations.

What, then, could subjectless critique—with its far-reaching analytical, ethical, and political scope and ambitions—have to say to citizenship?[1] For some queer readers, a subjectless queer lens might seem inimical to citizenship, at least as citizenship is normatively construed by nation-states, liberal identity politics, and discourses of respectability (and by critics of those formations—see, e.g., Cossman 2007; Brandzel 2005). Indeed, Jasbir Puar (2007) has mobilized subjectless critique to chart the provisional embrace of some queers as U.S. citizen–subjects worthy of privacy and life, and the simultaneous marking of entire populations of South Asians and Arabs for death—a move accompanied, crucially, by the figure of the putatively backward, perverse, patriarchal yet homoerotic terrorist. Likewise, Scott Morgensen (2011) has demonstrated how colonial discourse has dichotomously construed indigenous populations as sexually perverse, and thus marked for death, yet at the same time exemplary of authentic "premodern" sexuality, and thus the grounds for settler claims on sexual citizenship in the "modern" colonial nation-state. For these critics, citizenship is constitutively heteronormative *and* homonormative (see Duggan 2003)—productive of "normal" heterosexualities and homosexualities— while subjectless critique exposes how the racialized and/or indigenous noncitizen is rendered queer. This view of citizenship treats it as the

province of what Eng (2010) calls "queer liberalism"—identitarian, unre-
flexive, limited (if not silent) in its critique of state violence, tacitly (if not
explicitly) attached to militarism and settler colonialism, and rigidly ad-
herent to the very surety and homogeneity of identity that subjectless critique aims to dislodge. In short, as Isaac West (2014) insightfully observes,
in the wake of such important critiques of homonormativity (Duggan
2003) and homonationalism (Puar 2007), citizenship has become something of a "bad object" for queer theory, including for subjectless queer
critique.

Yet it must here be asked whether the nation-state and its constitutive
violences hold the ontological monopoly on or comprise the imaginative
horizon for citizenship. Genealogical and empirical work in human geography and citizenship studies seeks to open up historical and contemporary ontologies of citizenship, not "beyond" but perhaps "beside," in
immanent excess of, nation-state dominance. Investigating "live" experiments and struggles through this alternative conception of citizenship by
no means asks us to suspend critical scrutiny of the contemporary juridical nation-state citizenship and its at times violent consequences (Berlant
2011a; Varsanyi 2006). Rather, approaching citizenship through geography
invites us to consider the myriad, often ordinary ways in which people appropriate, retool, tweak, and exploit diverse technologies of citizenship—
and how they might engage with nation-states in ways that evince a critical
political consciousness (or indeed, a political unconscious) that is far from
beholden to the nation-state. Such strategic negotiations, which often borrow and rework technologies across multiple and overlapping spatialities
(Ridgley 2008; Painter 2006; Secor 2004), point to a multiplicity of citizenships that require careful analytical engagement. It becomes crucial to
refuse to permit "scalar thought" in queer critique (Isin 2007)—the normative representations that hierarchically order types of place—to simply
have the last word on citizenship; indeed, to do so would ironically serve
the very forms of nation-state power that queer theory and related critical formations aim to challenge. The alternative to permitting sustained
nation-state capture of citizenship that I am advocating—letting citizenship remain ontologically open and subjecting it to historically and geographically specific investigation—cannot promise to transcend nation-
state citizenship; but it can open up queer theory's vision to a proliferation
of already existing queer citizenships that gleefully flout the nation-state,
even and especially when they engage it.

Subjectless queer critique asks queer theory to be analytically capacious, to inhabit "rifted grounds" in the hopes of developing "more mobile, expansive mappings of power" (Butler 1994, 21) and confronting those "linked yet varied sites of power" (Cohen 1997, 462). And, just as queer theory refuses a proper object, so too might critical engagement with citizenship. If queerness cannot be known in advance and has no fixed referent, then perhaps the "goodies" that citizenship promises can be imagined and made manifest within an ever-thickening and -widening range of social relations. In proposing an improper queer citizenship, I aim to map queer practices, concepts, and spaces of solidarity, sympathy, redistribution, and rights-claiming that do not (necessarily) take the nation-state or LGBTQ identity as their exclusive or primary referents, even as they work within those idioms. What might make such ontologies of citizenship "queer" is not the involvement of LGBTQ-identified subjects per se but the force of pathologization by sexual norms as a departure point for alternative citizenship forms. As Wendy Brown (1995) and Dina Georgis (2006) contend, encountering loss, particularly in the form of repudiated desire, can lead to political practices that ossify or shore up a coherent identity. But engaging loss can also reinvigorate desire, leading political subjects to ask both "What do I want?" and "What do I want for us?" on more expansive terms (Brown 1995, 51; Georgis 2006).

Moreover, when "citizenship" is understood as ontologically multiple and open (Isin 2002)—as a "cluster of promises" (Berlant 2011a, 23) around rights, responsibilities, sympathy, redistribution, and solidarity at any one or multiple geographical scales—then it can powerfully answer the boldness and dexterity of an improper, subjectless queer political imagination. Subjectless queer critique's demand for capacious politics and analysis upends fixed identitarian referents for citizenship, while geographical accounts of citizenship point to the already present tremulousness in citizenship's ties to nation and to citizenship's potential for far-reaching, multiscalar solidarities. Simultaneously, mapping geographically specific scenes of citizenship—of political engagement and affective attachment—helps ground the analytical promise of subjectless queer critique and trace both the potential and limits of its realization.

By proposing a subjectless or improper queer citizenship, I am not advocating citizenship without subjects—a prospect that sounds either simply impossible or frighteningly Agambenian (see Agamben 2005). If anything, the concepts and practices of improper queer citizenship I map in this book are teeming with subjects and subject-forming processes—identification, transference, desire, solidarity, contestation, attachment. What makes such queer citizenships improper or "subjectless," rather, is their resonance with subjectless critique's call for a queer theory and politics without proper objects or subjects. Improper queer citizenship doesn't evacuate subjectivity; it exceeds LGBTQ and national frames on identity without transcending them. It thinks and feels its way beside the forms of nonrelationality and frankly miserable relationality entailed in the fetishes of LGBTQ identity and national identity, in the pursuit of better forms of relationality. As Nandita Sharma (2005) writes in her anti-identitarian critique of Canadian immigration law, "The goal is to recognize the modernist preoccupation with identities, most of which are imposed, and move *through* them so that we humans can reorganize ways of living that are not antithetical to continued life on this planet" (152 [emphasis original]). When church actors speak to agents of the nation-state or to national polities— as they do quite powerfully in chapters 2 and 4 of this book—the affects of improper queer citizenship, like loss, nonsovereignty, and reinvigorated desire for collectivity, impishly speak through them. Performative, proleptic, and affectively sophisticated, improper queer citizens conjure up citizenships in polities—churches, cities, nations, transnational communities, worlds—that don't exist yet. The analytic of improper queer citizenship traces how queerness—figured centrally as vulnerability—troubles and is invoked in practices of citizenship at a range of geographical scales.

To geographically pluralize citizenships, then, is not to eschew nation-state violence but precisely to contest it, by refusing to regard the nation-state as the only game in town, sustaining a critique of the nation-state, and asking what else might be going on. A multiscalar approach to queer citizenship, as Grundy and Smith (2005) put it, points to the richness of "multiple, overlapping and differentiated modes of queer citizenship" (389). This book takes affective, political, and ethical cues from work on diasporic (Walcott 2003) and decolonial (Sharma 2005; Simpson 2013) sensibilities that engage ironically and critically with the nation-state as needed, but always with broader emancipatory goals in excess of nation in mind. Where my project differs from diasporic and decolonial scholarship is less in sensibility or in politics than in focus; my objects of analysis are the moments of intervention, interruption, and surprise in queer polities that are normatively white and often implicitly framed by nation—moments when such polities catch up to and learn from the insights of movements like Idle No More or Black Lives Matter, or have an opportunity to do so, and moments when the lure of integration into national polity fails, or at least falters. Improper queer citizens critically engage with the nation-state; what makes their activism compelling is the terms on which they do so. A rich body of scholarship has argued that queer citizenship is haunted by the nation-state and complicity in nation-state violence (see especially Puar 2007). It is precisely because I find such work persuasive, and share in its outrage at such complicity (including my own complicity), that my aim here is to demonstrate how improper queer citizenship in turn exceeds and haunts the nation-state.

But queer reckoning with the bad objects of citizenship and religion requires more than better concepts and genealogies or more capacious political analysis; it requires grappling with habits of thinking and feeling. To begin to confront the affective difficulty that such bad objects can engender, I turn in the following section to the work of Eve Sedgwick and Melanie Klein. With their emphasis on people's capacity to integrate competing and contradictory affects in order to carve out nourishment and plenitude in a violent world, such work provides a supple language for theorizing the affective sophistication with which people negotiate the promises and the limits of citizenship and religious community.

Reevaluating Bad Objects

Queer scholars' calls for a politics without proper object have yielded powerful social and cultural analysis and given a signal boost to radical political projects that mobilize capacious understandings of queerness, solidarity, and belonging (see, e.g., Duggan 2003). But how might an improper queer citizenship *feel*? Under what affective conditions might it emerge? A subjectless queer analysis might rationally plod along, unfolding toward an expansive understanding of a wide range of subjects and objects as queer. But, as Martine's quarrel with the church demonstrates, citizenship—particularly the kind that I am arguing is recast by subjectless queer critique—is an affectively fraught and demanding scene: promising and menacing, hypocritical and ostensibly replete with potential, riven with desire. How do people feel their way through that scene? How does the subjectless queer "rubber" meet the affectively fraught "road" of citizenship? Under what affective conditions do people actually risk the surety of collective/individual identity, imagining more expansive grounds for solidarity and meaningfully enacting that solidarity (Brown 1995)?

My ethnographic inquiry into queer church has led me to embrace a particular understanding of *reparative* practices and affects. Given the growing uptake of Sedgwick's work on the concept, it proves crucial to clarify how I inflect the concept in this project. Much social and cultural theory, Sedgwick famously argues, seeks to expose the mimetic reproduction of the bad and the insidious, which it already knows in advance are lurking there, and which it presumes are hiding and need exposure. Playfully but frankly framing such ways of theorizing as "paranoid" enables Sedgwick to break up what she views as paranoia's monopoly on the critical interpretation of culture. Insisting that paranoia comprises only one kind of critical interpretive orientation, she proposes an alternative, "reparative" reading practice that shares paranoia's critical allegiances but not its conspiratorial pretensions.

Sedgwick's account of reparative reading is characterized by a productive tension between reparation as an ethically *chosen* reading practice, on the one hand, and reparation as an elusive, intermittent psychic *state,* beyond the scope of intentionality or progress narratives, on the other. She draws on a range of sources exploring the affective dynamics of paranoia and its alternatives, including the works of cognitive and affect scholar Sylvan Tomkins and object relations psychoanalytic theorist Melanie Klein. As sunnier, more voluntarist accounts of reparative practice as an "ethical choice for difference" proliferate in human geography (see Gibson-Graham 2006; Brown 2009), and as queer critics worry that the reparative lapses too readily into the sentimental (see Berlant and Edelman 2013), I find it particularly helpful to return to reparation's Kleinian genealogy, which is, in my view, insufficiently engaged by both human geography and queer theory (for exceptions, see Sibley 2003; Bondi 2008; and Eng 2010). Klein's distinction between paranoid and depressive psychic positions forms a crucial basis for Sedgwick's distinction between paranoid and reparative reading practices and has been central to my own process of making sense of how citizenship feels in church.

In Klein's theory of paranoid and depressive positions (1975), infants come to form attachments to external "objects" that they initially experience as uniformly and absolutely good, conferring plenitude and unwavering devotion (2). Inevitably, the infant directly experiences a loss of that object (however momentary or permanent), comes to feel anxiety at the threat of such detachment, or both. The real or potential unavailability of an object that conferred plenitude and was once thought to be constant precipitates a profound crisis for the infant. What is to be done now that the goodness and infinite availability of the object are not so certain? To foreclose the possibility of future loss, the infant negotiates the world as a universe of good and bad (mostly bad) objects and object fragments, and experiences a corresponding split in her own ego. Whether through advance "knowledge" of the badness of objects or through projecting phantasies of idealized goodness onto objects (hopes that are inevitably dashed), the child in the paranoid position thus cannot form or sustain durable attachments, making impossible what Klein calls love—emotional attachments to complex objects we come to regard, despite their limitations, as "good enough" (see especially Winnicott 1953). By failing to unite good and bad part objects into integrated, messy, complex whole objects, the infant remains safe but paranoid, negotiating a world that is profoundly fragmented but at least free from contamination.

In Klein's lexicon, the alternative to the paranoid position is the curiously named "depressive" position (14). Under certain (if not necessarily "ideal") conditions and over time, an infant in the paranoid position undergoes a surprising process of integration or reparation (21). As she comes to regard her objects as consistent, if not ever-present or perfect, the infant can reestablish the trust breached by that first painful loss of the good object. Growing accustomed to the complexity of her objects and piecing together good and bad part objects, the infant must also negotiate a corresponding internal complexity. Even though the infant can never feel the initial plenitude she did when she first saw her objects as perfect and good, she no longer so intensely undergoes the fear she did at that inaugural moment of detachment or loss. Concomitantly, her introjections stabilize and become more complex. On the one hand, her initial experience of detachment was not a result of something shameful or unlovable about her, and on the other, she can live on with her anxious fear of loss enough not to rigidly insist upon her own goodness or to project negatively onto her objects. Her objects, and her ego, become integrated and "good enough" (Winnicott 1953), and while the threat of pain and bad surprise remains soberingly ever-present, good surprise and love become possible.

Later in her work, Klein refined her thinking on the relation between the paranoid and depressive positions, situating paranoia as the condition of possibility of the depressive position but not simply its predecessor in a teleological narrative of development. Klein came to emphasize that the paranoid and depressive positions are recurring and nonlinear; that one slips in and out of depressive positioning in moments rather than stages throughout one's life (Sedgwick [1997] 2003, 128). Just as importantly, Klein views paranoia as the position in which avoidance of suffering trumps and excludes the possibility of seeking pleasure (Sedgwick [1997] 2003, 129). The depressive position, by contrast, remains acutely aware of suffering but risks identity and suffering in the pursuit of good surprises. Reparation, then, is far from a flaky or straightforwardly conscious ethical choice to love the world, but a "depressive" negotiation of a world marred by hierarchy and exploitation, on the one hand, and the necessity of pleasure and amelioration, on the other. Joshua Chambers-Letson (2006) puts it aptly: "Reparation is not about being able to repair oneself into some kind of mythical (and impossible) whole subject, as American ego-psychology would have us believe that we could do, but about finding ways to live and love in relation to the injuries of our pasts and futures" (173). Critical, though often playful, in its approach, reparative reading does not necessarily celebrate the scenes it investigates. Nor does it suspend critique or even contempt when appropriate. Reparation does not mark a clean break from paranoia. Indeed, Sedgwick ([1997] 2003) emphasizes, "It is sometimes the most paranoid-tending people who are able to, and need to, develop and disseminate the richest reparative practices" (150).

In staking out an alternative affective bearing toward citizenship in this book, then, I am not claiming to simply make a better ethical choice of reading practice than do other queer critics primarily concerned with mapping nation-state violence; to the contrary, I admire and am in wholehearted agreement with such critics. Thus, rather than counter queer paranoia about citizenship as always already national with a kind of bad-faith optimism about our capacity to choose to read reparatively, I am advocating a reparative reading of citizenship in line with Klein's depressive position. If there is a "choice" at play in reparative reading at all, then, it does not come ex nihilo. Nor does reparative reading entail a suspension of paranoid judgment—as if we could. Rather, I would suggest that the "choice" to read reparatively is possible only after reparative insights have interrupted the ordinary hum of our (understandably!) paranoid habits of making sense of the world. Indeed, in her account of the depressive position, Klein draws on the Greek tragedian Aeschylus, who describes learning as an affective process born of constraint:

Man by suffering shall learn.
. . . .
Wisdom comes against his will. (Qtd. in Klein 1975, 296)

It is only when reparative insights undo us—as critics, activists, brokenhearted queers, melancholic Lefties, people of faith, whomever—that we become aware of our *propensity* for judgment and can possibly hope to revise it. Good surprise here engenders less an optimism than an intermittent curiosity and an openness to having been wrong.

A reparative scholarly orientation toward citizenship in queer studies matters, because it reflects and catches up with the insights and practices of ordinary, extraordinary people who are leading, theorizing, and participating in critical social movements and engaging in everyday acts of citizenship. This orientation helps us read debates about whom "queer" institutions serve as affective scenes in which the always contingent line between good ("proper," ideal-typical) and bad ("extraneous") part objects for those institutions comprises a vector for both aggressive splitting and the prospect of integration (see Butler 1994, 6). Indeed, the informants whose insights ground my book are often directly affected by and profoundly critical of the constitutive contradictions and elisions of citizenship at multiple scales. As Martine told me that night over drinks, her attachment to the church and desire for the possibility of what it could be routinely elicited skepticism from other black queers in Toronto. The most common question she got, she told me, was "Why do you go *there?*"—an allusion to the church's overwhelming normative whiteness. "Why, indeed?" I asked her. Martine described at length the forms of solidarity and intimacy—around mental and spiritual wellness, black diaspora, feminism, and BDSM—that different affinities within the church nourished for her, and her simultaneous unwillingness to abide the structural privileging of white men's perspectives in the congregation. Hardly sunny about the church's limitations, Martine integrates good and bad fragments of the church together, sustaining a relation to the church that involves disappointment and violence but cannot be reduced to one of "cruel optimism" (Berlant 2011a). As I flesh out in detail in chapter 1, understanding the nuances and variegations in how people like Martine inhabit the church points to people's engagement with the church and other citizenship forms on reparative, or indeed depressive, but hardly "cruel-optimistic" terms. What makes such affective negotiations exemplary of improper queer citizenship lies in their visceral and urgent departure from the comfort and stability—the surety—of identity that characterize identitarian and homonationalist renditions of belonging, citizenship, and home. Martine's proleptic claims on belonging in the church—claims nourished by the promise of a "house of prayer for all people"—dispute the conceit of the church as an always already "welcome home," largely for white cisgender lesbians and gay men. That this affective and political work takes place in religious space is not incidental. People come to church in states of profound trauma, vulnerability, and pain. Indeed, religious spaces are sites of formative, inaugural sexual repudiation for many subjects, LGBTQ or not, in ways that can make a return both disruptive and generative. For many people, church as a good part object seems to promise a means of becoming coherent, being made whole, and finding home and comfort in community.

But as a space where people can work through the inaugural repudiation of the erotic impulse (Georgis 2006), church can also serve as a space where people desire anew, and on more sophisticated, integrative, and capacious terms. Indeed, Martine's approach to citizenship in and through church is less about "homeyness" than about coalition, a key idiom for subjectless queer critique. As black feminist artist, activist, and scholar Bernice Johnson Reagon ([1981] 2000) notes, coalition is life-giving, world-building and affectively rocky terrain. Speaking as a black woman at the normatively white West Coast Women's Music Festival in 1981 about differences and political potential within feminisms, she challenged her listeners and herself, positioning coalition as a crucial but uncanny process: "Coalition work is not work done in your home. Coalition work has to be done in the streets. And it is some of the most dangerous work you can do. And you shouldn't look for comfort. Some people will come to a coalition and they rate the success of the coalition on whether or not they feel good when they get there. They're not looking for a coalition; they're looking for a home!" (359). Reagon's insight about the affective difficulty of coalition resonates and remains profoundly salient across a range of political feeling practices that I am linking to improper queer citizenship. Through her account of the unhomeyness and discomfort of coalition,

Reagon helps direct us to the visceral and psychic facets of improper queer citizenship.[2] Likewise, Martine's claims on belonging in church disturb desires for church as a homey, homogeneous, gay white space, contesting and reinvigorating it as a more capacious, more coalitional site of contestation, of improper queer citizenship. Martine doesn't vacate identity in the way that worries E. Patrick Johnson (2001), but her interventions demonstrate how anti-identitarian sensibilities—the negation of "home"—can be put to emancipatory use.

Martine is a citizen of a church and a world that don't exist yet, a church and a world in which everyone might live, in Talal Asad's (2003) words, as a "minority among minorities" (180). Like those of many of my informants, Martine's practices and inflections of improper queer citizenship—contestation, solidarity, attachment, and desire—demonstrate a profound analytical and affective complexity, one that can help reframe queer theory's orientation toward citizenship as an always already bad national object. The task for subjectless queer critique—precisely because citizenship is so affectively fraught—is not to refuse citizenships (Brandzel 2005) as an analytic of power or a political category but to spatialize, (re)inhabit, contest, and work through them, as Martine and so many others do.

Why Church?

At first glance, the Metropolitan Community Church of Toronto—or any religious object, for that matter—may seem an unlikely choice for a study of improper queer citizenship and its affective dynamics. Formed in 1973 and tasked with the project of ministering to Toronto's "gay and lesbian community," MCCT has been at the forefront of a host of ostensibly identitarian, often nationally framed LGBTQ citizenship struggles: urban activism against police brutality and for improved police–minority relations, provincial and federal advocacy for sexual orientation and gender identity nondiscrimination laws, ministry and social services for people living with HIV/AIDS, conducting and suing for the right to conduct the country's first legal same-sex marriages, support programs for LGBTQ asylum seekers in Canada, and global Internet outreach to LGBTQ Christians, to name a few. Moreover, much of this activist work has been spearheaded by the church's charismatic longtime minister the Reverend Dr. Brent Hawkes. A cisgender gay white man born in the baby-boom generation, Hawkes circulates a public narrative that reads in many ways like a paragon of queer liberalism, a progressive, "it gets better" story (Eng 2010). Raised in a fundamentalist Baptist church by his family in the small maritime village of Bath, New Brunswick, Hawkes came to Toronto, joined MCCT, went to divinity school, and became the congregation's openly gay and unapologetically activist pastor in 1977. Though such activist ministry initially elicited hesitation from congregants, dismissal from gays and Christians alike, jeers, and police beatings, Hawkes ultimately rose to national fame, respect, and political influence. In 2001, Hawkes performed what are considered by many to be the first legal same-sex marriages in Canada, and in 2006 he married his longtime partner, John Sproule. The following year, Hawkes was named to the prestigious Order of Canada, the country's highest civilian honor of merit, by the governor general of Canada. In 2011, the pastor presided at the state funeral of his good friend the Honorable Jack Layton, the late leader of the Official Opposition and the New Democratic Party of Canada. At first glance, such activism would seem to position Hawkes as a model queer citizen, but not in the improper sense with which I am centrally concerned.

Yet as a church, MCCT's logics and geographies of citizenship overlap with but also substantially exceed national and identity-based framings of the political. To begin with, MCCT is one of the largest congregations in the Universal Fellowship of Metropolitan Community Churches (UFMCC), a small, pro-LGBTQ Protestant denomination that was founded in Los Angeles in 1968 by the Reverend Troy D. Perry Jr. It was Perry who, struggling to reconcile the twin queer attachments of homosexual desire and a call to ministry, first framed UFMCC as promising "a house of prayer for all people." In the nearly five decades since UFMCC's founding, that initial promise has circulated and ricocheted, theologically, politically, and geographically. Claiming status as the largest membership-based LGBTQ organization in the world, the UFMCC denomination now counts roughly two hundred congregations and fellowships in more than thirty nation-states on six continents, and continues to see robust internal debates and contestations over racism, sexism, ageism, ableism, polyamory, and U.S. imperialism.

The work of the UFMCC movement proves profoundly integrative in a psychoanalytic sense. For most in the MCC movement—not all of whom identify as Christian—religious community is intelligible as an object that, however vexed, is also worthy of repair. Religion is, after all, normatively framed as a bad object for feminist and queer struggles in Western secular liberal framings of faith—a characterization that accrues to Islam with particular intensity (Mahmood 2004) but is likewise attached to Christianity (Jakobsen and Pellegrini 2003; Scott 2011). But it isn't only a matter of religion's normative rendering by law, New Atheism, or "clash of civilizations" rhetoric that makes religion such a difficult object. Indeed, many very differently situated people's lives have been profoundly, and in many cases indelibly, marred by encounters with open hatred, toxic group bonding, groupthink, dogmatism, shaming, excommunication, and abuse in religious collectivities—forms of violence that are often accompanied all too easily by theological justification in concepts such as Christian atonement theology (see Parker 2006). Thus, the work of drawing together good fragments of Christianity and organized religion; articulating alternative, critical relationships to aspects of Christian theology or biblical text; and resisting the redeployment of spiritual resources to authorize homophobia, misogyny, racism, or neocolonialism comprises a massive undertaking. This effort is psychic, spiritual, and political. Rather than exhibiting a paranoid "manic denial" (see Alford 2001) of Christianity's historic imbrication in homophobia, misogyny, racism, and related forms of oppression, or a naive, willful insistence that Christianity can be unproblematically inhabited by queers on unreformulated terms, the MCC movement is productively troubled by Christianity's limitations and bad fragments, constantly working out relationships to those limitations in order to live with a "good-enough" Christianity, a "good-enough" church. Its theological and organizational project (see, e.g., Shore-Goss et al. 2013) is, in and of itself, profoundly reparative, in ways that contribute not only to many people's survival but to their flourishing.

Understanding the Toronto church in the context of the UFMCC denomination—a supranational and transnational locus of solidarity, intellectual and theological resources and rationalities, belonging, and community formation—points to some of the ways MCCT comprises a space of citizenship neither beyond nor squarely within, but *beside* the Canadian nation-state (Sedgwick [1997] 2003). This alternative spatiality became especially clear to me at a Sunday worship service in 2012 that celebrated the thirty-fifth anniversary of Hawkes's ministry. Recalling his appointment to the Order of Canada, Hawkes produced a box containing his Order medallion. Hawkes revealed that the box held not only the nationally conferred medallion but his business card, which listed both his denominational attachment to UFMCC and his pastoral role at the Toronto church.

While grateful for recognition from the nation-state, Hawkes said through tears, it was the latter item—a piece of cardstock naming his allegiances to the urban congregation, the global denomination, and the sovereignty of God—that pointed to the most significant loci of accountability and attention for his ministry. Recognition from within the church, at subnational and supranational scales, had the most profound affective and ethical stakes for Hawkes as a queer citizen.

Indeed, it is the specifically religious character of MCCT that makes the church an especially idiosyncratic, fecund site for understanding citizenship's affective dynamics. As a liberal Christian church committed to the ideals of diversity and pluralism, but also a congregation stubbornly resistant to a clear separation between religion and politics (neither the 1867 British North America Act nor the 1982 Canadian Charter of Rights and Freedoms makes such a distinction), MCCT both inhabits and vastly exceeds the conceits of secular liberal reason. The staff and laypeople I interviewed described a vast, chaotic, incoherent, and contradictory range of motivations and attachments for participation in church ministries and activist initiatives, some of which squared well with secular "queer liberal" (Eng 2010) visions of the good life, but many of which pointed to radical, visceral, theological attachments to social and ecological justice. Congregants framed their desires for solidarity with LGBTQ asylum seekers and international outreach to LGBTQ Christians, for instance, as propelled by both theological and ethical commitments and a sense of shared identity and differential vulnerability. People also highlighted their experiences of music, preaching, and prayer at worship services as at the core of their affective enmeshment in the church and its activist ministries. During my fieldwork, the morning worship services I attended, typically a little over an hour in length, tended to blend spectacle, showtunes, dynamic sermons mixing liberal Christian theology and self-help, and narratives of queer injury and repair, enacting an affective pedagogy of sympathy and celebration. While I often jocularly describe worship to outsiders as a hybrid between an episode of *The Muppet Show,* a New Democratic Party of Canada rally, and *Sister Act,* the church's playful engagement with musical theater and other forms of campy spectacle and the dazzlingly high production value of its musical guests and choral performances made up some of the core affective tugs that sustained people's attachment to the church. The psychic and spiritual valences of worship services also offered a powerful ground for contestation within MCCT. Indeed, as I will investigate in depth in chapter 1, congregants seeking more meaningful racial and gender equality in the church's leadership and worship services, for instance, referred both to the significance of representation and visibility and to the affective power of worship in making their claims on citizenship within the church.

The specifically urban geography of both the larger denomination and MCCT also proves crucial to understanding the church as a space of citizenship that engages, haunts, and exceeds the nation-state. The church's framing as and within a "metropolitan community" is hardly incidental. Indeed, UFMCC founder Rev. Perry (1972) flagged the denomination as both urban and collective quite purposely, aiming to build not only a church with an intimate sense of community—"a small area, a place where you knew everybody"—but also one that would serve an entire metropolis rather than a single neighborhood (117). With six hundred churchgoers attending across three services and hundreds (at times, thousands) of additional webcast viewers every Sunday, it would prove difficult to know everybody at MCCT. But the church's formation and location in "metropolitan" Toronto—within the religious and queer landscapes of Canada's largest city, in which half of all residents were born outside Canada—are central to its influence. From riots against police brutality in the early 1980s to international fracases over queer interventions against Israeli apartheid and antiblack racism in the 2010s, Toronto has a rich genealogy of contestatory LGBTQ organizing. Noting Toronto's coordinates on an imperial map—its siting as a destination for diasporic populations from across the ruins or remains of the British Commonwealth/Empire—Rinaldo Walcott (2009) astutely positions the city as a space of "creolization," a place and a process "between brutality and something different, something more possible" (170). Often framed as a foil or bête noir (I use that idiom advisedly) in Canadian federal electoral politics, Toronto has a multifarious relationship to the nation-state as at once an economic engine, a site of a bloated and gravely inequitable housing market, and a space in and from which racial and sexual ideals for citizenship are exceeded, contested, and defiantly spoiled. As Grundy and Smith (2005) suggest, urban queer citizenship in Toronto has sought to respond ethically to the city's profound transformation by recent immigration, prioritizing residence in the city over nation-state citizenship as the privileged geographical basis for affinity, solidarity, and intimacy. While MCCT leaders have maintained an ambivalent relationship to radical forms of transnational and urban queer citizenship, the church both owes and contributes a great deal to those same urban formations.

For Toronto's LGBTQ Christians, MCCT has historically served as a "revolving door," welcoming people whose faith community of upbringing rejected them, only to see some of those people return to their childhood faiths as attitudes about sexuality in many faith communities have liberalized. Importantly, MCCT also acts as a revolving door for people who are not necessarily Christian. In my nearly five years circulating through LGBTQ communities in this city—volunteering for organizations serving immigrant youth, marching, cruising, dating—I have been struck by the persistent framing of the church as a landmark, a place to perhaps make friends, meet a partner, or simply visit as a kind of LGBTQ point of interest. As my chat with Martine already suggests, MCCT is far from a comfortable, homey, canny space for all who move through it. But the church's ubiquity as a household name—including among Buddhists, atheists, and Muslims—points to its role, aided in part by Christian hegemony, as an ephemeral urban queer commons, and one that makes slightly different promises than apps, bars, or even community centers. Rather than a house of prayer that neatly contains all people, the church is a chaotic urban assemblage, a specifically religious queer space where people congregate in their vulnerability, nonsovereignty, and repudiated desires, perhaps in the hopes of being made sovereign but perhaps also desiring something more.

But if MCCT proves a rich study in the affective, spiritual, and urban dimensions of queer citizenship, what makes it "queer" in a subjectless or improper sense? As a denomination, UFMCC has been theorized (Warner 2005) as grounded in an essentialist rendition of LGBTQ identity—less "born this way" than "God made me gay," although choral renditions of the Lady Gaga anthem are certainly a staple at many UFMCC worship services, in and well beyond Toronto. Indeed, it is impossible to separate the denomination's history from its provenance in identity-based political movements. Yet such attachment to essentialism is by no means universally shared or unambivalent within the contemporary MCC movement. Indeed, denominational officials and congregational leaders have long and vigorously rejected labeling the UFMCC as "the gay church," which many regard as theologically delegitimating or a misconstrual of the church's more broadly inclusive promise. Both MCCT and the denomination espouse more wide-ranging ethicopolitical ambitions, as in MCCT's official vision, "to be Canada's leading progressive diverse community of faith" (MCC Toronto 2016). The denomination's mission statement, likewise, links UFMCC to a broad swath of human and civil rights concerns, addressing racism, ageism, and sexism alongside and intersecting concerns about sexual orientation and gender identity (Universal Fellowship of Metropolitan Community Churches 2014). In some of its transnational circulations, UFMCC is known not as "the gay church" at all but as "the human rights church." This theologically grounded political pursuit of civil and human rights, broadly conceived, has attracted a growing number of heterosexual-identified people to many UFMCC churches, a point of pride in some congregations eager to contest branding as a "gay church." While numerous critics of human rights have demonstrated the whiteness tacitly understood as the sum total of the "human" in much human rights discourse, such a pivot also needs to be understood as a fruitful negation of the church's identitarian proclivities and an intelligible way of permitting the church's social justice ministry to embrace concerns beyond the narrow scope of LGBTQ identity politics. A 2011 congregational survey suggested that 20 percent of MCCT members identify as heterosexual. Some congregations, such as MCC San Francisco, have openly embraced and branded themselves as "queer" in a subjectless sense, positioning themselves as welcoming a wide range of abjected and pathologized subjects—people without housing, national status, financial means, or sexual respectability, broadly conceived (see Gerber forthcoming)—within and beyond an LGBTQ idiom.

Queerness does not have the same institutionalized uptake or even vernacular purchase at MCCT as at MCC San Francisco, yet I refer to it throughout this project as "queer church" in order to frame the moments—scenes, acts, encounters—in and through church that enact an improper queer citizenship. Because people come to church in their nonsovereignty and incoherence, with repudiated desires they may hope to make legible or redeemable through religious space, church can act as a site that consolidates identitarian, homonationalist, and homonormative subjectivity. But my research also points to moments when ethical encounters with nonsovereignty and vulnerability breathe new life into political desire and subtly, impishly inflect debates within the church and the church's engagements with nation-state power and identitarian idioms. In its most critical and expansive moments, MCCT nurtures forms of political action and affective attachment that extend far beyond essentialized identity. The same can be said for the UFMCC denomination. While it remains indelibly shaped by its genealogies in identitarian LGBTQ politics, the MCC movement has been hailed within Christian communities, particularly the World Council of Churches, for two historic theological and liturgical developments with wide-ranging implications in excess of politicized identity: open communion and sex-positive theology (Wilson 2013). It is thus by coming back to church and returning to the repudiated sexual—an affect we might think of as "figurally" queer—that the MCC movement can make political and theological interventions that are profoundly improper (Georgis 2006; Edelman 2004). Much as in Sedgwick's insight quoted earlier ([1997] 2003, 150) that it is often the most paranoid-tending people who can experience the most reparative insights, I am arguing here that it is often spaces dismissed variously as "identitarian," "small," "fringe," or "(neo)liberal" that can nurture the most surprising, capacious forms of improper queer citizenship. It is precisely in ostensible "smallness," boundedness, and queer damage that church can, in its best moments, prove so capacious, "big," and subjectless. It is exactly because the church can be such a frustrating and unlikely object for subjectless queer critique that it illuminates the affective sophistication that improper queer citizenship requires—and the centrality of the depressive position, rather than voluntarism, to queer reparativity.

Just as I am arguing that citizenship needs to be approached as multiple and multiscalar, so too, then, does the work of repair. The subjects whose insights populate this book work to repair multiple objects—church and citizenship—simultaneously. The very mission of the MCC movement is one of psychic and spiritual integration—finding elements and fragments in Christianity, which long seemed almost overdetermined as a "bad" object for queers, that are worth repairing, and incorporating them into broader political world-building itineraries. The task of reconciling LGBTQ identity and Christianity can too easily be written off as liberal, identitarian, or in pursuit of a politics of respectability. Yet, because repairing religion also entails working through conflicting feelings of love and hate for the religious object, it can also productively give way to experiments in being collective that need not cling to the surety of marked religious or sexual identity. Donald Winnicott (1953) positions religion as exemplary of his concept of "transitional space," a space at the boundary of "me" and "not-me" that offers subjects a "respite from the strains inherent in coming to terms with a world that does not comport with one's wishes" (Parker 2012, 139). It is precisely in such a transitional—in this case, religious—space that people can enact a more playful relationship to the burdensome requirements of marginalized or politicized identity. In this regard, it is by being—and playing—in MCCT as a queer church that people can *become,* that possibilities for being collective can multiply. In repairing their relationships to religious community and to citizenship, in making room for multiple objects and making repair at multiple scales, people do the affective work that coalitional politics requires. Rather than approach MCCT through the schema of the oedipal triad—in which a relation to God or a religious authority figure inexorably reinstantiates a paternal relationship (Freud 1989 [1927])—I use the narrative lens of object relations to open up a multiplicity of objects here, precisely to map the alternative possibilities for affective citizenship and coalition politics that emerge in church. This project thus adds additional affective layers to the burgeoning literature on the ways that progressive faith communities recast normative understandings of both religion and citizenship (see Hondagneu-Sotelo 2008; Yukich 2013).

To date, scholarship on UFMCC churches has productively explored the persistent tension between the movement's essentialist historical trajectory and its more capacious or at least liberal universalist framings as a "house of prayer for all people" or a "human rights church." Largely focused on churches within the United States, such scholarship has traced the contradictions between the theological promise of inclusion and the limits to that promise imposed by everyday practice (see McQueeney 2009; Sumerau 2012). Without theorizing UFMCC in terms of citizenship, this work implicitly frames MCC's promise and limits in terms of U.S. sexual citizenship claims. Another strand of literature that includes (Wilcox 2003; Rodriguez and Oullette 2000) and extends beyond (Reid 2010) the United States charts how MCC churches inaugurate the possibility of integrating a range of sexual, religious, gendered, racialized, and ethnic identities—attachments that are normatively construed as discrete, if not irreconcilable. Building, then, on scholarship that approaches MCC churches either as sites of political contradiction *or* as sites of affective integration, this book brings the two strands together. By more fully theorizing the UFMCC movement as a space of *citizenship,* I aim to map simultaneously the contradictions of belonging in church and the ways people affectively negotiate, exploit, and work through those contradictions. Taking exposure of contradiction as a starting point rather than an end in itself enables me to map MCCT as a live, affectively dynamic and contested site of citizenship—open to interventions resonant with the spirit of subject-less queer critique. Moreover, given UFMCC's considerable transnational circulation and purview, an approach to the church as a space of multis-calar citizenship and multiscalar repair can help us better understand the multivalent character of contestations in and through church, within and beyond nation-state citizenship.

A *House of Prayer for All People* simultaneously contributes to a broader effort to dislodge the position of religion, alongside citizenship, as a default bad object for much feminist and queer scholarship and activism. As Ann Pellegrini (2009) persuasively argues, rigidly insisting on religion's univer-sally corrosive and irredeemable status comprises a key means by which feminist and queer social formations, particularly in the academy, remain normatively white and occlude alternative genealogies of queer and femi-nist inquiry and struggle. "Seeing religion as enemy (a seeing that is also a kind of structured un-seeing)," she writes, "produces a 'white' geneal-ogy of both queer and feminist studies by, among other things, leaving to the side the women of color and transnational feminisms whose relation-ships to religion have historically been far more complex and variegated. This is not the same thing as unambivalent" (208). Indeed, I would suggest that secular radicals of any stripe who are seriously interested in coali-tion among differently marginalized people but balk at the attachments to religion described by the subjects centered in this book, many of them racialized people, do so to their own detriment. My point is not to mobi-lize the figure of the religious person of color as a sign of authenticity or an untouchable trump card meant to bait secular queer critics into accus-ing that subject of "false consciousness." Rather, by reflecting on sustained ethnographic work in queer religious community, as opposed to a more functionalist or a priori analysis of religion (as mere opiate or vehicle of respectability), this book sheds light on the affective complexity and ca-pacity to tolerate anxiety and ambivalence, as well as the conviviality, that characterize many differently marginalized people's affective relations to church as an object.

Indeed, the turn toward affect in much contemporary scholarship, Pellegrini (2009) contends, inexorably demands a reckoning with reli-gion, because the secular discourse of "tolerance" often trotted out to defuse the fraught affectivity of the contemporary politics of difference is itself a "Christian sexual structure of feeling" (214). Whether in queer and/or religious polities, Pellegrini observes, people participate in affectively laden rituals and performances meant to secure injured or impugned identity. Crucially, in staging injury, such collective performance of identity simultaneously disavows *and* avows identity's fragility and nonsovereignty, making religious and identitarian spaces particularly fecund spaces for examining subject formation. In a related vein, Wendy Brown (2015) suggests that greater attention to nonsecular, nonsovereign affects—she points to the accounts of self-discipline and submission to higher authority in the works of the Reverend Dr. Martin Luther King Jr. and Socrates—proffers alternative genealogies and practices of freedom, genealogies that depart from liberalism's sovereign, rights-bearing acquisitive and atomized subject, which buttresses so much identitarian politics. Pellegrini's and Brown's more contemporary interventions resonate with the earlier observations of Winnicott, who held that while religion did in one sense comprise an illusion, that very illusory character could, under the right conditions, afford access to creativity, to improvised rather than imposed forms of ethics, more concerned with the play of belief than with the neatly delineated coordinates of identity (see Parker 2012, 140). Together, such scholars hold out the possibility of reading identitarian social formations, including both queer and religious polities, for nonidentitarian affects, affects that might provide the "groundless grounds" for more capacious ethical and political sensibilities and practices.

Indeed, such affective relations can provide an important environment for the kind of empathetic political engagement I am framing as vital to improper queer citizenship. I have long (and no doubt wrongheadedly) been resisting narratives about repairing the religious object—about integrating LGBTQ and religious identities—as always already identitarian. And indeed, many of the people I met at MCCT—those who advocate the tokenizing approach to diversity I recount in chapter 1 or a celebratory relationship to police, for instance—did come to the church primarily for identity affirmation. Yet, at the same time, the moments of improper queer citizenship in this book are significantly informed by religious affects: racialized worship leaders' sustained attachments, Rev. Hawkes's legible public authority as a faith leader, aspirations to a nonmissiological global ministry, and the prospect of nonidentitarian hospitality. Indeed, much of what makes MCC Toronto a potentially generative *and* often limited site for subjectless queer critique is that repairing religion and repairing citizenship are *not* always correlated—but sometimes are, to powerful effect. "There is," psychoanalytic religion scholar Eric Santner (2001) sagely remarks, "often a thin line between the passions infusing our engagement in the world and our defenses against such engagement, between what is genuinely enlivening in the world and what is 'undeadening' in it" (19). This book considers both the moments when repairing a religious object leads to a point of closure toward sovereign, liberal gay identity politics, and when repairing religion also enables a more creative and capacious approach to queer citizenship.

Likewise, this project derives inspiration from scholarship in religious studies and theology that seeks to critically reevaluate conservative Christians' synechdochic claims to stand in for and exhaust the legitimate possible permutations of Christianity. Such writing considers both (at times unwitting) Christian contributions to queer movements and the figural, affective queerness lurking in Christian theologies and practices of belief. Focusing on the United States, religious historian Heather White (2015) situates the sure-footed status of Christianity as a bad object for queers as a profoundly recent, and even then partial, event. Liberal protestants, White argues, show up unpredictably in the history of sexuality, popping up all over the place in twentieth-century debates: embracing a science of personality that helped consolidate the figure of the "homosexual" in dominant Bible translations, at first welcoming therapeutic "cures" for homosexuality, and campaigning vigorously against antihomosexual discrimination well before Stonewall. And Anthony Petro (2015) considers how sexual "puritanism" became a key foe for gay activists in the early years of the AIDS crisis—and how this either/or figuration ("queer" versus "Christian") attempted to render discrete religious and queer polities that in fact prove far more interpenetrating and intertextual. Petro performs an innovative reading of a bold and well-known 1990 ACT UP New York demonstration at Saint Patrick's Cathedral in which a protester decrying church homophobia and silence on AIDS crumbled and destroyed a sacralized Communion host, which in Roman Catholic doctrine literally comprises the body of Christ. Rather than fortify oppositional mappings of Christian versus queer, Petro points out that such a deliberate and particular form of "sacrilege" was born of intimacy with church doctrine and intended to make a protest that would be legible to Roman Catholics. What would it mean, he asks, to understand such protests as both adamantly secular and profoundly religious? These and other scholars encourage more careful reassessment of the potential for both painful intimacy and, at times, solidarity and conviviality at the intersections of Christian and queer ways of being collective.

But arguing against religion as an always already bad object for queers also requires careful situation of the religious community in question among other communities of faith and other sacred objects. My aim in this book is neither to redeem Christianity nor to endorse Christianity in general, or even liberal Christianity in particular, as somehow better positioned or suited to the task of fostering a capacious, nonidentitarian topos of citizenship over and above other faiths or practices of belief. Indeed, the history and historical present of Christianity prove gravely imbricated with the violence of colonial missiology; dominion theology; just-war doctrine and its genocidal consequences; disingenuous prosperity gospels; twisted justifications for enslavement; deep institutional misogyny and homophobia; complacency and complicity in the face of multiple genocides and genocidal occupations; and the practice, naturalization, and impunity of a wide range of forms of abuse. In the Canadian context, Paul Bramadat and David Seljak (2009) point to the centrality of bitter conflicts over race, gender, and sexuality in animating a general waning of interest in mainstream Christianities, notably including sustained battles about feminine submission, nonnormative sexual and gender identities, same-sex marriage, reproductive freedom, and women's leadership; ongoing practices of sexual abuse with impunity and, in many instances, tacit church assent; and church complicity in the deracination, cultural genocide, and rampant abuse of indigenous people through residential schooling. I am not an apologist for these atrocities.

Moreover, there are no doubt many political and spiritual communities—communities that anchor their ethicopolitical practices in a wide range of beliefs and empyreal object relations—that harbor or realize the potential for a capacious citizenship in excess of the idioms of politicized identity. In Canada alone, one need only turn to the hard work of non- and post-Zionist Jewish congregations and individuals, including many members of groups like Queers against Israeli Apartheid and Independent Jewish Voices Canada; or the capacious anticolonial and antihomophobic sensibility nurtured at the Toronto Unity Mosque; or the religiously diverse, deeply spiritual and proleptic work of Black Lives Matter Toronto; or the bravery in submission to her own ethical values of former Attawapiskat First Nation chief Theresa Spence, who went on a six-week hunger strike to demand reparation from a negligent and abusive

Canadian colonial state. There are many, many stories worth telling about the braiding of affect, belief, and emancipatory politics. Part of what motivates my especial focus on MCCT, however, is *precisely* its positioning as a large Protestant Christian church within Canada, a nation-state in which Christianity is normative. Indeed, MCCT, like all Christian churches, benefits from what David Martin (2000) has called Christianity's "shadow establishment" as a tacit state religion, and no less so in the era of "multiculturalism," in which public policy governing religion has largely been silenced and subsumed under the secular idiom of managing immigration and integration (Biles and Ibrahim 2009). I argue that MCCT's positioning as a liberal Protestant Christian church in a hegemonically Christian country is not unrelated to its broad political salience and intelligibility as a political actor. What makes MCCT particularly interesting, then, becomes clear in moments when the shadow establishment of Christianity in Canada, its axiomatic and (unthought but) felt normativity, produces unintended consequences—moments when Christianity's pretensions of universality, for instance, are repurposed to the ends of an improper queer citizenship. This study of MCCT, then, is in part a study of the queer, perverse, and ironic—and in moments, perhaps, ethically and politically emancipatory—legacies of Christian hegemony.

Finally, this book springs from my long-standing personal interest in, and attachment to, progressive churches as spaces where people go to feel political, and, as Lauren Berlant might put it, to feel possible. It is precisely my own ambivalent intimacy with liberal Christianity that makes me most compelled to contribute to an immanent critique of it. As Donna Haraway (1997) writes poignantly of the fraught work of immanent critique, "It is a rule for me not to turn a dissolving eye onto straw problems, not to 'deconstruct' that to which I am not emotionally and politically vulnerable" (348). Although the when, where, and why of people's attachments can often be hard to pin down, my attachment to liberal church can in some sense be dated to the fall of 2004, when I started attending a Unitarian Universalist church in Waukesha County, the heart of conservative Republican power in the state of Wisconsin. George W. Bush had just been reelected on a platform of preemptive war and family values, the state of Wisconsin was gearing up to enshrine a ban on same-sex marriage in its constitution, and then–Milwaukee County executive Scott Walker was wreaking havoc on public transit and mental health services in Milwaukee County. I was seventeen and had been out as gay for a little over a year, and shifting family dynamics afforded me just enough freedom to start going to a lefty church, despite the fact that some of my evangelical relatives considered it "cultish." Having been raised in a mainline Lutheran church that had always harbored warm individuals but ultimately felt tepid to me, I could have just as easily stopped going to church altogether. But perhaps precisely because I had been raised in a somewhat middle-of-the-road flock, both theologically and affectively, the UU church felt exciting and welcoming to me. This church had no doctrine or creed, but it did have antiracism and antihomophobia workshops, progressive sex education, peace conferences, and rallies against U.S. imperialism, the death penalty, and nuclear proliferation.

My attachment to church included but also went beyond the liberal preoccupation of reconciling LGBTQ identity with religious community. But the excitement also went beyond shared political projects. I'm not entirely sure why, but it mattered to me profoundly that this was not a political party or a community center but a *church*. Perhaps my attachment to church had to do with a sad, implicit sense of the constraints of the sociosymbolic order—a feeling that it was impossible to be politically intelligible in the United States without religion. But there was also a profound affective draw to this place that turned to metaphysical values rather than to nation or even God to actively affirm marginalized people, in contrast to the (then) lukewarm nondiscrimination of the Lutherans and of some secular liberals, or the active antipathy of a wide range of conservative Christians. Long before I ever read Winnicott, I would think of church as a place where I felt "held"—free enough to experiment. I'm sure that not everyone would feel that way there. The place was not without profound constitutive exclusions—particularly in terms of race and class. But, for me at the time, it was a good-enough object. In the middle of middle America, a landscape where homophobia, sexism, racism, arrogant class privilege, and bellicose Christianity seemed so consolidated, so sure, so airtight, there were also wise old dykes lighting candles, making protest signs, praying, singing about the divine spark in all beings, and befriending me. There was surprise. There was repair.

My undergraduate education—through coursework and through friendships—challenged me to account for the racial and class formation of my sexual politics, and my fantasies of repair in church. I brought my new preoccupations with intersectionality theory and Foucault's all-encompassing topography of power into worship with me at the next church I became part of, a small, scrappy South Minneapolis congregation called Spirit of the Lakes. Like the UU church, it was predominantly white, but it was also way more Christian, predominantly queer, and predominantly working-class. The congregation had an AA feel to it: we sat in folding chairs, facing one another in a circle in a warehouse the church board later learned was on a contaminated-waste site. The open, personalized Communion service at that church remains one of the most resonant spiritual experiences of my life. I formed friendships with the minister and several congregants, but mostly I struggled to integrate the critiques I was engaging with in class and with friends with what we were singing on Sundays. One Sunday, I gave an earnest, inelegant, pedantic guest sermon, calling out the character of this predominantly white queer congregation's use of black gospel idioms on terms that I worried were appropriative. The sermon's ambivalent reception in the congregation—particularly from some of my friends of color—invited me to confront the affective dynamics of white antiracism, which can prove self-serving, paranoid, and overly preoccupied with its own persecutory anxieties rather than answerable to the complexity of its neighbors.

My time at MCCT has felt different from the initial plenitude I experienced among the UUs and the heavy-handedness I brought to my time at Spirit of the Lakes. But many of the key elements from my relationships to other churches are present in this project: paranoia and repair, affective integration and its political potential, sexuality and race, faith and citizenship. While I have come to MCCT wearing a research hat first and foremost, I still carry my desires for specifically religious grounds for a capacious citizenship. Thanks in significant part to rigorous scholarly interlocution, though, I have become less interested in applying conceptual critiques than in understanding how I might better learn from and, if mutually desired, work with people contributing to an immanent critique of the church as a space of citizenship. I hope this book comprises a better attempt at an integrative relationship to church, both in the affective sense of piecing together contradictory fragments of the church as a political space and in the analytical sense of producing a more careful and gentle synthesis of critique and empirical engagement.

Methods; or, Walking to Church

My inquiry into MCCT and its potential to nourish an improper queer citizenship took me in all kinds of directions, but those lines of flight emerged from two primary research techniques: participant-observation in church and related scenes of being collective; and semistructured interviews with congregants, church leaders, and outsiders familiar with the church with relevant perspectives on faith and LGBTQ politics. While very little data from formal LGBTQ or public archives made it into the book, I also spent some time in archives—a process I describe at length in chapter 2.

First, and significantly, going to church was the departure point but not the limit for participant-observation. I attended church services at MCCT regularly (three to five times a month) for just under three years, from February 2011 through the Christmas Eve service in December 2013. I largely focused on the Sunday service at 11 a.m., rather than the services at 9 a.m. or 7 p.m., for two key reasons. First, the middle service garners the most attendance and the most attention from visiting public figures. More than any other service, 11 a.m. showcases many of the church's most explicit engagements—sometimes celebratory, sometimes prophetic—with state power at multiple scales. Second, and as I detail in chapter 3, the 11 a.m. service is also webcast live and followed by hundreds (in some cases thousands) of weekly viewers in dozens of nation-states, making for an interesting study in how visual technologies old and new recast and rescale the intimate and the social.

When I first began attending church services, I tended to focus my attention on the "lessons for life," or sermons, with a critical eye toward how they might consolidate or interrupt dominant discourses on sexuality, faith, and citizenship. Over time, however, I began noticing other layers of ritual and sociality: the way people held out their hands during a musical rendition of the Lord's Prayer; the two women who seemed so rapt as they signed "Amen" in American Sign Language during the closing song every Sunday without fail, and the way others also noticed and counted on them to do so; whether and how people clapped, or danced, or didn't; side comments in meetings, uttered by someone but reverberating as if thought by everyone or no one. Sunday services cued me in to some of the ways that group bonding works at MCCT—around the charisma and celebrity of the Reverend Dr. Hawkes, certainly, but also through music, ritual, intimacies cultivated in volunteer work, adult spiritual education, and retreats. In addition to Sunday services, I participated in a church men's retreat in June 2013, and regularly attended meetings of the MCCT Social Justice Network from the summer of 2012 through the summer of 2013. On the retreat and in committees, I made a point of letting people know that I was there as a researcher as well as a person with shared attachments and preoccupations. In church services, people who shared my pew occasionally asked me if I was a writer or a journalist, and I would take the opportunity to clarify who I was and why I was there. After services, I would linger in the social hall—a space that can feel alienating, awkward, chatty, friendly, cruisy, uptight, or crowded—chat, grab a cookie or two, and check out the church thrift store. Alongside church services and meetings in Toronto, I attended worship services and workshops at the General Conference of the UFMCC in Chicago in July 2013. Taking advantage of the occasions that academic conference travel proffers, I have also attended services at MCC churches in Chicago, Los Angeles, Minneapolis, San Francisco, and Washington, D.C.

But perhaps the simplest and most evocative way to describe my research process for this book, and to situate that work in the geographies of Toronto, is to give an account of my (at least) weekly walk from my apartment to church, the conditions that enabled that routinized journey, and the conditions it evinced.[3] I have always been something of a prolific walker—at just over 6'1" and usually at least lightly caffeinated during research, I find my strides get me around fairly expeditiously—a capacity only slightly attenuated as I have recovered from a nasty ankle fracture I experienced one month into drafting this manuscript. While I sought to privilege the convenience of my interview subjects over my own, and also relied on public transportation to conduct interviews, whenever feasible I tended toward walking all or part of the way.

But long legs are only part of the story. I had the privilege of being able to live on my own as a renter in a centrally located apartment in downtown Toronto over the course of researching and writing this book. Though I certainly lacked the resources of the one-bedroom-condo dweller who in many respects comprises the ideal-typical subject of much real estate development in downtown Toronto (Kern 2010), in other respects I indubitably comported with one prevalent profile of that subject: I was a single, childless, university-educated, gay, cisgender white man from a middle-class family, with the arbitrary, unearned good fortune of being able to call upon resources in times of need that most others simply cannot. Indeed, Toronto's soaring housing markets and escalating sociospatial polarization (Hulchanski 2010) would render impossible for most people in the city, especially those with dependents, the type of independent, quiet life I was able to eke out in order to read, conduct interviews, reflect, and write.[4] The mayoralties of Rob Ford—which provided more in the way of antics than administration—and his somewhat more sedate successor, John Tory, have done little to ameliorate the stark inequality in the city's property taxation scheme and housing strategy, and even their hands are tied by a governance structure that privileges Ontario provincial officials favorable to real estate developers over local and municipal control (Boudreau, Keil, and Young 2009).

During the time of my research, I resided in downtown Toronto's Ward 27, the city's most populous and fastest-growing ward and the top location for condominium permit applications at the time of this writing. I lived just south of Wellesley Street between Yonge Street and Church Street—two thoroughfares that have comprised important, though by no means sole, centers of gravity for (some) Toronto queers since at least the late 1960s (Nash 2006). My literal, concrete path from "the gay village" to MCC Toronto tendered a small but telling glimpse of the city's downtown east side, long the site of a swath of crucial social services and what one writer appositely calls "a cradle of low-income housing" (Spurr 2015), and of the steep contours of Toronto's landscape of class and racial inequality. (For many of my interview subjects, particularly asylum seekers who sought affordable housing farther from the downtown core, accessing the LGBTQ social services within a five- to ten-minute walk from my apartment would likely take well over an hour.) My walk to church took me south, to Carlton Street, past a posh supermarket seen as an anchor of gentrification in the neighborhood (Costa 2013), and the site of a high-rise condo development slated to go up where a gritty mixed-class gay bar used to be, and then southeast, through Allan Gardens, a ten-acre park containing six greenhouses. The gardens' frothy history—of uprisings against capitalism and fascism, first-wave feminist organizing, and a gay men's cruising area (Ball 2015)—remained palpable, if muted, in the nervous glances exchanged by middle-class condo dwellers at the dog park and precarious, street-involved folks napping or enjoying one another's company on park benches, sometimes over a beer. The southeast end of the gardens brought me to Gerrard Street, a key and idiosyncratic thoroughfare connecting the city's historically working-class East End with the street's terminus downtown. I remained on Gerrard, which curves slightly at Parliament Street and felt a bit like walking on a fault line, especially as I traversed the camber of the streetcar tracks at that intersection, a feature that can make cycling somewhat perilous.

Neighborhoods to the south, like Regent Park and, more recently, Moss

Park, have been the targets of controversial urban revitalization efforts that replace publicly subsidized community and affordable housing with mixed-income development (August 2008). So-called priority neighborhoods, these and other zones of working-class, racialized sociality have been subject to disproportionate policing by the controversial TAVIS, or Toronto Anti-Violence Intervention Strategy, and have seen organized resistance to redevelopment by antipoverty and neighborhood groups (Walcott 2014; Martínez 2011). The neighborhoods lie somewhat uncomfortably adjacent to Cabbagetown, a historically working-class Irish neighborhood that has seen a slow gentrification since the 1970s, where small Victorian row houses chock full of leaded glass now sell for well over a million dollars, and where strollers the size of small tanks and designer bicycles crowd hip espresso shops that don't serve decaf. Gerrard eventually transects the Don Valley Parkway and the adjacent lower Don River, a somewhat grim, gray trickle that one environmental historian aptly described as "an ugly and neglected place" but that paradoxically animates much athletic and social life for downtown East End residents, perhaps simply because it's what one has to work with (Pitman 2011). The east side of the Don at Gerrard features a gate announcing the upcoming commercial strip around the nexus of Broadview and Gerrard as one of the city's six Chinatowns. Though the main streets are lined with Chinese and Vietnamese food and clothing retailers, duplexes, and doctors' offices, if I took just a few steps off the major streets—say, a block north to Simpson and a block east to Howland—the largely residential environment felt considerably whiter and more affluent. MCC Toronto sits at precisely that pleasant junction.

I recount this journey at length in order to place MCCT, on social, political, geographical, and affective terms, within a city hailed for its multiculturalism and embrace of sexual minorities but also made tense by rapid gentrification and marred by harrowing racial and class inequality (see Catungal 2013). The destination of MCCT might feel comfortably middleclass and normatively white, but the itineraries through this city that eventuate at church—on foot or by any mode of transit, or in the lives of anyone who worships there—traverse more complicated histories and geographies of violence, despair, blight, and desire.

I began formal interviews in March 2013. All told, I conducted about sixty interviews—a drop in the bucket for a congregation with a combined online and in-person weekly attendance of more than a thousand. Indeed, both because MCCT is so large (for a progressive church, at least) and because I came to church with a particular set of intellectual, political, and spiritual stakes, I deliberately sought out interview subjects I thought could perhaps tell me something about citizenship: participants in the church refugee program and Social Justice Network; congregational and denominational leaders, especially leaders of color; and volunteers and staff engaged in the church's global outreach efforts. For outside critical perspectives, I also interviewed a handful of Toronto and religious LGBTQ activists who were familiar with MCCT or the MCC movement and engaged it from the outside, either as friends or as somewhat wary or ambivalent coalition partners. In many of these conversations, I regarded it as my task to push interview subjects to go beyond "preaching to the choir," encouraging them to get specific about their visions for social justice and inviting them to become articulate about their political desires and desires for the church.

My interview scenes included bourgeois homes with granite countertops, cramped restaurants, wan and sunless cafeterias, cluttered social service offices, busy hotel lounges, unassuming benches in malls and parks, and so many cafés that the scent of scorched coffee beans continues to waft from one of my bags. Within the amalgamated city of Toronto, my interviews took me from the affluent Beaches and Leslieville neighborhoods in the southeast to Jane and Finch, a low-income, racialized neighborhood on the city's northwest side that is home to some of the asylum seekers I met. When participants agreed, as all but a handful did, I used a voice recorder so as to retrace our conversations later. In all of these encounters, I also took notes by hand, as I have found that a pen and paper can prove less of a bar to eye contact than a screen. Some interviews were hilarious, jocular encounters with what felt like fellow travelers. Others felt awkward, haunted by what Dionne Brand (2005, 5) incisively limns "the certainty of misapprehension" in a city that, as Rinaldo Walcott (2009) observes, is both colonial and postcolonial. As I note in chapter 4, people at times read me as an extension of the church rather than an independent scholar engaging in immanent critique. This impression, likely mediated by my whiteness, university affiliation, middle-class affectation, and residence in a legible downtown gay neighborhood, seemed to bubble up with particular frequency in my conversations with asylum seekers. Still other interviews, though, conformed a bit too closely to an "it gets better" narrative in which the church, the city, and the nation-state are sites of sunny repair. It is certainly possible that my lack of "spark" in response to some interview narratives is symptomatic of my own predilection for paranoid reading—and that the "complex personhood" of those interview subjects continues to haunt my limited vision because I have failed to adequately apprehend it (Gordon 1997, 5). Indeed, it is my intention not to belittle or write off the integrative, reparative spiritual work that the project of reconciling homosexuality and Christianity—identitarian or otherwise—entails in the world, but merely to flag the sets of concerns that most animated my attention at church.

I include this reflection on which interviews I prioritized because it leads me to one crucial remaining caveat. Readers of this book expecting an authoritative or comprehensive history of MCCT, the MCC movement, or queer religious organizing in Canada will likely both find ethnographic material that intrigues them and be disappointed. I am not, strictly speaking, a Canadianist, religious studies scholar, theologian, or historian, but a cultural geographer interested in theoretical and political questions about affect, citizenship, race, and sexuality. Much as Rinaldo Walcott (2003, 15, 26) brilliantly turns to Canada not as a container for blackness but as a site from which to think about the political sensibilities of black diaspora, I find that Canada, and especially Toronto and MCCT, are good to think *with* and *from* about the intersections of racial and sexual politics, in an immanent, unbeholden, and excessive relationship to nation-state citizenship and disciplinarity. Thus, the preoccupations I bring to MCCT both embrace the church's spiritual work of integrating sexuality and religion, and ask after the transgressive affective and political force of repair— wondering, in a sense, "What's queer about queer church now?" I have sought in the chapters that follow to present and work through a series of ethnographic vignettes that simultaneously do justice to people's multiplicity and nontransparency, and support a theoretical inquiry into the kind of affective capacity and sensibility that I contend an improper queer citizenship requires.

1

Too Diverse?

Race, Gender, and Affect in Church

You can't do no coalition building in a womb.

—Bernice Johnson Reagon, "Coalition Politics: Turning the Century"

"Goldilocks" Diversity

I met Grace, a deacon at MCCT and divinity student in her early fifties, near her office for a midday meal on a brittle November day in 2013. Grace had responded to an e-mail I sent to the collective church address for deacons (spiritual leaders who are not paid clergy), seeking interview participants. We ended up at a ramen place just east of Toronto's downtown Chinatown (the greater Toronto area claims at least six such enclaves). Like other MCCT deacons, Grace provided voluntary affective and spiritual labor, leading worship services at the church, serving at MCCT's remarkable weekly open Communion, anointing people for healing, and providing pastoral care (spiritual counsel and witness). Yet Grace also differed from the vast majority of other deacons in her relationship to normative whiteness and Canadian birth citizenship. As J-pop reverberated around us that afternoon and more harried customers shuffled in and out, Grace and I had a rich conversation traversing her upbringing and early adulthood in the Philippines and her experiences as a pro-democracy activist and community development worker during the Marcos dictatorship, all of which ultimately informed her call to ministry as a deacon in a queer church in Toronto. She recalled her first experiences at MCCT, which moved her to tears and ultimately led her to leave the Roman Catholicism that had formed her and sustained her in diaspora.

But the story Grace told that most affected me spoke to one of the key conflicts over citizenship *within* MCCT, one I that had heard about over and over during my research. At the center of this controversy was a mundane but crucial liturgical practice: the selection and scheduling of deacons to help lead worship each Sunday. More specifically, Grace told me, agonism coalesced around which deacons could colead worship together—around which configurations of racialized, gendered, queer bodies most appropriately embodied "the church":

> I remember there was one issue that became so big at that time, at least for us in the deaconate. Because one time, someone said, "OK, [the Reverend Dr.] Brent [Hawkes] always needs a man and a woman assisting him in worship service." So that's fine. "But the man and the woman need to be white and of color." And Adrian [another deacon, who is a black man] and I said, "Well, we'd both like to go on the third Sunday. We'd both like to serve together." And then somebody told us, "Well, you can't do that. That's too diverse."
>
> So the question now of having a conversation with people who are making this decision is, what do you mean by diversity? And what to you is "too diverse"? We cannot have a black man and a brown Asian [woman] together with Brent. It has to be a white woman.
>
> Okay, let's talk about that, because that is not acceptable for me. So it became an issue, and it's still an ongoing issue. I think those things don't go away overnight. People have a comfort level of accepting change, even in their ideology, even in their liturgical worship and the symbols behind the worship. For them, conservatively, it just has to be a man and a woman, and it's preferably white and black or a person of color. So . . . all the more I felt, wouldn't it be more clear for people to see how diverse we are and how welcoming, if they actually see Adrian and me in front?

Grace encountered what I call a "Goldilocks" representational schema for the management of racialized and gendered bodies in worship planning. In Goldilocks representational thinking, the absence of deacons of color is perhaps "not enough diversity," two people of color constitute "too much diversity," and the pairing of one white deacon and one deacon of color is "just right." Likewise, two men leading worship seem too reminiscent of a good old boys' club, two women seem to portend a menacing lesbian feminist takeover, and a man and a woman combination is rendered appropriate—a formula that not only ironically reiterates the heteronormative logic of binary gender but contradicts the church's aspiration with respect to enfranchisement of trans and genderqueer worshippers. Critically identifying such policing practices as unacceptable, but mindful of the persistent character of people's attachments to normative whiteness, Grace marks out the debate over representation in the deaconate as an ongoing avenue of political struggle within MCCT.

The act of policing that Grace recounts—the dubious effort to delineate between diversity's putatively excessive and reasonable variants—evinces the spatial character of political struggles over race, within and well beyond MCCT. Goldilocks logic demonstrates how normative whiteness takes concrete and embodied spatial form. Thinkers such as the Indian Marxist historian Vijay Prashad (2002) and the British antiracist feminist sociologist Avtar Brah (1996) have theorized a politics of "horizontal" or "lateral" encounter and solidarity among differently constituted racialized subjects and collectivities. These writers contrast such sideways solidarities, in which distinctly formed "minor" bodies engage and forge political relationships with each other, with "vertical" relationships between different racialized groups and normatively white forms of authority. In the late-modern Canadian context, the key mechanism for maintaining the primacy of such siloed, vertical relationships between racialized groups and normative whiteness has been the discourse of multiculturalism. Himani Bannerji (2000) points to a white supremacist logic that underpins national multiculturalism and its discourse on "visible minorities." "The construction of visible minorities as a social imaginary and the architecture of the 'nation' built with a 'multicultural mosaic,'" Bannerji insists, "can only be read together with the engravings of conquests, wars and exclusions" (92–93). Bannerji's insight—that multiculturalism manipulates the distribution and juxtaposition of racialized bodies in order to efface difficult histories and keep whiteness at the center—reverberates in Grace's insistence that a Goldilocks approach to diversity is "not acceptable." Such a "gridding" (Puar 2007; see also Massumi 2002) of identities—their intersections and representations—serves to freeze race and gender in place, securing the church as a beacon of liberal tolerance while foreclosing more open-ended proliferations of gender and race. Even though Goldilocks diversity accords a place to racialized people, even idealizes that place, it also delimits the acceptable proportions and parameters of racialized embodiment—an accounting for difference in identitarian queer politics that Judith Butler (1994), with echoes of Melanie Klein, might describe as "an idealization which is not without its aggression" (6). By contrast, the kind of "horizontal" or "lateral" solidarity that Grace advocates—a multiplicity of differently racialized and gendered bodies alongside one another next to the altar, leading worship—comprises a powerful challenge to a more vertical form of engagement that maintains normative whiteness and heteropatriarchy.

I begin with Grace's account of the Goldilocks diversity schema because it throws into relief the braiding of affect and representation in citizenship struggles over race and gender within MCCT and the fraught character of belonging in the congregation for many queers. Perhaps the most "microscalar" in its focus on the politics of church life, this chapter considers what binds and sustains people I refer to as MCCT's "minor" subjects—particularly worship leaders of color and dissident, social justice–oriented queers—in their attachment to this avowedly liberal, normatively white, big-tent institution. Promises of citizenship—material support, social solidarity, sympathy, recognition—can sustain people's attachments to institutions and spaces in which they also experience sometimes-devastating social exclusion. I have begun to demonstrate that MCCT as an LGBTQ institution, though it promises a "house of prayer for all people," is a profoundly contradictory space with respect to the myriad forms of social difference that encounter, collide with, and co-constitute sexuality. Thus, if racialized and radicalized queers have emerged as the idealized subjects of much of contemporary queer critique, the subjects I center in this chapter also sustain what many readers of queer theory might consider almost axiomatically "bad" attachments—to liberal religious community and to a sense of substantive citizenship within it. Seeking to make sense of such attachments, the chapter responds to the question I mentioned in the Introduction, the one my friend Martine described hearing repeatedly from her fellow black queers in Toronto: "Why do you go *there?*"

In endeavoring to understand such vexed attachments, the chapter simultaneously weighs in on leading and ongoing debates among queer, feminist, and antiracist scholars over the relationships among affect and representation. For both psychoanalytic and new materialist strands of affect theory, identities that are capable of being intelligibly represented are only ever a provisional achievement, a momentary coherence, an ephemeral and iterative articulation (Oliver 2004; Massumi 2002). From such perspectives, the project of giving voice to or representing marginalized identity proves contradictory, because representation and recognition tend to crystallize identities that are not organic or solid but both historically contingent and internally incoherent. Though indispensable, critics warn, the reification of politicized identity—even identities at the intersections of multiple forms of oppression—can lead to toxic forms of group bonding; synecdochic slippages whereby dominant elites within a marginal group come to stand in for the entire population; the consolidation of niche markets; and the demarcation of populations as targets for state projects of surveillance or development. Scholars have turned to affect, then, to understand the more complex histories of injury, bodily encounters, and constellations of desire that are only retroactively (or preemptively) narrated through the lens of identity (Georgis 2014). Thus, if politicized identity (e.g., the intersection of Asian, Filipino, woman, lesbian, and Christian) operates ambivalently as both a crucial means of resistance and a complicit vehicle for capture and co-optation, what work can affect perform in troubling, exceeding, or inhabiting identity politics (Puar 2007; Eng 2010)? I venture a reading of claims on and within identitarian political formations like MCCT for affects and political sensibilities that both inhabit and exceed identitarian terms—affects and sensibilities that I argue provide key conditions of what I am calling improper queer citizenship.

Answering both my empirical and my theoretical questions—why some racialized and radicalized people stay attached to MCCT, and what work affect can do to both move and trouble identity politics within the church—requires more sustained engagement with the substance of critiques like Grace's. For many of my interview subjects, claims on racialized and gendered citizenship within the church stem from more layered and multifarious spiritual and political itineraries and praxes beyond it. My interview subjects respond to complex histories and geographies of injury with only tactical recourse to identity as a kind of shorthand, and proffer visions of a "capacious" church—not simply in the liberal sense of making more room for difference but in the sense of affective *capacity* for empathy, play, irony, and solidarity, for being changed by sharing a relationship to the church as a "public thing" (Honig 2013). Such affective capacities, I suggest, are central to practices of improper queer citizenship, which simultaneously engages in concrete politics that requires tarrying with identity *and* displaces the primacy of LGBTQ identity and nation as bases for affinity or solidarity.

Attending to the affective dynamics of people's relationship to the church, I argue that what sustains minoritized people's attachment to MCCT is neither "cruel optimism" nor paranoid identity politics but a complex, integrative form of love, in keeping with Klein's depressive position (Berlant 2011a; Klein 1975). At stake here is not the redemption of "minor" queers' fraught attachments to MCCT nor a disavowal of their conviviality with the church's institutional project. Nor, indeed, do I suggest that MCCT is the only or the privileged site of subjectless queer engagement, including in faith communities. My point in this chapter is not simply that objects of attachment that could, on first glance, be dismissed as "bad"— religious, identitarian, conservative, cruel-optimistic—are (like all objects of attachment) stand-ins, but that some such attachments are imbued with profoundly coalitional political and spiritual sensibilities. Reading identitarian spaces for their nonidentitarian potentiality is a reparative practice that can emerge only from immanent critique, in this case one buttressed by the slow work of ethnography. In contrast to the excessive solipsism with which identity-based politics is often tagged, people contending with racism and sexism within MCCT take what they can from a promising but fraught environment in order to nurture a generous spirituality and an extensive approach to queer citizenship that embrace a wide range of social justice struggles. Even when the church's minor citizens mobilize identity categories such as race, gender, and sexuality to make claims on belonging, I contend that attending to affect enables a more supple understanding of what might otherwise be wrongly dismissed as "mere" identity politics or a "bad" attachment to MCCT, Christianity, or religion writ large. But first: What's so "mere"—or so vexed—about identity politics, anyway?

Who's Afraid of Identity Politics?

Identity-based political movements and tactics have long been subject to criticism in many corners of the humanities and social sciences concerned with radical, progressive, or left-wing politics. Thus, Wendy Brown (1995) theorizes identity political movements' worrisome tendency to impoverish the political by making politics a proxy for unexamined or unprocessed trauma. Brown argues that, at its worst, identity-based politics fetishizes injured social identities, transforming them from contingent effects of historically specific forms of political economic exploitation and cultural domination into stable, traumatized attributes. The productive effect of such a process of fetishization is that a subject consolidates a self-understanding as injured—what Brown calls a "wounded attachment"—and treats the revelation of that injury as the horizon for political action, to the exclusion of contending with the beauty and difficulty of desires for alternative modes of being collective. Brown links political formations that become indissociable from (or indeed, dependent upon the citation of) their injured identities to Friedrich Nietzsche's concept of *ressentiment,* which describes an injured subject's will to vengeance against the self, the Other, and even the passage of time itself. As an alternative to the *ressentiment* of identity politics, Brown calls for a politics of desire: "Given what produced it, given what shapes and suffuses it, what does politicized identity *want?*" (62 [emphasis original]).

Building on Brown, Jasbir Puar (2007) proffers a critique of identity politics informed by more Deleuzian-Guattarian currents in affect theory. Puar (2007; Puar, Pitcher, and Gunkel 2008) critiques what she reads as the mainstreaming of an intersectional (see Crenshaw 1991) approach to identity politics that takes gender, race, class, sexuality, and other vectors of subject formation and social ordering as always already convergent and mutually constitutive. Puar notes that intersectionality initially emerged from the capacious and coalitional sensibilities of U.S. black feminist movements in the 1970s, in response to the profoundly racialized and classed character of violence against women (Puar, Pitcher, and Gunkel 2008). Yet since its formal introduction into academic parlance, in the late 1980s and early 1990s (Crenshaw 1991), Puar notes, the term *intersectionality* has been embraced on terms that depart from those dexterous, emancipatory sensibilities—taken up by state actors as a tool for managing difference and mobilized by well-intentioned activists and students as a seemingly transparent, formulaic diagnostic of "gridded" identity. Drawing on the work of Gilles Deleuze and Félix Guattari ([1980] 1987; see also Massumi 2002), Puar proposes the "assemblage" as an alternative framework for understanding chaotic, violent, or pleasurable encounters among bodies—encounters that are only retroactively narrated through identity categories and politics. Puar prefers the assemblage, a chaotic metaphorical machine in which many component parts affect and are affected by other parts, with no singular or predictable causal agent, to the conventions of intersectional politics because the latter seem only to reinstantiate the same categories and intersections of categories (Puar, Pitcher, and Gunkel 2008).

No modular matrix of identity (at the corner of gender, race, sexuality, class, etc.), Puar insists, can adequately tell us in advance about the interchange of affects, the collision of bodies and sensations that constitutes a given social scene. Intersectional matrices—marked by their "unrelenting epistemological will to truth"—work on essentialist terms, securing or fixing knowledge about populations at the crosshairs of multiple vectors of difference—feminized and queered brown populations framed as objects of "rescue" by the War on Terror, and sexualized brown terrorists whose perverse "mind" the national security state claims to understand (Puar 2007, 216). Yet, in her turn to assemblage and affect, Puar concedes that one cannot scuttle the project of representation or identity-based politics altogether. Rather, she simultaneously avers the necessity of intersectionality and representational, identity-based politics and points out their inadequacy and worrisome hegemony (see also Thrift 2007).

Such critiques of the occlusions and inadequacies of representational politics prove incisive. The domain of representation and subjectivity is indeed both belated and anticipatory, inadequate to an understanding of affective encounters as they actually happen. Yet, as Puar (2007, 207–14) points out, representations of injured identity also take on their own materiality, their own agency, their own life beyond the emancipatory or oppressive intentions of the component or actor that first generated them in a social assemblage. Thus, the co-optation of intersectionality, and its perverse departure from the richly coalitional and imaginative black feminist thinking and movement that generated that term toward an essentialist "gridding" of identities to be targeted for development, salvation, or exploitation, is indeed distressing, and points to the limits and the wiliness intrinsic to representational projects, like all elements in any chaotic assemblage. But if the representational domain remains inescapable, as both Puar and Nigel Thrift suggest, what these scholars ultimately advocate is not simply a "turn" to the realm of affective or the nonrepresentational but an effort to carefully scrutinize the relationships, interchanges, and slippages between and among affects and representations.[1] Indeed, in an important recent rebuttal to Puar, black feminist scholar Tiffany Lethabo King (2015) calls for a project of carefully tracing the affectivity that imbues intersectional and representational politics. King argues that intersectionality theory itself must be read as a critique of representation, that by pointing to the intersections of identities, black feminist theory gestures toward spaces of aporia, where dominant identitarian movements organized around a single signifier break down and where a rich, nonidentitarian "Black feminist love politics" (see Nash 2013) might be fostered.

With these debates at front of mind, I aim here to offer an affective and more-than-identitarian reading of ostensibly identitarian claims on citizenship within MCCT—claims that I argue are too easily dismissed as "merely cultural" (Butler 1998) identity-political demands for recognition. This chapter seeks to add empirical and affective layers to scholarly debates on politicized identity in general and racialized queer affect in particular. It develops an argument for MCCT as a space of ambivalent, complex, loving attachment for racialized and politicized congregants. I pay especial attention to debates about gendered and racialized representation—in worship services, in theology, in leadership—as vectors not simply for identity-based politics but for affectively and politically sophisticated forms of claims making. Reflecting on my fieldwork, I demonstrate that MCCT should be understood not simply as a "bad" religious, conservative, or normatively white object of attachment but as a chaotic assemblage through which possible affective and ethical horizons for social justice movements and possible futures for queer and progressive world-building projects are being debated and recast. Crucially, I do not assume that all instances of identity-based claims making are created equal. Indeed, the claims of people of color and especially women of color work to unsettle the sense of "comfort" or "homeyness" required by a normatively white, bourgeois, and male identitarian queer citizenship. As I argue throughout this book (and I am hardly the first to do so; see Sandoval 2000), one of the forms that resistance to identitarian queer citizenship can take entails tactically trafficking in identitarian idioms in order to enact forms of solidarity in excess of identity politics. Likewise, attending to the affective dimensions of people's identity-based claims points to identity-based politics as shorthand for more complex trajectories and chaotic assemblages of injury and desire (Georgis 2014). Moreover, that worship leaders of color remain attached to the church on the basis of its potentiality, I contend, invites openness to lines of flight and alternative temporalities that might yet recast the politics of difference and citizenship within and beyond the church on representational *and* richly affective terms (Deleuze and Guattari [1980] 1987).

Simultaneously, the chapter participates in debates on race and gender within the MCC movement, providing additional support for complex antiracist and feminist citizenship claims that some in the church habitually disregard or treat as mere complaint. Leaders of both MCCT and the wider denomination have avowed the necessity of ongoing collective work on race, gender, ability, and other vectors of subject formation, and the value but also insufficiency of past efforts.[2] I hope this chapter helps highlight the affective richness, the urgency, and the political vision of the work of church leaders of color, and especially women of color, to realize the church's promise as a space of improper queer citizenship. For many of these leaders, the spiritual and psychic work of making a "good-enough object" out of MCCT both nurtures and is informed by broader political and spiritual itineraries and labors in the city of Toronto.

The bulk of the chapter draws on interviews with worship leaders of color, and particularly women of color, who sustain complex, integrative, loving, and critical attachments to the church as a site of promise, of immanent "queer potentiality," through and despite conflicts over racial representation in worship planning (Muñoz 2009). I focus on longtime worship leaders of color because I found in my fieldwork that leaders simultaneously exhibited strong attachment to MCCT and were able to draw on long histories of the racialized and gendered limits of the church's promise of a house of prayer for all. I also found that leaders' conscious choice to make themselves visible as queer Christians of color in a predominantly white space reflected considerable deliberation and ongoing affective negotiation, and tended to lead to intensified contact with and insight about the experiences of people of color whose contact with the church was (understandably) more ephemeral. My focus on church leaders surely also comprises a limitation, in that it means my interview subjects are on board with the overall project of MCCT, even as they sharply critique it. But one of my key claims in this chapter is that there is no singular project or "point" of MCCT—that, as a queer, religious, and political object, it stands in for a wide range of needs, desires, and possible futures, and is appropriated to a wide range of ends, by people who are also willing to be inconvenienced by being collective in church (Seitz 2013). The question throughout this book becomes one of performativity: what differently situated actors are able to *make* of citizenship within MCCT, what they inhabit its ministries in order to *do*.

I conclude the chapter by briefly discussing another ministry, the church's Social Justice Network, which takes improper queer citizenship beyond the worship space. Many in this small but scrappy group of volunteers, which acts as the church's critical advocacy arm, frame the network as unsettling complacency among churchgoers in a homonormative moment. I demonstrate how the network members conceptualize their faith-based activism not on the basis of identitarian "wounded attachments" (Brown 1995) but in terms of queerness as "not-yet-here"—as continuing to place new ethical and affective demands upon them (Muñoz 2009). At a moment when religious institutions and mainstream LGBTQ institutions routinely have their utility and progressive potential questioned by queer and left-wing critics, the activism of the Social Justice Network is taking on such pressing concerns as global climate change, immigration, settler colonialism, police brutality, and racism—at times breaking ranks with church leadership to articulate more critical positions. Such discernment and critical deliberation over possible horizons and possible futures for LGBTQ and progressive faith movements take on particular significance in the context of Canada, where legal victories on antidiscrimination and same-sex marriage are cited to authorize both teleological claims to have reached the "end" of LGBTQ struggles and complacency among many queers, particularly the most privileged (see Aguirre-Livingston 2011). Approaching queerness as potentiality, as incomplete, as never fully accomplished—as "not-yet"—is crucial to an improper queer citizenship, because it unsettles the homeyness and triumphalism of identitarian queer citizenship and redirects attention to the work that remains, haunting any claim of progress (Muñoz 2009). Activists and worship leaders within the church work to realize improper queer citizenship at multiple scales within and beyond the church, through critical, integrative relationships to religion and citizenship as compromised but potentially good-enough objects.

On Sacred Object-Choices

One consideration seems crucial before proceeding further, however—a caveat that is helpfully illustrated by way of an example. Most of the subjects who populate this chapter have, to paraphrase Margaret Cho (2006), "chosen to stay and fight" at MCCT. But many other people of color in the city have left, or would never desire to engage with MCCT to begin with. I will revisit the question of who stays and who leaves in chapter 4, which examines the church refugee peer-support program and takes on the racist, xenophobic debates within MCCT over whether asylum seekers' attachments to the church are "instrumental" or "authentic." For the purposes of the current chapter, however, suffice it to say that marginalized, politicized, and racialized queers experience the sacred in a whole host of object relations that trouble lines between "religious" and "secular"— from the powerful viral intimacy of barebacking subculture (Dean 2009) to holy community on the black and brown queer dance floor (Allen 2009; Cervantes 2016). MCCT is an important sacred object for many queers, including some queers of color, in the greater Toronto area, but it is not the only one. And for many, it is a place that elicits hesitation, disdain, and skepticism.

For still others, the church is a friend, an institution worth visiting, and perhaps even a pleasant surprise, but not a spiritual home. El-Farouk Khaki, a prominent Toronto immigration lawyer and queer Muslim leader, told me he had a positive but arm's-length relationship to MCCT, largely because he had religious communities and commitments of his own. Toronto's Unity Mosque, a Muslim faith community open to all which was cofounded by Khaki in 2009, had received a community-outreach grant from MCCT to improve its technological capacity to connect with Muslims around the world. Having spent his early childhood in Tanzania and the United Kingdom and come of age in Vancouver, Khaki was mindful of the largely axiomatic "shadow establishment" of Christianity as a hegemonic presence in Canadian life, and leery of the way this establishment scripted Muslims as "minorities," expected to account for their difference and managed by the multicultural state (Martin 2000). Khaki told me that on a visit to Sunday-morning worship at MCCT to accept the grant, he had appreciated the relatively open theology and liturgy of MCCT, the way in which prayers were easily amenable to recitation—at least by a person of any Abrahamic faith—because of their focus on God rather than Christ. "One of the things I like about the church," he told me, "is that it's not so suffocatingly Christian"—so unchecked in its presumption of theological universality. Moreover, given Christianity's history of homophobia, he said, "the sense of queer liberation that is manifest in MCCT is really beautiful."

At the same time, Khaki reflected, there were limits to the similarities between the Unity Mosque and MCCT, and not simply because they represented different faith traditions. In particular, he described to me how Canada's quiet Christian shadow establishment positioned non-Christian organizing around questions of sexuality rather differently from the work of congregations like MCCT:

MCC in Toronto can afford to be seen as "the gay church." We can't afford to be seen only as "the gay mosque." It actually defeats our purpose. Because all it does is, for us it serves to isolate queer Muslims from other Muslims. And what we need to do is we need straight Muslims, or the larger Muslim community, to actually embrace us, or at least accept us, or tolerate us as a beginning step, so that we can start to break down those barriers that remain within those larger communities. And they're not going to be broken down if we are seen only as a gay mosque. MCC can afford to be seen as the gay church because it's not "just the gay church" in other places [i.e., outside the United States and Canada] and because there are churches in Toronto that are queer-inclusive without being queer. It's part of a spectrum. And right now, Unity Mosque is not part of a spectrum. We're it. There is one other congregation in Toronto where open queer folk are welcome. But it's more about, "Well, you're welcome to be here," as opposed to "We're going to actually incorporate you into our theology."

Khaki's point here is decidedly not to put Islam behind Christianity on a teleological, Eurocentric path toward acceptance of gender and sexual diversity; indeed, he is a trenchant critic of colonialism, racism, Islamophobia, and Christian dominance under the guise of secular multiculturalism. Rather, Khaki suggests, in a hegemonically Christian landscape—one in which Muslims are already isolated—the pressures of racism and Islamophobia make solidarity within Muslim communities all the more urgent. Moreover, if shoring up heteropatriarchy in contemporary Muslim communities is understood in significant part as a *reaction* to the painful ongoing legacy of colonial encounter (Georgis 2013), then it will not do "to isolate queer Muslims from other Muslims," because doing so does not address the key conditions that animate conflicts over gender and sexuality within Muslim polities. By contrast, the relative maneuverability of MCCT—its dexterous capacity to break away from other Christian institutions but still inhabit Christian norms, to begin with an identitarian mandate but simultaneously insist on going beyond it, and to toggle between "gay church" and "human rights church"—thus in part comprises a privilege, a perhaps ironic legacy of Christian hegemony.

Focusing on those who stay at MCCT proves important, then, not because the church is the most self-evidently radical or represents the most marginalized constituents, nor because it comprises the horizon for the queer sacred (if the sacred isn't already queer), but precisely because MCCT is in some sense a hegemon, a behemoth, a big tent—a dominant yet contested sacred space where people struggle it out over matters of spirit and citizenship. MCCT remains an object of attachment for thousands of people in the city of Toronto, in Canada, and globally. It is the largest predominantly LGBTQ faith space in Canada, and among the largest on the continent. The church functions as a kind of urban commons for queer people of a range of faiths (and some of no faith), an adaptability or open-endedness that owes not to universality nor even to a strong music ministry or charismatic leadership, but in significant part to the synechdochic slippage between Christianity and faith writ large in the Canadian context (Martin 2000). In an interview I conducted with the queer theorist Lauren Berlant (Seitz 2013), Berlant reflected that she "started working on citizenship in the first place, not because I loved it but because I saw that people saw it as a state where they could imagine being collective, and being willing to be collective in ways that were also inconvenient for them." One might make a parallel claim about MCCT: it proves compelling not because it is predictably subversive but because it magnetizes a vast and heterogeneous public, and thus is perpetually liable to subversion and creative inhabitation.

For the thousands of people attached to it, MCCT comprises what Bonnie Honig (2013) might call a religious variety of a "public thing." For Honig, attachments to commonly shared "things" (anything from public telephones to Big Bird) can work to substantively confer a relation of equality among differently situated people. MCCT is not a public thing in the same sense as a public asset like the Canadian Broadcasting Corporation or Canada Post. But its promise of universal welcome—a culturally and theologically particular, situated Christian message rendered default by the "shadow establishment" of Christianity as normative (Martin 2000)—also opens it to contestation in unexpected ways, among people who may not have previously understood themselves as peers. Honig further suggests that marginalized members of publics might seize hold of common attachments to beloved public things in order to make demands on equitable redistribution. Honig calls for a politics of "catachresis," whereby minoritized subjects deliberately mix metaphors, shuttling back and forth between the particular and the universal, external public thing and internal object relation, in order to legitimate their claims on public infrastructure. What makes following those who have chosen to stay and struggle it out at MCCT compelling is not that the church exhausts the political potential of queer religious polity but that it provides a case study in catachresis vis-à-vis Canada's largest and most dominant LGBTQ religious polity. As we will see, the measure of the church's "pull" comes in how actors within it leverage the church's both marginal (queer, progressive) and privileged (large, Christian) position to emancipatory ends.

"No Rose-Colored Glasses"

As Grace's encounter with the Goldilocks diversity schema evinces, the promise of congregational citizenship, of "a house of prayer for all people," has a highly uneven geography within MCCT—a geography that breaks down in many ways, including and especially along the lines of race. For instance, MCCT and the larger UFMCC denomination often proudly tout a remarkable policy of "open Communion," whereby people may share in the elements of Communion (historically understood as the body and blood of Christ but differently inflected by each participant) without membership in MCCT or any Christian congregation and without passing any litmus test of belief of any kind (Shore-Goss et al. 2013). Yet the question of who performs the labor of serving Communion, or anointing people for healing, proves profoundly fraught and significant, particularly but not only in terms of race, gender, and other vectors of social difference. This promise of universality and the controversies attending that universality's uneven realization comprise the central object of this section. Indeed, many of the self-identified people of color involved in MCCT's ministries described to me a pattern of racialized alienation and burnout. More intense than the routine attrition at play in any volunteer-based nongovernmental organization, this burnout affected congregants and prospective congregants of color with particular acuteness. Many people described concern about limited leadership-development opportunities and cycles of overwork, exhaustion, and alienation for people of color within MCCT. In different ways, whether they are asylum seekers attending the church refugee program and seeking support as precarious people (an experience I center in chapter 4) or Canadian citizens seeking active involvement in church, people of color in the church are scrutinized and shut out by many of their white fellow congregants. Aside from a few core black congregants who had consistently taken on lay (i.e., volunteer, nonclergy) leadership roles, one woman told me, most of the black people at MCCT left within a matter of a few years. Likewise, I heard concerns about limited leadership opportunities for women in the congregation. While the church board of directors formally requires gender equity (a formula that can and should be complicated by nonbinary and genderqueer claims on citizenship in church) and one of the two pastors on the paid staff identifies as a woman, several women I spoke with described concerns about women's roles in leading worship—not behind the scenes but front and center.

Many of my interviewees located experiences of burnout and alienation for congregants of color within a deeper and more structural affective, material, and representational contradiction in congregational life. For instance, Martine, who had been involved in planning and leading worship services for several years, described the church as an organization that put on a moving "show" for visitors but that had difficulty nurturing or making room for the leadership of people of color or white women among its more regular attendees, members, and volunteers. Martine yearned for a day, she told me, when "anyone but gay white men got a chance" to lead at MCCT. While she described her profound appreciation and enjoyment of the church's "good show" and the ideals espoused within it, Martine told me those high ideals of love and social justice held out a promise that was unevenly realized within ordinary life among dedicated churchgoers: "We might sing the right songs or say the right things, but it never applies to our own congregation." When I asked what sustained her involvement at the church, Martine paused. "I'm seeking to find reasons to stay," she told me over a tea break she took from working at Toronto Pride, "but it's exceptionally difficult. There are no rose-colored glasses." Martine's candor and grimness—the absence of rose-colored glasses—made me wonder what kept her at the church, a question we discussed routinely. As I noted in the Introduction, Martine described the church as fitting within her own larger itinerary of creative and spiritual practices, practices that incorporated a range of spiritual traditions within and beyond Christianity, as well as the erotic and spiritual dimensions of BDSM. The space of the church, and Martine's agency within it, seemed to hold out some kind of potential for her to nurture practices of sustenance and transformation, amid and in excess of the norms and hierarchies she described. I remained curious about this potentiality as I interviewed more people involved in worship leadership who identified as people of color.

Likewise, my conversation with Grace about her call to ministry within MCCT, against and despite practices like Goldilocks diversity arrangements, ultimately returned to the theme of potentiality. When I asked Grace how she had heard of MCCT, she replied that another Filipino queer couple had invited her, along with her partner. This answer elicited curiosity for me about the history of Filipino presence at the church. Filipinos comprise the fourth-largest of what the Canadian government calls "visible minority" groups in the greater Toronto area, and Tagalog is the fastest-growing language in Canada (Coloma et al. 2012). Moreover, Filipino and Vietnamese diasporic communities in Canada have been cast as a revitalizing force in Roman Catholicism (McGowan 2008). Finally, I had heard allusions to a short-lived but briefly quite voluminous Filipina lesbian meet-up group at the church that had been popular sometime in the 1990s or early 2000s—allusions that were meant to attest to the church's "big-tent" capacity to nurture and reflect Canadian ideals of multiculturalism. But I had found little concrete evidence of such a group. Grace, who began attending church in the mid-aughts, had no idea what I was talking about. For her, MCCT had always been a space nearly devoid of Filipinos, save for a few gay men, most of whom were in relationships with white men. "Why do you think so few Filipinos come to MCCT?" I wondered aloud.

Acknowledging "Catholic guilt" and its sustained hold on even her own "liberal" psyche, Grace pointed to the persistence of the trauma of expulsion and renounced desire in making MCCT both an enthralling and a guilt-inducing space for many Filipino diasporics, herself included. I didn't doubt the lingering salience of Roman Catholic strictures, sacraments, and silences in the lives of Filipino queers (among many others, including at the church). Still, I was leery of culture-based explanations that chalked up the invisibility (and also the presence) of queer Filipinos at MCCT to the grip of Filipino Catholicism (itself a legacy of Spanish and U.S. imperialisms) alone. I remained equally curious about barriers to participation coming from *within* the church.

So, I tried a different approach, inquiring about the climate for people of color and immigrants at MCCT. Grace launched into a narrative connecting her personal experience at the church with a broader set of concerns and ethical obligations around race, gender, and representation:

> I think it automatically became a responsibility for me to make sure that there is visibility, there is representation, and that there is

active participation. Just like you said, I look around, there's no one else who looks like me. Especially no one else who looks like me in front of the church. And that made a lot of difference for me in the later years of my going more seriously into my spiritual journey as a deacon. I felt that it was important that people see a representation of themselves or somebody who can represent them, or just to encourage more people of such diverse cultures to just come out and play—you know, just come out and play. Let's do this together. Let's create and re-create. But I can't do this alone. And I just felt so much of a responsibility.

And that actually became a challenge for me, in the deaconate that was so white. Save for Adrian and then later on Karen, who was [in] the same batch [of candidates for the deaconate] as I was, when we were discerning for the deaconate, there was no one else. So, I'm the only Asian person of color.

Grace recounted an immediate feeling of self-consciousness; an acute awareness of her visibility as a Filipina Canadian, a person of Asian descent, a woman, and a lesbian in her role as a deacon at MCCT; and a sense of obligation to engage in that representation within a major LGBTQ and spiritual institution. An overwhelmingly white MCCT deaconate, she suggested, lent especial ethical and political urgency to her visibility project.

In moments, Grace's story about her spiritual journey would seem to resonate with the kind of representation-based identity politics that contemporary affect theorists (Puar 2007; Thrift 2007) both acknowledge as politically valuable and find deeply troubling. On the one hand, the underrepresentation of people of color in church leadership, when contrasted with the makeup of the church (to say nothing of that of the city of Toronto), attests to the concrete effects of atmospheric racism within the church, the alienation and burnout described by my friend Martine in the Introduction. On the other hand, a preoccupation with optics, representation, and leadership risks eliding the more diffuse, structural, and affective character of racialized and gendered exclusions within the congregation. (After all, history is littered with racialized people and white women at the helm of institutions and polities that nevertheless remain constitutively exclusive.) As Grace continued, I wondered about both the affective potential and the limits of her visibility project.

However, as she elaborated on her sense of obligation to represent in worship service as a Filipina Canadian lesbian, Grace chronicled robust debates over race and gender in the deaconate—debates that trafficked in but also vastly and rapidly exceeded the domain of representation. In her rendition of the Goldilocks controversies, Grace sought to upend the very multicultural and homonormative logics of representation that trouble critics of identity politics, instead envisioning a more complex distribution of bodies and affects. In the remainder of our conversation, Grace sought to stake out an affective *and* representational alternative to the Goldilocks logic for managing and representing diversity. She described to me where her pastoral and visible role as a deacon fit into a broader, more extensive spiritual and political imaginary, and within the geography of the church and the city:

> How many Asians do you want to attract in a place [Toronto] that is so predominantly Asian? I mean, that is little Chinatown out there [MCCT is located in Toronto's East Chinatown], and do you get Chinese, Asian people [at MCCT]? No. Right?
>
> This is what it means to be radically welcoming. This is what it means to be radically diverse. This is what it means to be having a woman with all of my social locations up there [before the congregation]. Without saying a word, that is a strong symbolism for worship. It's a strong symbolism for liturgy. It's a strong symbolism for spirituality. It will talk on so many levels of what is possible. What is not understood before can now be understood in a whole new way and actually welcome.
>
> So, it has become a responsibility for me. I take it very seriously. When I'm up there, I know that I am able to do—that I am doing that because some people can't. And some people are uncomfortable because of retaliation or, "Grace, you're too forward," or, "Toe the line." . . .
>
> Whether I talk, whether I open my mouth or not, if I occupy that space, it stands for something. It's important, and I take that seriously. And I think that that is a direction that we need to put more focus on. Let us, as we shape our denomination and try to articulate who we are, well, open your eyes a little bit more, why don't you? Because the lenses are different. The way we will give meanings to things might have changed. And so, we have to reshape that as a church.

Grace articulates a theological and ethical vision—a vision with significant
political implications—that necessarily includes, but also necessarily goes
beyond, a "wounded attachment" (Brown 1995) or a reaction to racism and
sexism in LGBTQ institutions. Throughout her narrative, Grace describes
a strong sense of responsibility to represent historically invisibilized identities and communities within a normatively white religious and LGBTQ
context. Yet her description exceeds a liberal economy of representation
that prioritizes making the invisible visible. I read gestures like Grace's invitation to "come out and play," to "create and re-create," as calling for a
spiritual collectivity marked by a more transformative, receptive, dynamic,
and ludic ethos, irreducible to a straightforward rendition of identity politics. "Without saying a word," she explains, the embodied presence of diverse bodies leading worship harbors a different kind of potentiality in
relation to worship, liturgy, and spirituality. Recalling Donald Winnicott's
(1953) appreciation of religious spaces as, at their best, creative and transitional spaces, Grace points to the religious space of MCCT as one in
which the rigid identitarian idioms of "me" and "not me" and the need for
a (homogeneous gay white) home *could* be suspended. Such affective work
within the church, she suggests, could also make the church a more live
site of urban citizenship, a space more responsive to its neighbors and its
difference from itself (Kristeva 1991), not simply more inclusive but more
"radically diverse." At issue, then, is not simply which identities will surface in the church's representational economy but which forms of potentiality, not fully knowable in advance, might be generated in an encounter
among differently racialized worshipping and playing bodies (Lim 2009).

Grace's insight about the potentiality of predominantly nonwhite deacon configurations also struck me in a series of conversations I had with her
colleague Adrian, a deacon and a black gay man with whom Grace is occasionally paired as worship leader (much to my defiant delight and that of
many, though unfortunately not all, at MCCT). In a series of conversations
in coffee shops and more informally after worship services, I asked Adrian
about his reasons for remaining involved in a congregation where he described feeling marginalized yet overworked, particularly when it came
to organizing for people of African descent at the church. Adrian framed
his ministry as a deacon as answering a call beyond the scope of MCCT,
the MCC movement, or any institutional church. His work as a counselor
and provider of pastoral care, he told me, enabled him to provide mentor-
ship and spiritual support, particularly for young queer men of color. His

visibility on Sunday mornings as a worship leader, he suggested, helped underscore not only that the church was an affirming, welcoming space for people of color but that he and other deacons of color were institutionally vetted and supported, and available to provide affective resources to meet the common and unique needs of people moving through the church— people looking for a mentor, a friend, someone to talk to, someone to help them reconcile seemingly incommensurable corners and contours of their lives. My participant-observation experiences at the church persistently bore out Adrian's claims. Sunday after Sunday, when Adrian co-led worship and the time came for Communion, for anointing, for healing, or for informal after-church sociality, people I took to be people of color, including friends of mine, particularly young men, made a beeline for him—in Communion, sometimes walking across the worship hall and interrupting the orderly flow of people just to get in Adrian's line. This observation, like Grace's call to "come out and play," points to the affective *potentiality* immanent in the encounter staged through worship. Adrian's efforts to enact a relationship to the church on terms that felt "good enough" took place within a more multifarious set of affective geographies and practices of citizenship—within the African diaspora, within the greater Toronto area, within queer communities of color.

Adrian's and Grace's encounters with Goldilocks racism in worship service planning and their accounts of the value and significance of their visibility as racialized queer deacons underscore the power of worship at MCCT as a site of material and affective encounter. At a moment when many corners of critical social theory are productively engaged with the more-than-representational and nonrepresentational dimensions of sociality and agency (Thrift 2007; Puar 2007), and when other, less generous corners chide representational politics as insufficiently engaged with questions of political economy (Fraser 1996), engagement with the question of representation may variously register as retro, identitarian, or "merely cultural" (see Butler 1998). Yet I would submit that debates over race, gender, and representation in the configuration of the deaconate in fact point us to an affectively rich and materially distributive struggle. In my conversations with deacons, several people noted that the two key facets of service in the deaconate—worship assistance and pastoral care—could also support each other, because the visibility of deacons at Sunday services can contribute to their recognition by and rapport with congregants seeking emotional and spiritual support. Thus, far from a "merely" symbolic item, the question

of deacon selection can convey an important message about the range of
types of life experiences the deaconate might be capable of helping congregants work through. Visibility in this regard is a matter not simply of
representation, recognition, or identification but of the kinds of encounter
that might give way to more emancipatory and equitable circulation of
the congregation's material and affective resources of sympathy, spiritual
solidarity, and emotional nourishment.

Importantly, Adrian and Grace tell a story that is also about an ambivalent yet *sustained* attachment to MCCT. Both deacons told me it matters to
them to remain at the church in defiance of assertions of normative whiteness that work to foreclose lateral connections among differently situated
people of color, because of the potentiality of the church to nurture alternative means of distributing solidarity and sympathy. Karen, a worship
leader and a black woman, described her state of ambivalence to me by
recounting both moments of violent misrecognition, on the one hand, and
an expansive potentiality for ministry and politics that she locates within a
church she considers a "truly loving place," on the other.

> *Earlier you mentioned—when you were discussing Black History
> Month—representation and the idea that it really matters to see
> people of color who are in positions of leadership. . . . I wonder if
> that has come up for you being a deacon as well, that other people
> see you.*
> Karen: How do people see me?
> *Yeah, like the significance of you being there as a woman of color,
> and being visible in front of the whole congregation and leading.*
> Karen: I know one time I shared my story, and actually it was a
> Caucasian woman who came to me who was raised in Africa,
> who was touched by it. In terms of other—see, when you're
> talking about the black community, you're talking about many,
> many different layers, right? So, some may look at you as
> [though] you've turned whitewashed, right? Some may look at
> you as, "Okay, my sister, thank you, you're representing," right?
> Some may look at you as that.

Karen differentiates between two types of affective encounter, and two
interchanges between affect and representation, in church space. The
first—"I shared my story"—refers to a formalized representational practice

of testimony, of narrating racialized, gendered, sexualized injury and citizenship within a normatively white LGBTQ congregation, a practice Lauren Berlant (2000) describes as participating in a "structure of sympathetic normativity" (43). Yet she also describes more multifarious affective encounters and reading practices among black queers in the pews, fraught encounters with "many different layers." What struck me about Karen's typology—"sharing my story" versus "many different layers"—was its unflappable tone. Karen maps the contours of the variegated structures of legibility and sympathetic normativity that characterize her engagement in the church. Though attached to the church and in sync with many aspects of its stated project, Karen is by no means Pollyannaish about its affective and representational limits.

Karen then directed her critical reflection on representation in church back to the white gaze:

> Karen: Some may not see your face, [they] just see a person of color. For example, Jennifer, who's in the choir, and I are the two black women in the church who are quite visible. Jennifer is very much—we look totally different. Different height, different whatever, different hair. And people who've been going to the church for years and years and years still confuse the two of us together.
>
> *Really?! I mean, I'm surprised, but I'm not surprised. You have such difference voices and different everything. . . .*
>
> Karen: Mmm-hmm, yeah! So, they confuse Jennifer and I. Even with my son. My son has different coloring and I was holding another child, black child, and he was a baby, my son's like seven, and someone who's been at the church for a long time said, "Oh! Is that your baby?" And I thought, "Wow. . . . But you haven't even looked at the face. You're looking at the skin color here."

Karen's experience of the persistent racialized misrecognition or nonrecognition of her face reverberates with long-standing debates across disciplines about race, recognition, and intimacy. Throughout his oeuvre, the Lithuanian-born French Jewish philosopher Emmanuel Levinas (1969) famously emphasizes the primacy of the face as the basis for ethical relation and obligation. For Levinas, the face is reducible not to the human face as such but to an apprehension of anything that reveals the vulnerability of the other—the slump of the shoulders, the small of the back (Butler 2004). It is precisely the recognition of such vulnerability—and the simultaneous recognition of one's capacity to exploit the precariousness of the other— that obligates the subject not to harm the other, even when fear of the other invites her to do otherwise. In *Precarious Life* (2004), Judith Butler engages and expands upon Levinas's thought to map how certain representations of faces might circulate in ways that do not engender attention or ethical response to the vulnerability of the Other. Thus, encounter with the face of the Other is socially and politically organized to enable or foreclose an answer to the Other's vulnerability. In Karen's experience, some white congregants at MCCT reduced her to a generic (non)being at the intersection of "woman" and "black" in the gridded logic of representational politics. Such reduction forecloses engagement with Karen's *face*, her vulnerability, as well as her singularity and specificity—her contributions to the church as a deacon, her spiritual and intellectual offerings to the life of the congregation.

The socially organized character of Karen's experience of nonrecognition also recalls Frantz Fanon's pathbreaking ([1952] 2008) earlier scholarship on the psychic and social dimensions of racial alienation, and prospects for disalienation. Building on Jean-Paul Sartre's ([1946] 1995) work on hate and anti-Semitism in the wake of World War II, Fanon theorizes the role of the white gaze in shaping the collective psychic life and sense of agency of black people. While articulating solidarity with Jewish people's experiences of a range of violences, Fanon also uses the experience of anti-Semitism as a departure point for thinking about how blackness is apprehended and rendered as Other, on terms distinct from Jewishness:

The Jew is not liked as soon as he has been detected. But with me things take on a *new* face. I'm not given a second chance. I am overdetermined from the outside. I am a slave not to the "idea" others have of me, but to my appearance.

I arrive slowly in the world; sudden emergences are no longer my habit. I crawl along. The white gaze, the only valid one, is already dissecting me. I am *fixed*. Once their microtomes are sharpened, the Whites objectively cut sections of my reality. I have been betrayed. I sense, I see in this white gaze that it's the arrival not of

a new man, but of a new type of man, a new species. A Negro, in
fact! ([1952] 2008, 95 [emphasis original])

Fanon describes the alienated, wrenching, yet banalized experience of
being "fixed" by the white gaze, locked in place, alienated from his sense
of individual subjectivity by social entrapment in his racialized positionality (Oliver 2004). Yet, even as he decried the dehumanizing effects of
racism, Fanon was equally leery of efforts to recuperate and romanticize a
black past or pan-African identity, which he regarded as largely useless to
the struggle against capitalism, racism, and colonialism. An anticolonial
revolutionary, Fanon was just as committed to humanism and universalism, and he wanted the struggle to eventuate in a world where he could
"already see a white man and a black man *hand in hand*" ([1952] 2008,
196 [emphasis original]; see also Shohat 2006). The traumas of racism
and colonialism become departure points for Fanon for alternative concepts of the human, alternative forms of relationality, collaboration, and
solidarity.

In a similar vein as Butler and Fanon, Karen critically recognizes that
not all forms of visibility or representation are equal in their power to center the agency of marginalized people or repair historical injuries, particularly when it comes to race. Karen is mindful of the heterogeneous, often
reductive or violent lines of flight (Deleuze and Guattari [1980] 1987) that
might emerge from an experience or affective encounter in church while
she leads worship: she could be dismissed as a "whitewashed" race traitor
at a normatively white institution; she could be affirmed by other black
people as a "sister . . . representing" in a normatively white queer faith
space; or she could be violently fixed by the white gaze, her subjectivity
overdetermined by positionality, rendering indistinguishable her unique,
individual contributions as a deacon.

These experiences of racialized and gendered overdetermination make
Karen less surprised to hear about other people's experiences of exclusion
within the church. But this unsurprised affect is not quite paranoid, nor
does it lead to a resentful, identitarian politics of representation. Instead,
Karen's history of injury and misrecognition by some of her fellow congregants leads her to envision a more capacious church—not only to redress
her own injury but to enfold everyone who longs for "a house of prayer for
all people":

And I know there's been, when I was doing some work with the
refugees, they did talk about how they experienced a lot of racism at the church, which I was surprised at. But considering how
some people don't even see the difference between Jennifer and I,
I thought, "You know, I can see how that could happen." So within
our own walls, we have to do a lot of work. . . .
   I still think there needs to be more of a place for people of
diversity. I don't see one transgender person who stands out in our
community, and we're supposed to support them, right? I see few
Asians. People with disabilities, I don't see. What I see in terms
of majority is what you'd see anywhere else, which is Caucasians,
able-bodied Caucasians, which I think is sad, because we are supposed to be a diverse community.

Karen envisions the church as providing "more of a place"—not for an essentialized group at an intersection of representational categories but for
"people of diversity," broadly conceived. Karen does not stop at decrying
her own violent misrecognition but uses the idioms of politicized identity to imagine a church that embraces more possibilities for embodiment
and for citizenship, rather than a church that boasts "Welcome home"
but ultimately feels homey only for cisgender, middle-class, "able-bodied
Caucasians." Karen's encounters with forms of loss, repudiated difference,
and exclusion in church prompt a reinvigoration of desire for more expansive forms of citizenship within the congregation. The point here is
not to valorize loss as such nor to naturalize the forms of exclusion Karen
and others experience, but to highlight her creative and ethical responses
to conditions (like racism) that produce nonsovereignty, responses that
proffer a radical vision of improper queer citizenship that departs from
the performance of sovereign identity-political subjectivity (Berlant and
Edelman 2013).
   Still, given her mistreatment, and the persistent burnout among leaders of color she and others identified, I wondered what sustained Karen
at the church. Much like Fanon, Karen told me she remains passionately
attached to the prospect of better forms of relationality across multiple
forms of difference, a prospect she describes experiencing in church in
the form of potentiality. Karen continues to see—and to performatively
conjure—possibilities within the church for queerer, more reparative,
more subjectless forms of congregational and global citizenship:

What keeps you at MCCT, given the kinds of barriers that you've talked about to people staying for a long time?
Karen: So what's kept me there. . . . The other part of what I've done is I used to hold wellness workshops. So, I'd have a wellness day, I'd have all different kinds of alternative therapists coming in, just to show people there are other ways of healing beyond the traditional sense, right?
 So, what keeps me there is the possibilities. And the social justice work that we do. I think we reach a lot of people. I do think we do good work, I just think we need to do more *of* it, and have our voice heard in different settings and not just *one* voice, but *many* voices. So, it's the possibility that keeps me there.
 And it truly is a loving place. If you walk in there, you feel the love, right? And I know for me, through all my stages of healing, MCC's always been there. However I've wanted to let MCC in, it's always been there. I think any church, any system, has their problems.

Karen's commitment to practices of affective repair in a racist, sexist, heteronormative world—practices of healing in excess of hegemonic secular scientific idioms—drives her engagement with MCCT. The church makes space available for the kinds of wellness most central to Karen's own spiritual practice, and the availability of that space informs her ability to integrate the good and bad fragments of the church. It is important to note here that Karen does not simply take what she can from the church; she experiences it as a "truly . . . loving place," an object worthy of repair, even as it is a space of disappointment and exclusion. This relation to the church reverberates with Klein's (1975) depressive position, in its loving integration of profoundly disparate fragments of an object, including vile or contemptible ones. This integrative process does not keep Karen from contesting her experiences of exclusion at the church; Karen simultaneously desires and demands a pluralization and proliferation of the church's conceptions of social justice and citizenship. Though identity-based politics is often reduced to the negative, to grievances of an isolated group that lacks a comprehensive or cosmopolitan vision, Karen's imagined proliferation of social justice work points to a more open-ended, unfixed relation between injury and desire.

Because Karen had brought up her own desires, for "more *of*" the church's social justice work, I decided to take a cue from Wendy Brown's (1995) query about what politicized identity *wants* (62) and follow up:

> *I've asked a little bit about the past and the present—things you think could be changed for the better, things that keep you there—but my last question has to do with the future. As you think about where MCC Toronto is going, what are you worried about and what are you hopeful about?*

Karen: Wow, that's a broad question [laughs]. . . . I would hope that we would see more women in positions of power at MCC. There are women in some positions of power, but they're behind the scenes. I'd like to see women in front of the scenes as well, right? In the past couple of years, there's been reverends who have come, but it's been mostly male that we really see. So, what do we do? How do we ensure that we have a diverse group of people around?

I remember when [former MCCT director of congregational life and director of education the Reverend] Jo Bell came to MCC Toronto. The women of the congregation were so excited, because they had a woman who was going to represent them. I think everybody wants to be represented in one way or the other, right? I think that needs to be seen.

Yes, I love Brent, yes, I support him all the way. But there are different lenses. You see the world through different lenses when you come from a different perspective. Like, I sent Brent an e-mail one time and I said, "Just one day of your life, go through your day, imagining you're a black person. See how many images you see around you. See how many positive messages you have about being black. Who is 'okay'? 'Loving'? 'Normal'? And see when you come home how you feel about yourself and why you would think it would be a good thing to see someone of your own race in front of you talking to you." I was trying to say, "You are coming from a very privileged viewpoint. For me, I would walk into a room, and because of the way I've been raised and because of my color and I'm a woman and I'm gay, it's like, I've got a whole bunch of things internalized that I've had to work through because of those things. For you, you are a white male who's gay, you have one thing, but imagine having more than that to work through, and how that affects you. And when you're coming with your lens, and you're portraying life with your lens, you have to understand that not everything is gonna deal with things from your lens."

Here, Karen appears at first blush to engage in the same kind of representational logic that Puar and Thrift regard as necessary but limited. Like Grace, she traffics in the metaphor of "lenses," which seem to describe preexisting categorical views or standpoints on the world corresponding with vectors of identity.

But, following black feminists like King (2015), can we push a reading that would simply dismiss intersectionality and "move on" to affect here, without hearing the difficult affects that propel people to make recourse to intersectional or identitarian idioms? Karen is corresponding with her pastor, after all! What else is going on here? I would argue that when Karen invites Hawkes and other white people involved in MCCT to imagine what it would be like to take her steps, to fight her fight, on an ordinary, quotidian basis, she is not attesting to an isolated experience of trauma or making recourse to testimony as a singular, disruptive political event (Badiou [1988] 2013). Her invitation exceeds the representational, precisely because she is asking the reader or listener to depart from tidy liberal narratives that testify to bounded, knowable and reparable injury. She invites the listener to attune not to the kind of discrete, ameliorable injury represented in liberal race discourse but to what Lauren Berlant (2000) tentatively describes as *suffering:* "a constantly destabilized existence that monitors, with a roving third eye, every moment as a potentially bad event in which a stereotyped someone might become food for someone else's hunger for superiority . . . [connected to] the subjective effects of structural equalities that are deemed inevitable under national and transnational conditions" (43). Karen continued:

I was just trying to encourage him [Hawkes] to see that it's fine to look at things in one manner, but when you are dealing with how many different isms out there, how you walk into a room or what you do with your life can be very different. I know [that] Jennifer, Adrian, and I, we've all had to put up with it. We've all had our "own people" turn on us because they think that we're behaving a certain way or we shouldn't do certain things, or even Caucasian people would say, "You're stepping out of line." . . .

So, it's like we're constantly fighting for something, and someone's trying to tell you, "All you have to do . . ." It's like, "Wait a minute, no. You have not taken my steps, you have not fought my fight." I want to hear someone who's fought my fight to talk about that. We fought the same fight about being gay, but you haven't fought the same fight as being a woman, black, and gay. So, I think those things are important.

So, I'd like to see more representation, because when someone comes to that church, yes, Rev. Brent has an image, he has a name. Seeing someone else that day say something may be the thing that gets them. Like, "Oh, you're one of me, you get where I come from." . . .

Other wishes? I'd like BEAT [the Black Education and Advocacy Team] to come back. I would like HOLA [worship services and fellowship for Spanish speakers] to be more visible within the church, not just for social functions. I'd like to see the transgender group more visible, doing more things within the church. I'd like to see not just the people who have the money be honored sometimes. Because I think, yes, we rely on people who have the money to keep our church going, but [also on] a lot of people who do a lot of work and volunteer who can't give the money. . . .

Concerns? I think if we continue on the same path, with the same kind of agenda, that in terms of diversity, I think we're going to start alienating more people. Our church is changing for the better. Before, we were known as the "gay church," where now we're everyone's church. But if we don't start seeing representations of all those different people, I think we're gonna start losing some people.

Karen responds here to acts of exclusion so routinized they no longer become occasion for surprise—yet, again, her affect is far from paranoid. Though sober about the limits on her church as a space of citizenship, she seems animated by a sense of the immanent potential at MCCT for better forms of relationality in and beyond queer and religious collectivity. Karen describes *something* immanent in the promise of a predominantly LGBTQ church oriented toward social justice—an indeterminate but perceptible something that she senses could yet nurture more diverse, relational, motile, and responsive forms of religious and political collectivity. The very same worship leader who described being consistently misrecognized, glibly confused for another black woman as if the two individuals were interchangeable, simultaneously described the church as a "truly loving place," a space of "possibility," and saw the task of the church as doing more of its good work for more people. Rather than reiterate zero-sum or resentful approaches to politics (Brown 1995), Karen yearned for an expansion and a recasting of the church's ministry, for the congregation to continue to make good on the promise of moving from a "gay church" to "everyone's church."

Karen's account of the church as a space of "possibility" and prospective expansiveness thus spatializes what the late cultural theorist José Esteban Muñoz (2009) called "queerness as potentiality," queerness as an orientation to futurity. Unsatisfied with presentist and pragmatic approaches to politics that take what they can get under neoliberal conditions as the best that can be expected, Muñoz called for attention to the already embedded, already immanent character of potentiality for worlds beyond and within this one. Muñoz's figuration of queerness as "not-yet-here" alerts us to a richer future that is both here and not-here. For Muñoz, the here and not-here are primarily temporal markers. Yet, as Doreen Massey (2005) reminds us, "For the future to be open, space must be open too" (12). That Martine, Grace, Adrian, and Karen can sustain a critical, loving attachment to a church that at times frustrates them deeply and intimately on matters of race and gender directs our attention to MCCT's heterogeneity and incompleteness in both time and space. MCCT can be a space of misrecognition, inclusion, and policing that aims toward a normative distribution of bodies. Yet "it is always in the process of being made. It is never finished; never closed" (Massey 2005, 9). That radical spatiotemporal indeterminacy, coupled with its utopian, loving theological, ethical, and political promise, grounds my interview subjects' complex affective orientation toward the church, and my own.

That Martine, Grace, Adrian, Karen, and others find the church to be a site of devastating exclusion yet sense its potential and choose to stay and fight, as it were, also tells us something important about the affective dynamics of improper queer citizenship. Like Klein's (1975) depressive child, these leaders of color have no illusions about the limits on the church's capacity to provide an ideal environment for them. They remain committed to practices of repair, healing, amelioration—practices that take place in, yet extend far beyond, the church and that integrate the good and bad fragments of the church as a space in order to weave it into their broader spiritual and ethical itineraries. They confront the violence they experience with strength and alacrity, but they do so not as part of a paranoid exposure project, a resentful fantasy of sovereignty, or a provincial identity politics, but in order to transform the church and hold it accountable to its promise of "a house of prayer for all people." In demanding that the church proliferate and pluralize its approach to worship and spiritual support across a range of markers of "diversity," these leaders unsettle the homeyness, homogeneity, and comfort that identitarian queer citizenship and faith community requires, and articulate an improper, subjectless practice of faith-based queer citizenship. Improper queer citizenship, then, is a work of love, in the Kleinian sense.

Just as importantly, the work of sustaining a relationship to the church does not take place in a political or affective silo. As Adrian, Karen, and Grace work to integrate the church's good and bad fragments, to move through it and love it on terms that confer plenitude rather than abide the terms of toxic nonreciprocity, they work simultaneously to recast citizenship at other geographical scales. All three describe forms of spiritual and citizenship praxis—within diasporic communities, within the greater Toronto area, and within queer communities of color—that have complex and multifarious geographies. Geography matters here, because it helps us understand the affective work of "integration" on rather different terms. Rather than cast these leaders as simply seeking to integrate in the sense of "fitting into" a predominantly gay white male church, we come to see that the church in fact also fits into their more wide-ranging goals and itineraries. The work of integrating and incorporating a good-enough religious object, then, takes place within and at the same time as a broad ensemble of political, social, and spiritual practices in various theaters of citizenship. Adrian, Karen, and Grace work to integrate the passions, love and hate, in relation to multiple objects simultaneously, as citizens of the church, the city, and more.

I have just developed an argument for the affective and political significance of church leaders of color contesting their management by representational logics of diversity in worship services. I have demonstrated how such contestations exceed representational identity politics, and how these leaders articulate more dexterous, prolific, and wide-ranging visions of the

church's ministries and of an improper queer citizenship. In what remains
of this chapter, I want to turn to another church ministry that has likewise
sought to challenge the church from within to live up to its promises of
citizenship: the church's Social Justice Network.

"David, and Not Goliath"

Launched in the spring of 2012 after several attempts at creating such a
ministry, the MCCT Social Justice Network was convened to give the
church a visible and broad-based advocacy arm independent from
the highly activist but highly overextended senior pastor, the Reverend
Dr. Hawkes. As an intermittently active (but by no means founding) member in the network during my fieldwork, I participated in marches and
walks opposing neoliberal austerity and xenophobia; engaged in collective
deliberations about directions for the group over e-mail and shared meals;
helped organize a workshop on environmental justice and decolonization led by an organizer from the indigenous protest movement Idle No
More; and interviewed most of the network's small but highly active core
of members at the time. Hardly an objective outsider or a benign ethnog-
rapher (Haraway 1988), I found myself drawn to the Social Justice Network
precisely because of its recourse to spirituality as an alternative ground for
political engagement and because of the broad swath of political issues it
addressed. Over the course of my fieldwork, the network repeatedly took
visible stances on the rights of undocumented people and environmental protection, and organized workshops on the criminalization of HIV
transmission and federal attacks on funding for faith-based social justice
and development organizations working in occupied Palestine. Yet it was
curiosity about people's motivations, stakes, and attachments—about how
people in the network related to MCCT as a space and an ideal, how they
understood the connections among spirituality, sexuality, and citizenship,
and why they moved with/in this congregation as a particularly dense node
for such conceptual and practical connections—that pushed me beyond an
activist identification with the network and piqued my scholarly interest.

In contrast to the worship leaders I interviewed for the preceding section, it might be tempting to gloss over the potential ethical and political significance of the Social Justice Network—a group of predominantly
white, middle-class, and, intriguingly, mostly heterosexual progressive
people taking up a range of political causes at an LGBTQ church. After all,

such people often have the time and the means to learn about the struggles of others. Yet if we take queerness in general and improper queer citizenship in particular as generous, messy, coalitional, and anti-identitarian or more-than-identitarian, then it strikes me that the sometimes quite strange people who show up in church basements—people who care earnestly about (and work savvily in solidarity with) people with life courses radically different from their own; whose descriptions of their own motivations and politics cite all kinds of metaphysical paradigms unapologetically out of sync with secular liberalism; who have no hesitation about being the only middle-aged, middle-class white people at a rally against migrant detention or austerity measures; who get into fights about things like whether their church permits bottled water or the use of Styrofoam cups; and who proudly sport flare for LGBTQ causes but get annoyed with others for getting bogged down exclusively in liberal gay identity politics—might hold some valuable insights for queer studies and coalition politics. Indeed, while the ideal of social justice can be linked to multifarious genealogies and resonances in diverse religious and secular traditions, it should also be situated as a kind of sacred object attachment in and of itself, one that at times but by no means necessarily coincides with an attachment to a religious object. But what happens when the desires for the sacred objects of church and of social justice do intersect and condense? How do improper queer citizens work through disappointments in the promises of their objects, and under what affective conditions might they conjure up more expansive ways of being collective?

Consider my conversation with Herman, a Canadian citizen who immigrated from a small village in Switzerland as a young man and has been part of MCCT for much of his adult life. This kind, thoughtful, unassuming man was a regular presence at rallies organized by No One Is Illegal, one of Toronto's forerunning and most innovative and radical migrant-rights organizations. Sometimes Herman was the Social Justice Network's only representative at such demonstrations, a fact evinced in photographs on the network's listserv. In my experience as a participant in the Social Justice Network for over two years, I noticed that the political concerns Herman brought to the group's attention reflected a candidly agonistic view of politics, particularly with respect to the rights of migrants and unjust forms of state power over migrants' lives. My impression of Herman's orientation to the world was further solidified when I interviewed him in the Leslieville home he shares with his longtime partner. Passionately attached to MCCT, Herman described a great deal of frustration with the congregation he also loved:

> *When the formation of the Social Justice Network was announced, you told me you were, like, "Finally—this has been a long time coming!" . . . Say more about your reaction to the announcement for me.*
>
> Herman: When that was brought up, it was also about more international issues, issues with the environment, not just the gay issues that were previously [addressed], because I think previously, social justice was gay issue–related. We're not supposed to be a gay church anymore, but in social justice, I think there was just gay issues, and that was the breakout point of, okay, it's going beyond just gay issues, because really, when you think about it, we haven't had any gay issue at the [Social Justice Network] meetings. You know, it's funny. . . . Sometimes I'm sitting at the table, we are "a gay church," we have a social justice meeting, and out of the five people, only one is gay.
>
> *What do you make of that?*
>
> Herman: I think it's a little bit sad.

Herman speaks of his displeasure with narrow, identitarian conceptions of social justice that seem to haunt MCCT even though, as he says, the church's promises mean "we're not supposed to be a gay church anymore." He notes the irony—both "funny" and "a little bit sad"—that the church ministry committed to a vast range of social justice issues generally attracts the church's small minority of heterosexual-identified churchgoers. On the one hand, I was mindful during my conversation with Herman that many people within the church whose work was indisputably political had other battles to fight; asylum seekers and worship leaders contesting racism and sexism in worship planning, for example, were unlikely to have or to make the time for meetings to take on "causes." On the other hand, I shared Herman's sentiment that the lack of LGBTQ-identified people at the church who were curious about social justice advocacy was "a little bit sad." Had the modest gains of affirming churches, antidiscrimination laws, and same-sex marriage—a modicum of a respectable good life for some mostly white, middle-class queers—really rendered so many at our church so complacent, so solipsistic, so depoliticized? I had to follow up with Herman.

Do you feel sometimes about gay politics that it's . . . too focused on itself, and then it doesn't connect with broader political issues . . . ?
Herman: Yes. I know some of my friends at church—I was at a party, we were socializing, and a question about immigrants came up. And I was totally shocked what some of the comments were. Like, "When we came to Canada, nobody helped us, we had to do it all ourselves, now they get everything." And I'm sitting there—are these the same people I see every Sunday? [laughs]
    We come home and [my partner] says, "Did you hear that?" I said, "Sure I did," because the both of us were just sitting there like, "I can't believe this." I'm not saying this is just an MCC thing, I'm sure it isn't. But you kind of expect more. Like me personally, I would expect more compassion from gay people. A lot of them, maybe not as much the younger generation, but the older generation had to struggle. It was not easy. And then you expect them to be a bit more compassionate to other people. That's surprising.

Herman confronts a disappointing, ugly, xenophobic articulation of identitarian queer citizenship: one that is narrow, unimaginative, bereft of compassion, ahistorical, and affectively closed off to both the vulnerability and the agency of the Other. Yet, faced with such a bad surprise—a lack of compassion on the part of a fellow queer Christian whose experiences of struggle or repudiated desire do not seem to engender empathy or solidarity with the losses endured by (more) recent immigrants—Herman still holds out a set of potentially productive provocations for a congregation he views as "finally" turning toward a more expansive and supple vision of politics. At stake in Herman's frustrated call for the church to embrace a wider range of ethical and political concerns is a sense of potential within the church for capacious, improper queer citizenship—a sense that conditions many people's sustained attachment to MCCT.
    Indeed, Herman's vision resonates with those of other members of the church's Social Justice Network I interviewed. Take my conversation with

Ben, a genderqueer thirtysomething whose upbringing in Ontario's Catholic school system made them leery of connecting with anything religious for much of their young adult life until they came to MCCT. Proudly and publicly bi, HIV-positive, sober, and into leather, Ben described a desire for a politics that confronted injustice—against First Nations people in particular—on a basis other than that offered by identity politics. They told me of their excitement that the Social Justice Network was reconceptualizing horizons for LGBTQ movements, even if its numbers were small:

> *What does it mean for a faith community—and not just a faith community but a predominantly and historically queer faith community—to kind of weigh in on issues of social justice that are not what we traditionally think of as LGBT issues, but are connected?*
>
> Ben: I think we start asking more tough questions. We start educating ourselves more on issues that not just affect us as the queer community but [affect] us as the human race. I think that's the direction that I see us going in, and I think that there's evidence of that already. And some of the issues that are taken up will not necessarily be well received. We've seen that in recent years with Pride Toronto and the representation of QuAIA [Queers against Israeli Apartheid] in the parade.
>
> So, I think there will be issues that won't necessarily at first seem connected, for lack of a better term, on a superficial level. They won't be connected very easily, but ones where we can use our skills and everything we've learned throughout years of advocacy to help others, and to outreach. That's why I think it's so wonderful that we at least do have a network that's attaching itself to issues like environmentalism and clean water.

For Ben, pain and pleasure endured as a result of the mark of LGBTQ identity comprise the genesis of social justice consciousness, but not the telos. Queerness might well be simultaneously something instructive, something painful, a basis for empathy, and something worth reveling in and celebrating. But for Ben, a broader and more complex vision of social justice necessarily goes beyond LGBTQ identity and community, even going so far as to appeal to humanism and universalism. They acknowledge that a more expansive progressive politics will continue to conflict with prevalent identitarian understandings of LGBTQ politics that isolate

LGBTQ identity from other relations of difference and power, as has been the case in the controversy over the rights of QuAIA to participate in the Toronto Pride Parade (see Kouri-Towe 2011). Recognizing such inexorable difficulty, Ben nevertheless identifies this more multifaceted vision of social justice as the endless task that remains ahead.

Intriguingly, this sense of MCCT as a site of potential for improper queer citizenship also showed up in interviews with heterosexual-identified congregants. Chris and Ann, a couple I interviewed who were active in Toronto politics and the New Democratic Party, described their affiliation with MCCT and its social justice advocacy as a matter of living out spiritual commitments to confront politically and affectively "messy places." Part of what struck me about my conversations with Chris and Ann was their simultaneous firm commitment to solidarity with LGBTQ people as heterosexual and cisgender-identified people, and their lack of hesitation in subjecting the contradictory dimensions of the church and its ministries to critique where necessary. Where more polite straight liberals connected to the church might hold the church to a lower standard, not remarking upon silences, contradictions, or unfulfilled promises, Chris and Ann, like several other heterosexual members of the MCCT Social Justice Network, continue to push for what they understand as progressive and critical engagement on a range of social justice concerns, including and beyond LGBTQ issues, however conceived. Significantly, MCCT's roots in gay and lesbian social and political formations are not incidental to Ann and Chris's engagement with the church—the couple do not march in with their heterosexual positionalities and attachments unchecked. Nor, however, do they hold LGBTQ institutions like MCCT to a less rigorous critical standard out of politeness or guilt over heterosexual privilege (see Raphael 2010 for an excellent critique of the tacit homophobia of straight left-wing failure to ask more from LGBTQ politics).

At times, this rigor has led Chris, a lawyer with a history of pro bono work with trans people and asylum seekers and a fierce critic of racism, transphobia, brutality, and torture within the Toronto Police Service, to openly disagree with his friend Rev. Hawkes, whose long history of work on police–minority relations has led him to cultivate relationships with controversial former Toronto Police chief Bill Blair and current chief Mark Saunders. Significantly, the Social Justice Network's commitment to a copious vision of social justice has even led it to depart from the position held by others within the congregation, including Rev. Hawkes, on the question of police–minority relations. As I will discuss in greater detail in chapter 2, on pastoral "diva citizenship" and activism, church leaders acted as prominent critical voices against homophobic police brutality, particularly in the first two decades after the congregation's founding (Berlant 1997). In the late 1970s and early 1980s, Pastor Hawkes was among the leaders of the Right to Privacy Committee, a coalition that formed in critical response to massive police raids on gay men's bathhouses and nurtured strong ties in communities of color and lesbian and gay communities. After a massive set of raids in February 1981, Hawkes went on a twenty-five-day hunger strike to demand a public inquiry into police misconduct (McLeod 1996). By contrast, the church's more recent engagement with police has taken an increasingly celebratory tone, as formal police commitments to non-discrimination and education in the police force have proliferated, and as some LGBTQ people have become ordinary urban citizens and thus have receded as obvious targets for scrutiny and abuse (at least provisionally; see McCaskell 2016). This laudatory tone is most evident in the annual Emergency Personnel Sunday worship service, which features fire, police, and emergency medical personnel in uniform and has even seen the chief and other police officials address the congregation from the pulpit in uniform.

Many within the congregation, particularly in the Social Justice Network (myself included), have responded negatively to this celebration of putatively improved police–minority relations, citing the Toronto Police Service's record of racial profiling, humiliation and abuse of transgender people, torture, and pattern of excessive and at times deadly use of force with mentally ill people, particularly mentally ill people of color (see, e.g., Kane 2014; Sankaran 2012; Reid 2014). When I have sought to address my own and others' concerns in interviews with Rev. Hawkes, he has indicated he was neither unaware of nor unsympathetic to sustained criticism of the police. Hawkes described a willingness to organize meetings between police liaisons and trans and racialized congregants for an airing of grievances, but he also highlighted the kinds of change he feels he could help bring about as a friend to the leaders of Toronto Police Services.

By contrast, members of the Social Justice Network opted to make more public criticism of the Toronto police. In February 2014, after stories about patterns of illegal strip searches and the use of torture in interrogation came to light, the Social Justice Network publicly reprimanded then-chief Blair in a letter, calling on "the Toronto Police Service to state publicly and unequivocally its commitment to protect the rights of every citizen of Toronto, even those suspected of a crime" and demanding an outline of "specific steps that the Toronto Police Service intends to take to ensure that people are not subjected to torture inside Toronto's police stations and that they are not humiliated and degraded unnecessarily by unlawful strip searches" (Dick 2014).

Critical interventions like the Social Justice Network's critique of police brutality serve to thicken the notion of social justice at a historically identity-based "gay church" (Warner 2005). Moreover, it is particularly striking that the letter opts for the urban idiom "citizen of Toronto" rather than making recourse to Canadian nation-state citizenship. Such a choice suggests an alternative locus of belonging and grounds for rights claims that may or may not converge with nationality or legal status. Such improper forms of activism, which recognize issues like immigrant justice and police brutality *as* queer issues, strike me as resonant with Muñoz's (2009) reframing of queerness as futurity, queerness as immanent yet "not-yet-here." For participants in the church Social Justice Network, the specific content of political struggles is in constant flux, but there remains a queer affect, a feeling, that compels members to respond to the ethical and political demands of the Other. At a time when some in Toronto and within the congregation have publicly championed an assimilated and depoliticized "postgay" sensibility, the Social Justice Network recognizes both the sustained political salience of LGBTQ identity and community, and the imperative of an improper queer citizenship. And crucially, among the forces nurturing this capacity for self-reflexivity and for critical recognition of one's own privilege under changing historical circumstances is religious faith. As another member of the Social Justice Network active in local movements around mental health, affordable housing, and trans rights told me, "We always have to be on the side of David and not Goliath." The gesture to the biblical king David is both apt and ironic here, not simply because David is such a homoerotic figure in ways that sometimes propel identitarian investment and identification (see, e.g., the classic Horner 1978) but because David, once an underdog in a battle of epic proportions, of course ultimately became a king. Amid his power and privilege, David managed to retain God's favor—but only because of his capacity to repent and to reflect on his critical and abiding flaws and capacity to do harm, his ability to integrate and live with good and bad fragments of the ego as well as of the objects that populated his psychic world.[3]

Improper Congregational Citizenship

Together, the ministries of worship leaders of color and the Social Justice Network point to two rather different ways in which people act as improper queer citizens within MCCT, working within but also exceeding the idioms of representational identity politics. Worship leaders of color recognize that the configuration of racialized and gendered bodies leading prayer, song, and Communion is a matter of recognition and representation—but it is not only that. By challenging the dominant idioms for who counts as a citizen of MCCT through embodied and spiritual encounter, these leaders do material, affective, and redistributive work, nurturing alternative possibilities for sympathy, solidarity, intimacy, and identification. Worship leaders of color, particularly women of color, may mobilize idioms that could be read as intersectional and identitarian—yet, as with the black feminist praxis that King (2015) recounts, reading these gestures for their affectivity points to more complex histories and much more wide-ranging, more-than-identitarian sensibilities. Both these worship leaders and the Social Justice Network work to unsettle the comfort, familiarity, and homogeneity demanded by an identitarian queer citizenship, whether by challenging the church's Goldilocks approach to diversity management or by displacing the complacency and celebratory liberalism of church members in a city that remains menaced by racialized, antipoor, and transphobic police brutality. Both the worship leaders and the network members describe frustration and pain over the contradictions between the church's promises of "a house of prayer for all" and the reality they are presented with in everyday church sociality. For worship leaders, this pain emerges from experiences of racialized and gendered exclusion; for network leaders, most of whom are white and comparatively privileged, it registers differently, as disappointment in untapped potential. But all these leaders share a sense of the church's potentiality to be something more, for its ministries to go further in a commitment to faith-based social justice—a sense that the church's queerness is immanent but "not-yet-here" (Muñoz 2009). Yet, as reparative citizens of the church who find that their sacred object-choices conflict with some of the church's tacit micropolitical norms, these subjects do not simply take what they can but work to integrate the good and bad fragments of the church, sustaining a relationship to a "good-enough church" on terms that they make work for them (Winnicott 1953). Working through conflicting affects in relation to the church, these congregants labor on an ongoing basis to conjure a good-enough, improper queer church into being. Crucially, this reparative work on the church as an object both nurtures and exists alongside work to repair and recast citizenship at a wide range of geographical scales. Such sophisticated affective and political struggle, grounded in faith, should invite curiosity much more broadly about what other surprising, reparative practices and affective encounters might quietly play out under the maligned banner of so-called representational identity politics.

If promises of citizenship sustain people's attachments to institutions and spaces that also exclude them and marginalize their values, the church leaders whose ministries inform this chapter critically respond to that contradiction not with identitarian resentment but with "improper" queer love. That love is not merely identity-political, nor is it "cruel-optimistic," on Berlant's (2011a) terms, because these leaders do not hesitate to contest and transform the terms of their relation to the object promising congregational citizenship. Rather, such love imagines queerness as a more challenging, more uncomfortable, and more expansive mode of relation in spiritual and political community. Careful attention to such loving praxis can help MCCT live up to its promise of better forms of relationality and help queer theorists better understand the affective work that a dexterous improper queer citizenship necessarily entails.

2

Pastor–Diva–Citizen

The Reverend Dr. Brent Hawkes, Homonormative Melancholia, and the Limits of Celebrity

> *Another defence . . . is the preoccupation with the past in order to avoid the frustrations of the present. Some idealization of the past is bound to enter into these memories and is put into the service of defence.*
>
> —Melanie Klein, "On the Sense of Loneliness"

A Tale of Two Apologies

On June 22, 2016, Toronto Police chief Mark Saunders delivered what was meant to comprise a historic apology. Some thirty-five years after dramatic raids on four Toronto gay men's bathhouses, among the largest mass arrests in Canadian history, Saunders conveyed official "regrets for those very actions." He then rapidly consigned any of the affective trouble that regret can entail to the past, insisting the anniversary was "also an occasion to acknowledge the lessons learned about the risks of treating any part of Toronto's many communities as not fully a part of society" (CBC News 2016c). In a deft oscillation between a 1981 police attack that mostly affected white gay men and "any part of Toronto's many communities," Saunders quietly converted all concerns about police violence—whether animated by race, class, gender, or sexuality—to lessons already learned, already past, left in the "dustbin of history" (Eng 2010, x) on the path to putatively enlightened policing.

Saunders's gesture was widely panned by queers of various genders and sexualities who survived the 1981 raid and many others, and especially by the city's queer of color organizers. Indeed, only two days later, Black Lives Matter–Toronto (BLMTO), an organization led by queer and trans people of color, interrupted the unveiling of a mural in the city's gay village that was intended to celebrate improved police–minority relations and denounced the ongoing pattern of killings of unarmed people of color, particularly black men, by police in the city (Vendeville 2016).[1] Just over a week later, BLMTO made international news by stopping the Toronto Pride Parade (which it had been invited to lead) for twenty-five minutes, bravely demanding the restoration of black and brown queer programming at Pride and an end to the celebration of uniformed police at the event, and refusing to move until the demands were met (CBC News 2016a).

Given the atmospheric racism that suffuses many normatively white LGBTQ spaces in Toronto, as evinced by the Goldilocks diversity schema I relayed in chapter 1, it should come as no surprise that BLMTO's interventions were met with scrutiny and dismissal by many whites and conservative people of color, including many queers. I was dismayed, but not shocked, to be invited by a friend from MCCT to support pro-police content and organizing on social media, and to see another church acquaintance publicly and quite evocatively repudiate BLMTO and its supporters. Equally fraught was the presence of MCCT's senior pastor, the Reverend Dr. Brent Hawkes, at both the official police apology and the subsequent mural unveiling. Indeed, Hawkes went so far as to thank the chief and to attempt to mediate between police and BLMTO at the latter event (CBC News 2016a). At the apology, Hawkes told reporters, "Today not only helps to heal, here in Toronto, it also helps to avoid hurt. While the hurt remains, the healing can begin" (CBC News 2016c). While Hawkes made a point of acknowledging the persistence of historically organized and inflicted pain, he also gestured to a path to healing that proves decidedly more accessible for some queers than for others.[2] When questioned by BLMTO protesters at the mural unveiling about his support for police despite ongoing police harassment of homeless people, trans people, sex workers, and black Torontonians, Hawkes apologized to BLMTO for not having done more to stand in solidarity with them (Houston 2016a, 2016b, 2016c).

For those who dismiss Hawkes's activism as always already conservative, as tainted by a bad religious object relation, Hawkes's mix of celebratory and contrite rhetoric comes as unremarkable and expected. But, as we saw in chapter 1, for those who sustain attachments to Hawkes or to MCCT, faith leaders and faith community can work as stand-ins, proxies for more capacious political and affective itineraries that refuse to make a forced choice between religion and radical politics as sacred objects. Indeed, as became clear in chapter 1, for subjects like Ann and Chris, who

Top: *As the Reverend Dr. Brent Hawkes speaks at the official police apology for massive raids on gay men's bathhouses in Toronto in 1981, Toronto Police chief Mark Saunders looks on. June 22, 2016. Photograph courtesy of John Gordon.* Bottom: *As organizers in Black Lives Matter–Toronto decry the unveiling of a pro-police, pro-gay mural, Rev. Hawkes attempts to intercede. June 24, 2016. Photograph courtesy of Andrea L. Houston.*

are equally compelled by the idea of church community and by capacious, radical, and improper approaches to queer citizenship, celebrating police in church is an occasion for discomfort and disappointment. Moreover, what makes Hawkes's presence at events celebratory of police particularly contradictory—and symbolically significant—is that Hawkes himself had a major, if controversial, role in Toronto anti-police-brutality activism in the 1970s and 1980s. So, what happened?

This chapter seeks to address the affective quandaries that arise when an object—in this case, a religious and political object—that one wants to be "good enough" nevertheless disappoints. While Hawkes is illustrative for my purposes in this chapter, from another vantage, all of us sustain attachments to contradictory objects, institutions, and idealized communities. Such objects routinely disappoint us and at times throw us into crisis about whether our object relations are worth sustaining. As Klein (1975) observed so astutely, when an object disappoints, it is extremely tempting—and perhaps unconsciously irresistible—to split it in two. Living with a whole object, by contrast, means living with the pain that comes in de-idealizing it; as one of Klein's patients once put it, "The glamor is gone" (305).

One of the forces that accompanies and facilitates splitting for Klein ([1935] 1998) is a kind of nostalgia, a desire to protect the object's fondly remembered good fragments from contamination by its bad ones. Such nostalgia is palpable in contemporary efforts to memorialize the radical queer past in Toronto and in Canada. Indeed, the 2010s have seen a proliferation of efforts to enshrine or memorialize the historic activism of *The Body Politic*, a collectively operated gay liberationist newspaper based in Toronto in the 1970s and 1980s, which has been the subject of a conference, a play, and dozens of articles and books. Likewise, critical responses to the 1981 bathhouse raids—activism in which Hawkes played an important role—are the object of a documentary film, numerous public panel discussions, and, again, dozens of articles and books. The legacies and impact of *The Body Politic* and the bathhouse raids are indisputably important—and indeed, the events remain open as long as people produce new interpretations of them (Isin and Nielsen 2008). And alongside more identitarian or defensive cultural productions, there are many innovative, critical recountings of these events and people's contemporary relationships to them that cannot be reduced to nostalgia. For instance, in the recent debates over BLMTO's activism, queer black and antiracist writers have aptly situated the 2016 intervention at Pride within a much longer tradition of protest and opposition to state violence. As an open letter written by black scholars and activists puts it, "In the decades since Pride began, other communities have seen their spaces disappear while a white gay male dance party has proliferated and grown. If that is your tea then sip it, but this year Black Lives Matter Toronto took Pride back to its roots, with fabulous success" (CBC News 2016b). I speculate, however, that important among the many conditions animating this contemporary turn to radical queer pasts is an affective one: a deep malaise about the limits of contemporary neoliberal LGBTQ politics.

Homonormative Melancholia

A gesture to a radical past in activist debates resonates across contemporary queer scholarship, which at times positions the contemporary moment in LGBTQ politics as haunted by the ghosts of more daring, far-reaching, and expansive visions of erotic and political emancipation. In her now paradigmatic writing on the neoliberalization of U.S. sexual minority politics, Lisa Duggan (2003) traces a turn from sexual liberation movements, broadly connected to civil rights, black and brown power, antiwar, feminist, and socialist organizing, to a glossy, largely depoliticized "Equality, Inc." ethos. Such a "homonormative" LGBTQ politics, Duggan argues, seeks little more than comfortable envelopment in dominant social institutions. Within Canada, Patrizia Gentile and Gary Kinsman (2015) have similarly charted the rise of what they call the "neoliberal queer," which they likewise contend forecloses the more coalitional and radical queer politics that prevailed in previous moments. Tim McCaskell (2016) and Catherine Jean Nash (2006, 2014) chart ideological and discursive shifts in Toronto gay activism across the second half of the twentieth century, from ostensibly bolder and often Marxist-liberationist idioms to more liberal civil rights and human rights framings. And OmiSoore Dryden and Suzanne Lenon (2015) have highlighted how neoliberal forms of LGBTQ politics contribute directly to the reiteration of racial hierarchy, white fantasies of innocence, and nationalist conceptions of Canada as beneficent, enlightened, and exceptional (see also Lenon 2005, 2011).

Particularly striking are the affective dynamics of how such transformations in LGBTQ politics are narrated. Reflecting on a collective oral-history project documenting LGBTQ movements in Minneapolis–Saint Paul,

Minnesota, historian Kevin Murphy (2010) describes the experience of grappling with interviews that lament the usurpation of an optimistic and radical liberationist sensibility in the 1970s by something at once less subversive and, thanks to a liberal politics of recognition emphasizing visibility, more exposed. Murphy combines Duggan's work (2003) with that of queer affect scholar Heather Love (2007) to propose a notion of "homonormative melancholy," describing "the psychic and political costs of moving from a position of exclusion to one of belonging in a realm that Gayle Rubin has described as the 'charmed circle' of sexual normalcy" (Murphy 2010, 315; Rubin 1984).

It is important to stress here that neither Murphy nor Duggan, nor critics of homonormativity in a Canadian context, embraces a straightforward declension narrative in which neoliberalism need form the total and indomitable horizon for LGBTQ politics. Indeed, such scholars point to past and contemporary instances of queer politics that are expansive, coalitional, creative, grassroots, and far-reaching, and BLMTO certainly comes to mind as exemplary in that regard. At the same time, however, I would argue that critiques of contemporary homonormativity at times engage, perhaps inadvertently, in an affective pedagogy of melancholia, relaying a fraught and persistent relation to an ungrievable loss in order to model an ethical relationship to that loss. In Freud's early work on melancholia ([1917] 1953), he understands it as a pathological state. Yet, as Judith Butler (1997) observes, in his later work Freud came to regard melancholy less as a pathology than as a necessary, inaugural moment in any process of mourning. For Butler, melancholia both comprises an ordinary response to loss and brings about the possibility of an ethical relation to the ghosts (of genders, people, intimacies, ways of being collective) violently foreclosed by the current contours of sociosymbolic order. These writers find value in an affective orientation that remains haunted by progress's constitutive exclusions, particularly in a neoliberal moment.

This chapter grapples with and seeks to work through (at least momentarily) one potential consequence of homonormative melancholy: a tendency, not always conscious, toward a Kleinian splitting of time into "good" radical past and "bad" depoliticized present. I contend that such splitting can, at its most dramatic, result in an externalization of agency to a phantasmatic radical past, foreclosing engagement with immanent radical potential in the present. For me personally, this kind of melancholy can be especially acute in liberal and progressive religious spaces, which have long felt to me like spaces of promise. As I mentioned in the Introduction, in my coming of age and coming out in the midwestern United States at the height of the neoconservative nightmare of the George W. Bush administration, the local Unitarian Universalist congregation was a space of respite and hope, a space where familial conflict and despondency over war and emerging queer sexuality felt as though they could all be held and worked through in music, friendship, and prayer. In my most utopian longings, I continue to yearn, like many of the subjects whose insights I shared in chapter 1, for a church that is robustly, improperly queer in the sense imagined by subjectless critique: a church that is critically diverse and substantively feminist and antiracist, both compassionate and relentless in its prophetic witness for social justice, and accessible in myriad senses. I want a church that continues to reflect and engage the rich genealogies of contestatory LGBTQ organizing in Toronto in the present. I yearn for a church that refuses to rest on its laurels ("Welcome home") but instead acts as though empire and capitalism are themselves the apocalypse, the ruins from which people might yet build something more heavenlike, or at least less hellish, on earth ("My house shall be a house of prayer for all people"; see also Parker 2006). And I remain stubbornly attached to the potential in faith-based queer community for a nonsecular, nonrational critique of liberal progress and a proliferation of desires for other worlds.[3] On psychoanalytic terms, then, my relationship to MCCT might be described as one of transference, which psychoanalyst and education theorist Deborah Britzman (2000) helpfully encapsulates as "the capacity to bring new editions of old conflicts into present relationships" (41). I elaborate on this longing and disappointment at length not because I expect all readers to identify with all of it; rather, I do so with the hope that more explicit and situated accounts of disappointment and frustrated political investments might prompt further reflection and debate about the ways in which a wide range of people consume and yearn for radical pasts, pasts they may or may not have personally experienced—and that such discernment and discussion might help to open up people's relationships to the impurities and thus the potentiality immanent even to the neoliberal present.

Thus, throughout the process of research and writing on MCCT and the MCC movement, I have had to contend with the frustrated desire to have my romantic, redemptive, utopian desires answered, both in my ethnographic work with the church's contemporary history and also in my archival engagement with its past. Indeed, MCCT and the MCC movement are in many instances, both at first glance and even after sustained scrutiny, at odds with improper queer citizenship, investing in liberal, essentialist, and universalist political projects. This book is largely populated with moments of affective and political difficulty in the church—conflicts over xenophobia, police violence, racism, sexism, and neocolonialism—and with the ways differently situated actors within the church confront or fail to confront and work through such difficulty. In moments of disappointment with the church's present, I found myself prone to speculation about the church's history: Had the church always operated as an avowedly "big-tent," mainstream institution? How had its theologies and ideologies shifted? If MCCT and the broader denomination were now, as prominent denominational leader the Reverend Elder Darlene Garner once famously put it, "middle-aged," had the church had a feisty, messy youth with which I (and others) could perhaps identify?

My curiosity and my yearning led me to correspond with, and in some cases visit, a range of formal archival institutions in the United States and Canada: the Canadian Lesbian and Gay Archives in Toronto, the Manitoba Gay and Lesbian Archives in Winnipeg, the Montreal Gay Archives, the Toronto Reference Library, Library and Archives Canada in Ottawa, the City of Toronto Archives, the CTV Archives in Scarborough, and the One National Archives in Los Angeles. This research also took me to the perspectives of longtime church members and clergy, to longtime Toronto LGBTQ activists who'd worked with the church, and to documentary films, such as the oeuvre of Canadian filmmaker Nancy Nicol (2002, 2006, 2007). I also consulted extensively with the prolific Canadian LGBTQ chronologist and archivist Don McLeod (1996, 2014) at the University of Toronto Libraries. Yet even as I wondered about the possible radical queer churches of the past that might inhabit archives, I found myself productively challenged by psychoanalytic and queer scholar Valerie Traub's (2002) warning that desires for community themselves propel identifications (qtd. in Love 2007, 41). Like Love (2007), whose initial desire for community led her to investigate pre-Stonewall queer subjects, in my frustration with the LGBTQ present, I sought in my work on MCC history to "touch across time" an imagined radical church of the past (Dinshaw 1999, 1).

My formal archival exploration did yield exciting glimmers of the kind of obvious radicality of my fantasies—an MCC prison ministry and fleeting moments of collaboration, as well as conflict, with ACT UP in the United States and *The Body Politic* in Canada—but it also flouted the transferential expectations with which I had saddled the church. An archive of past and ongoing difficulty proves productive, however, in that it unsettles notions of a redemptive past and a closed present—a psychic split between good and bad part objects neatly partitioned across time. In working through my own nostalgic relationship to yearned-for radical pasts, my aim in this chapter is to confront the affective and political impurity and indeterminacy of the past, such that the present and the future might be recognized as likewise impure but might also feel more open. This process of working through the loss of a fantasized redemptive past is fundamentally conditioned by melancholia as an ordinary response to loss. It is, in Klein's (1975) sense, depressive—traumatized by past disappointments and sober about the limitations of its environment. Yet precisely by integrating good and bad fragments of the church's past and present, and suturing the paranoid split that cleaves past from present, this chapter aims to offer a more reparative account of the church's impure but significant political potential. Rather than splitting history between a "good" radical past and a "bad" homonormative present, it pieces together a "good-enough church" in different yet profoundly connected pockets of time and space. Crucially, such an integrative affective process is at once individual and social; the process I describe has been inspired and nurtured by the reparative work of many within MCCT and within the denomination, many of them antiracists and feminists whose accounts of their layered, loving, vexed attachments to the church have helped me make sense of my own. Though there are no guarantees, such an affective process can help differently situated people work simultaneously to both repair the church as an object and to imagine and practice citizenship otherwise.

Central to a process of integrating conflicting aspects of MCCT's history is the figure of its longtime pastor, the Reverend Dr. Brent Hawkes. A charismatic preacher and celebrated activist, Hawkes circulates in a range of publics as a rather complex and chaotic object of desire. Because both the church and various state forms are not monolithic but chaotic assemblages in which a range of actors bring their own desires and preoccupations, Hawkes as a celebrity-activist pastor functions as a stand-in, a pivot point for a kaleidoscopic range of projected intimate/political fantasies. In some instances, Hawkes may stand in for the very possibility of reconciling nonnormative gender or sexual identity with Christianity or religion, broadly conceived—a possibility that may register as absurd, surprising, foolhardy, naive, pointless, unthinkable, epistemically violent, or deeply desirable. In other cases, often instances of activism, Hawkes has stood in for LGBTQ community much more broadly conceived, a framing that has at once resonated powerfully and dismayed his queer political critics and those who have difficulty identifying with his life course or political and theological positions. Within the congregation, Hawkes's activist itinerary often works synecdochically to index the church's understanding of its work in the world, a tendency that worries many in the church and has led Hawkes and others to push for devolution of activism and other ministries to include lay volunteers. The kinds of personal stories that populate Hawkes's sermons—his trajectory from a fundamentalist Baptist church as a child in Bath, New Brunswick, to a successful pastorate at a predominantly LGBTQ, theologically liberal Toronto congregation—offer an "it gets better" narrative that can spur a range of identifications and disavowals.

Two historical moments in Hawkes's activist ministry helpfully illustrate the affective and analytical process by which I as a researcher first split present from past and then came, anxiously and without glamor (Klein 1975), to reintegrate them. This chapter focuses on representations of two key activist interventions in Hawkes's ministry, both of which have circulated widely in the production of collective memories and feelings about LGBTQ activism and history in the MCC movement, Canada, and especially Toronto. The first scene focuses on mass critical response to the 1981 bathhouse raids, when mass arrests of hundreds of gay men at bathhouses led to widespread condemnation of police and calls for accountability from a broad coalition of Torontonians. The second, more recent moment is the state funeral for New Democratic Party leader and Official Opposition leader Jack Layton in 2011. The bathhouse raids have long been positioned by sexuality scholars in Canada as a landmark event (Kinsman 1987; Nash 2014; Jackman 2015). By contrast, the Layton memorial service—which resulted in a significant upsurge in visibility, attendance, and web viewership for MCCT—is just beginning to be engaged by scholars of sexuality (Rayter 2012). The selection of these two episodes is closely related to the investigation of the contemporary politics of MCCT that I conduct throughout this book. Both moments have proved important in how people apprehend possibilities for contemporary LGBTQ politics in Canada, and particularly in Toronto. Both events prominently feature Rev. Hawkes operating as an activist pastor–diva–citizen (Berlant 1997), an idiom for critical urban and national citizenship that transects liberal boundaries between the intimate and the political, the religious and the secular, the private and the public.

Lauren Berlant (1997) formulates the concept of "diva citizenship" to describe the constitutive limits and political potential of public testimony by a member of a historically marginalized population. Fundamentally pedagogical, the diva attests to her "imperiled citizenship," teaching and seeking empathy from a privileged audience (222). Significantly, diva citizenship relies on both the success of the diva's capacity to performatively conjure sympathy and the failure of her (albeit moving) individual account of structurally induced pain to bring about structural change in and of itself—leaving that unfinished business to a collective audience. In this chapter, I argue for an understanding of Hawkes's key historic political interventions at the urban and national scales as comprising an archive of a specifically religiously inflected queer diva citizenship. But where Berlant's (1997, 12) "archive"—black women's slave narratives and the congressional testimony of Anita Hill—posits *resonances* across time between accounts of racial and sexual exploitation, my analysis of gay white pastoral testimonies also highlights historical *disjunctures*. If Hawkes began inhabiting the gay pastor–diva–citizen idiom in the 1970s and 1980s with agonistic outrage at homophobic police violence, more contemporary pastoral narratives increasingly valorize themes of success, teleological progress, and harmonious LGBTQ community. Juxtaposing these two episodes of pastoral activism, separated by thirty years, throws into relief powerful historical and geographical transformations in Toronto and Canadian LGBTQ politics. Yet I seek to avoid connecting the two moments through a linear narrative of liberal progress ("it gets better") or a paranoid account of homonormative decline ("it got worse"), endeavoring instead to work through the contemporary affective dynamics of a desiring relation to the past, exploring impurities and contradictions in both moments, in the modest but crucial hope of a more depressive, integrative relationship to the politics of the church across time.

Track Two: Enough Is Enough

On Thursday, February 5, 1981, police raided four separate gay men's bathhouses, arresting nearly three hundred men under Canada's rarely enforced "bawdy-house" law. Popularly known as the bathhouse raids or bathhouse riots, Toronto police "Operation Soap" and the critical response it provoked have been productively analyzed by activists and scholars as a key moment in histories of state violence and urban queer citizenship struggles in Canada (Hannon 1982; Kinsman 1987; Warner 2002; Nash 2006, 2014; Guidotto 2006; Jackman 2015; McCaskell 2016).[4] The raids comprised the largest mass arrest in Canada since the invocation of the War Measures Act (suspending habeas corpus) during the Quebec October Crisis in 1970, though both events were later eclipsed by mass arrests during the 2010 G20 Summit in Toronto. If the extent of police abuse of power in the bathhouse raids is understood as exceptional, so too is the power of the mass critical response to the attacks. While long histories of antigay police violence—and organizing against it—preceded the 1981 raids, the demonstrations that followed are framed in popular media as singular, at times rendered as the Canadian equivalent of Stonewall. And indeed, critical response saw broad swaths of radical, liberal, and mainstream Torontonians—spanning and transecting gay and lesbian, labor, black, arts, francophone, and religious communities and even some elected officials—denounce the raids in a remarkable collective display of resistance to state power. It is important to note that despite the unprecedented extent of the 1981 attack, police complacency in the face of informal homophobic violence and active police raids on gay institutions had been a feature of the ordinary in gay Toronto in the late 1970s and early 1980s. Many have noted an escalation in police harassment of gay communities after the death of Emanuel Jaques, a Portuguese Canadian shoeshine boy whose indisputably brutal sexual assault and murder by adult men in 1977 was also unfortunately invoked to legitimate a homophobic and classist "cleanup" of Yonge Street and Toronto's gay village (Cotroneo 2005). The chilling, invasive effects of smaller episodic raids throughout the late 1970s—including a 1978 raid on The Barracks bathhouse, which led to the arrest of nearly thirty men—had already led to the formation of the Right to Privacy Committee, a gay group dedicated to challenging police abuse that enabled provisional alliances between more liberal and more liberationist activists.

Fully apprehending the ethicopolitical significance of the raids and their aftermath for contemporary queer citizenship struggles, however, requires more than plotting a timeline of key events; it requires exploring the affective contours of their framing. My analysis in this section focuses on the mediation of contemporary relationships to the bathhouse raids through Harry Sutherland's documentary film *Track Two: Enough*

Is Enough (1982), which chronicles the raids and collective responses to them.

Contemporary interest in *Track Two* resonates deeply with Heather Love's (2007) and my own desire to touch and experience community in the queer past, as well as a broader collective desire for intimacy with seemingly foreclosed revolutionary pasts. The film was "rescued" and put back in circulation by Pink Triangle Press after decades of obscurity in order to mark the thirtieth anniversary of the raids in 2011—a recuperation that situates contemporary consumption of the film in the broader cottage industry of knowledge production about Toronto's radical gay history. The documentary frames the bathhouse raids as a parable of (mostly white male) gay community formation, as well as the formation of political alliances across race, sexuality, gender, and class. As I will explore in greater detail, Hawkes played an important part in the critical response to the bathhouse raids, including the Right to Privacy Committee, and his accounts of activism play a key role in *Track Two*'s pedagogy of gay politicization and community formation. At stake in my reading of *Track Two* is not simply the film's content nor even the historical truth of "what really happened" in the bathhouse raids, topics that have been quite competently addressed by film reviewers and historians, respectively. Rather, I follow Miranda Joseph (2002) in making what she calls as "classic cultural studies move" (viii): asking after the contemporary terms on which the text is consumed. Working through my own desires for a radical and romantic church and gay movement of the past, my analysis reveals both the subjectless, improper queer potential of *Track Two*'s framing and the film's constitutive exclusions and appropriations.

Throughout my engagement with MCCT and the history of gay and lesbian activism in Toronto and in Canada, I have struggled with the overwhelming overrepresentation of gay white men in formal institutional archives. Both Tim McCaskell (2016) and Catherine Jean Nash (2006, 2014) note that much of the activism that circulated under the sign of "gay" in Toronto in the 1960s, '70s, and '80s, was predominantly, if not exclusively, organized around the desires of gay men, and often bracketed the question of gender. Nash (2006) describes a complex, iterative process whereby lesbian and bisexual women's groups in the period strategically associated with gay men's groups under particular political exigencies, lending the appearance of a coherent "gay and lesbian" movement to some outsiders. The historical record is also populated by women who worked strategically within predominantly gay male organizations, such as *The Body Politic* or the Coalition for Gay Rights (eventually Lesbian and Gay Rights) in Ontario (see, for instance, Nancy Nicol's [2007] tribute to the prolific activist Chris Bearchell).

Moreover, such negotiation between gay men and lesbians played out in a context in which whiteness was profoundly normative. Activist and scholarly accounts of race in 1970s and 1980s gay and lesbian Toronto foreground the themes of marginalization, alienation, and robust contestation and organizing (Fung 1986; Churchill 2003)—themes that echo, albeit differently, in a contemporary city marked by rapid immigration and structural racism (Brand 2005). It may be objected here that the urban politics of race was surely different in 1981, when only 13.6 percent of Toronto residents identified as visible minorities (Doucet 1999), as opposed to the 2006 figure of 47 percent (City of Toronto 2014). Yet recourse to the putatively transparent truth claims of demography will not do here.[5] The demolition and displacement of racialized neighborhoods in Toronto in the 1950s (Lorinc et al. 2015), increase in anti-Semitic violence throughout southern Ontario in the 1960s (Bialystok 2000), long history of fraught relationships between Afro-Caribbean communities and Toronto police (Henry 1994), and contentious debates over racialized sexual desire and fetishism in gay communities in the 1980s (Churchill 2003) all point to the long-standing significance of race and ethnicity as key preoccupations animating urban politics and atmospheric life, including in gay communities. Given that this book is a project that is largely engaged with queer of color critique, I focus principally on race and sexuality in my reading here, but such scrutiny is indissociable from considerations of gender and class.

That *Track Two* continues to exist at all is something of a happy accident. Documentary filmmakers Harry Sutherland, Gordon Keith, and Jack Lemmon initially sought to follow the historic November 1980 City Council candidacy of George Hislop, an openly gay business owner and activist and the first openly gay person to seek elected office in Ontario (Mills 2011b). Hislop's campaign had received a boost from then-mayor John Sewell, whose vocal support for gay rights was thought by many (including Sewell himself) to have cost him politically (see Sewell 1985, 198). Both Sewell and Hislop lost their respective races that fall. The electoral defeat left Sutherland, Keith, and Lemmon burdened with reams of footage chronicling a valiant loss, and unsure as to the future of their production. Then, within a period of several weeks, the three suddenly found themselves called upon to film the vast spontaneous demonstrations triggered by the 1981 bathhouse raids. The documentary that ultimately resulted is considered the most comprehensive film record of the response to the raids from a social-movement perspective (Mills 2011b). *Track Two* interleaves the defeats of Sewell and Hislop with a powerful, optimistic story of bonding in outraged response to state violence, politicized community formation, the formation of alliances across multiple modes of difference, and the increasing intelligibility of gay community as an unjustly marginalized but increasingly influential minority group.

Just as I framed Hawkes's circulation as a public figure as that of a stand-in for a complex and chaotic mix of desires, it is important to situate the film itself as an object of consumption, a stand-in, that takes on new meanings with each contemporary viewing. Though initially subject to quite favorable reviews in the gay (Wade 1982) and industry (Eames 1982) presses, the film was unsuccessful at the box office and left Sutherland, Keith, and Lemmon with a debt of more than $40,000 (Mills 2011b). By 2010, only two copies of the film were known to exist: one at Library and Archives Canada in Ottawa, and a second at the Bibliothèque et archives nationales du Québec in Montreal. Thus, Pink Triangle Press executive director Ken Popert's successful effort to recuperate and recirculate the film comprises a touch across both time and space—cultivating intimacy with a seemingly irretrievable past and bringing a film back to Toronto, the very city it so incisively re-presents. That gesture has resulted in thousands of private/public, intimate/collective viewings. Pink Triangle Press and other organizations hosted a series of screenings of *Track Two* throughout 2011 and 2012, and the film is available to view for free on YouTube, where it has attracted about fourteen thousand views at the time of this writing.

Much of *Track Two* is preoccupied with the role of police violence in facilitating the emergence or consolidation of gay community in general, and gay community as a "legitimate minority" in particular. The film is rooted in Toronto's gay district, which at the time included a commercial strip on Yonge Street and side streets between Yonge and Bay from Bloor to College. Even the title is a manifestly spatial reference, to a route informally designated by police for harassing and arresting male sex workers and "homosexuals," a route that paralleled "Track One," a nearby site of (presumed) heterosexual sex work. Scholars have fruitfully explored links between the space of the gay village, the salience of gay identity as a minority group, and claims on political enfranchisement that the film's title proposes. Nash (2006) and McCaskell (2016) have described how spatial practices such as neighborhood formation informed the emergent conceptualization of "gay" as a minority community; the crystallization of gay community identity became a key basis for rights claims in Toronto in the 1970s and 1980s. This spatial and political process saw liberal and liberationist Toronto gay activists, themselves ambivalent about gay "ghettos" for their own divergent reasons, at times strategically making common cause (Nash 2006). Although it is (perhaps deliberately) less sensitive to substantive ideological differences among gay activists and lesbian activists, and between liberals, assimilationists, and liberationists, the film powerfully points to the bathhouse raids as a pivotal moment in the forging of coalitional alliances in response to egregious state violence.

Race, Religion, and a Critique of State Violence

Such provisional unity in outrage is particularly evident in the film's use of excerpts from Hawkes's interviews and speeches. Throughout *Track Two,* Hawkes differentiates between "moderate" and "radical" approaches to activism, a formulation that he echoed in my contemporary interviews with him regarding his practices of citizenship. Where "radicals" adamantly decry and shed light on structural injustice and demand transformation through a creative range of often vehement tactics, Hawkes explains in the film, "moderates" use the discursive space opened up by radicals to make themselves available to negotiate concrete demands with agents of the state. What makes Hawkes's performance of pastoral activism in *Track Two* remarkable for my purposes here is that he confesses that the extent of his own outrage leads him to abandon his general preference for a "moderate" political role. In fact, Hawkes goes so far as to indict moderate leadership, including his own, as leaving a "legacy of failure for the gay community." Hawkes concedes that "it's only when there are moderates but also people who are willing to take stronger action that people in power listen."

Hawkes's rhetoric powerfully positions the bathhouse raids as a galvanizing event. "No longer will we stand idly by," he tells a cheering crowd that braved bitter cold to rally, "while the politicians ignore us, the police abuse us, and the right wing lie[s] about us." Perhaps Hawkes's most memorable scene of testimony, at a hearing in front of the Toronto Police Commission, gives us the activist pastor–diva–citizen Hawkes at his most openly critical of state violence. In his clerical collar, as always, Hawkes

Protesters, including Rev. Hawkes (right) and noted gay activist and political candidate George Hislop (left), demonstrate against police raids on gay men's bathhouses in Toronto, February 20, 1981. An estimated four thousand protesters marched from Queen's Park, the site of the Ontario Provincial Legislature, to 52 Division of the Toronto Police. Photograph courtesy of Gerald Hannon and the Canadian Lesbian and Gay Archives.

joins hundreds of others in demanding an independent inquiry into police relations to gay communities, and positions himself as expressly abandoning moderate gay politics: "Because of the brutal and Nazi-like actions of some of the police force last Thursday and Friday, I am no longer able to pursue the moderate approach. Where are your priorities? People of Toronto need protection, not harassment. We ask—we *tell*—you to get out of our clubs, get out of our homes, get out of our bedrooms and get back to fighting the crime in the streets."

Importantly, Hawkes describes this professed outrage, solidarity with the arrested men, and embrace of political radicality as stemming precisely from his theological and ethical commitments. He calls on gay Christians to join in the coalition opposed to police injustice and abuse entailed in the bathhouse raids:

It's a very strong history in scripture, and throughout the history of the Christian church, where ministers and leaders of the church have been called to stand up to political authorities who are being unjust, and I felt that this was my call to stand up and to speak very, very loudly. I think it's important that gay Christians take a very, very strong stand. And I continually say this to my church, that we, of all people, should be speaking out. If we believe that God is supporting us, if we believe that if we're within the space that God would have us to be, that we will be okay.

Contesting stereotypes that gay Christians are too prudish, repressed, or self-loathing to support men arrested for cruising the baths (as though the categories of "gay Christians" and "gays who cruise" were discrete!), Hawkes insists that gay Christians, "of all people," should stand against police violence. As with almost all of his appearances in the public eye, he seeks implicitly to demonstrate the possibility of integrating passions— homosexuality and Christianity—that are normatively construed as antithetical to one another. Moreover, Hawkes intimates, such passions can be integrated in the service of a radical critique of state violence. While Hawkes still allows for the legitimacy of the police function to "fight . . . crime in the streets," he also calls on faith as a resource for defying the contingent and arbitrary injustices legitimated by state actors who claim a monopoly on organized violence. Here, Hawkes's critique echoes, though only in part, Walter Benjamin's (1986) account of "divine," justice-seeking violence, a force that militates against "mythical," power-seeking, law-founding violence. Benjamin locates divine power not only in certain facets of "religious tradition" but also in an "educative power" that "stands outside the law" in its call to atonement for injustice and its negation of the legitimacy of the prevailing social order (297). Benjamin's formulation of divine power, of course, would be unsatisfied with the reformist course that most police–minority relations advocacy ultimately took in Toronto; still, the outraged Hawkes of 1981 proves worth returning to, because he brings us into contact with a glimpse of the force of divine violence's educative, justice-seeking power—and likewise enables an appreciation of the "divine" character of BLMTO's 2016 intervention.

Hawkes invokes the lineage of faith leaders standing up to a wide range of injustices—one immediately recalls the role of black clergy in the U.S. civil rights movement—to authorize his participation in the Right to Privacy Committee and demonstrations denouncing the raids. This convergence of sexuality and race through performances of Christian moral authority has long roots and ambivalent political consequences in a Canadian context. David Martin (2000) uses an umbral metaphor to make sense of Christian hegemony in Canada, describing the sustained "sense of rightness" (Berlant and Warner 1998, 554) attached to a Gregorian civic calendar, constitutionally mandated funding for Protestant and Catholic schools, and the public credibility of some clergy as a kind of "shadow establishment." This establishment's manifest claim on power has diminished over the past half century, in significant part because of the national racial and sexual traumas that Paul Bramadat and David Seljak (2009) argue have animated the waning of Christian institutional moral authority: the role of Canadian Christian churches in the culturally genocidal residential schools inflicted on indigenous people through the 1990s and in the routinized child sexual abuse by clergy. Yet Hawkes's gay Christian protest against police brutality took place in 1981, several years before efforts to politicize the trauma of residential schooling or clergy abuse emerged in public view. Thus, for Hawkes to don a clerical collar in his activism, including in his interview in *Track Two,* is to step into a preexisting "structure of sympathetic normativity" (Berlant 2000, 43), invoking Christianity as an axiomatically credible ground from which to make claims on the moral organization of the social.

As Hawkes sought to inhabit a religious idiom in order to gain intelligibility with a broader urban public, his faith-based gay activism was not uncontroversial in the city's gay communities, on behalf of which he spoke to mainstream media. On the one hand, Hawkes's position as a gay *faith* leader, and his self-professed preference for playing a "moderate" rather than a "radical" role in movements that, in his view, require both, drew the ire from more radical gay liberationist activists, with whom Hawkes sometimes also collaborated as a provisional coalition partner. At a national annual gay conference in Toronto in the mid-1970s, Hawkes, then a student minister, told me he was spat on by a prominent gay activist who chastised him for having "sold out to religion" and opined that Hawkes "had no right to be there." In a not dissimilar vein, the noted gay liberation publication *The Body Politic* (Body Politic Collective 1974) dismissed the founding of MCCT under Hawkes's predecessor, the Reverend Bob Wolfe, on the grounds that "Christian belief and gay liberation are contradictory." Hawkes, for his part, feuded with the editors of the publication, somewhat glibly criticizing a controversial article on sex between men and boys that led to obscenity charges and a major freedom-of-the-press case, and clashing over strategy for challenging homophobic policing (see, e.g., Popert 1979). At other moments, *The Body Politic* (Body Politic Collective 1981) reported on MCCT as it would any other gay organization, and when Hawkes went on a hunger strike in 1981 to demand a city inquest into the bathhouse raids, relenting only when the province of Ontario agreed to conduct an investigation, he received sympathetic coverage. Yet an on-again, off-again relationship with secular gay liberationist activists is not the only important axis of conflict that characterized the early years of Hawkes's ministry; indeed, he and his partner quite candidly refer to the years of 1976 to 1983 as "hell." This period saw considerable antipathy from Christians, including even mainstream churches. As Hawkes's husband, John Sproule, recalled in one interview, "When we were trying to buy a church building, we were looking at one church building, and when the pastor of it figured out that we were gay, he said, 'I would rather burn this building to the ground than sell it to you.'" Even within MCCT, Hawkes told me he has struggled to balance a commitment to social justice activism and an internal focus on tending to the flock. When he went on his 1981 hunger strike—a protest he framed as a personal "spiritual response"—he deliberately didn't consult the congregation so as to spare MCCT from liability. When the UFMCC held its general conference in Toronto in the sweltering summer of 1983, disenchanted members of MCCT formed their own congregation. Thus, even among gay Christians, to say nothing of secular gay liberationists, Hawkes's brand of (primarily) "moderate" social justice activism was not without its ardent critics.

Yet, despite such bitter conflicts at the nexus of sexuality and religion, part of what made Hawkes's early activism so evocative and effective was precisely his use of a rich, simultaneously racialized and religious language of moral injury. Such rhetoric was circulating across borders and informed by recent world-historical events, such as World War II and the U.S. civil rights movement. As Michael Cobb (2006) demonstrates in his insightful work on James Baldwin and sympathy, visceral Christian language has long been a principal idiom for making black political suffering intelligible in the United States, and this language has in turn served a wide range of political grievances over intersecting vectors of subject formation, such as gender and sexuality. By calling upon the figure of righteous Christians standing up against injustice, Hawkes also recalls more historically proximate iterations of that figure, particularly black Americans engaged in nonviolent civil disobedience, leaving themselves vulnerable to various forms of unfreedom in the service of a higher ideal of freedom (Brown 2015). As Laud Humphreys (1972) notes, such racialized and religious structures of moral authority were far from lost on early UFMCC clergy, who fashioned frequent—and fraught—analogies between founder Troy Perry and Martin Luther King Jr., a claim that led Perry to quip that "Martin Luther Queen" proved more apt (151). In interviews, Hawkes, too, describes a profound admiration for King, cultivated at a distance during his teens in New Brunswick, an admiration he says inspired and informs his ministry. I will revisit the problem of the race/sexuality analogy shortly. My point here, however, is that the key conditions of a Christian shadow establishment in Canada and the transnational salience of racialized U.S. Christian rhetorics of pain afforded additional legibility to Hawkes's and other gay activists' controversial claims about gay people as an oppressed minority community. Throughout *Track Two,* Hawkes's testimony makes repeated references to shared minoritized experiences across race and sexuality in the face of violent police authority.

It is not only Hawkes who gestures to race in *Track Two.* Indeed, the film's central concern with race, and with the prospect of coalitions formed across myriad vectors of difference, but especially race and sexuality, is palpable. *Track Two* includes interviews with two leading black public officials and a speech by a black advocate for police accountability, all of whom attest to feelings of identification with a (normatively white male) gay community in response to routinized forms of state violence against racially and sexually marked subjects. Indeed, *Track Two* is, in many ways, as much a film about race as it is one about sexuality. Thus, perhaps not surprisingly, when I first viewed *Track Two,* I found myself given over to a flight of fantasy about the radical gay Toronto, MCCT, and Brent Hawkes of the 1970s and 1980s. Here was the radical critique of police violence I had wanted to hear in the contemporary church![6] Here were coalitions across race, gender, sexuality, and class, coalitions among differently formed subjects who shared not a discrete identity but an estranged relationship to police power. I thought (and hoped) I'd found what I had wanted to find: the very brand of improper queer citizenship called for by Cathy J. Cohen (1997) and demanded by decades of queer theory without "proper object" and queer "subjectless critique" (Butler 1994; Eng, Halberstam, and Muñoz 2005). Robyn Wiegman (2012) writes with disarming candor about the emergence in feminist and queer studies of intersectionality as an object of desire, a theoretical framework that promises to address more far-reaching desires for amelioration and radical world building. If not robustly inter-sectional in its analysis, *Track Two* at the very least seemed to open a win-dow onto a more capacious, coalitional, and contestatory moment in To-ronto cultural politics—the very thing I had at times found lacking in the contemporary city and church.

Analogy, Intersectionality, Affectivity

Yet upon repeated, closer viewing and investigation, it became clear that *Track Two*'s framing of questions of community, coalition, and race is bet-ter understood as both rich and profoundly contradictory. Coalition is a clear object of desire in the film, but whether that coalition is understood as forming among a messy web of interleaved differences or between dis-crete and analogous groups is less obvious and less consistent. *Track Two* is littered with race/sexuality analogies that appear to presume discreteness among essentialized communities. White gay men, including Hawkes and Hislop, draw upon notions of ethnoracial "identity" and "community" to provide a rough template for making gay collectivity intelligible in terms of the "truth" of its experience of oppression, its cohesion, and the legiti-macy of its claims on rights such as privacy. Such analogical thinking is, of course, deeply problematic, having been critiqued at length by a num-ber of antiracist and queer scholars in the United States for its eschewal of historically and geographically contingent intersections and complici-ties between modes of subject formation and social ordering (see Bérubé 2001; Joseph 2002; Jakobsen 2003; Halley 2000; Eng 2010; Ferguson 2003). Moreover, framing relationships between race and sexuality (or race and gender, or between any two modes of subject formation), such scholars point out, is not only analytically unclear but politically dangerous. Trite analogies—such as the U.S. gay publication *The Advocate*'s infamous 2008 claim that "gay is the new black" (qtd. in Eng 2010, ix)—can actually serve to dilute and chip away at solidarities, insinuating that some political struggles are "complete" and triggering backlash from people for whom it is crucial, and indeed lifesaving, to continue to engage in those struggles (see Hancock 2011). As Allan Bérubé (2001) trenchantly writes of gay MLK analogies, including those made through the MCC movement, "If the gay rights movement is already part of the ongoing struggle for the dignity of all people exemplified in the activism of Dr. Martin Luther King Jr., then there is no need for gay equivalents of Dr. King, racial segregation, or the civil rights movement. If the gay rights movement is not already part of the civil rights movement, then what is it?" (246).

Sympathetic to but departing from this line of argument against analogies, Cobb (2006) suggests that the proliferation of race/sexuality analogies might be approached not only as trite, abstract, or appropriative but as historically conditioned and constrained by race's centrality to American structures of sympathetic normativity (Berlant 2000). American public narratives about structurally inflicted suffering, Cobb argues, are so bound up with stories about racism and racialized pain—especially black pain, and often using religious rhetoric—that other modes of critique and complaint inexorably inherit, inhabit, inflect, and tweak such narrative structures. Cobb's point is not to deny the analytical limitations, historical inaccuracies, or strategic disadvantages of race/sexuality analogies so much as to direct attention to the specific historical conditions that enable and constrain their emergence and mobilization. It is precisely because of the historic and sustained centrality of blackness and antiblack violence to any understanding of American citizenship, Cobb suggests, that analogies to race are so prolific. While Cobb's argument is drawn from studied engagement with the circulation of affects around difference in U.S. publics, his analysis of the ways that "different" differences encounter each other proves of more general value, particularly in his attention to historical and geographical specificity.

Thus, it can productively be asked what different figurations of race and sexuality *do* in the historical and geographical context that *Track Two* mediates. On the one hand, the film and many of its principal subjects, most of them gay white men, are invested in a project of securing a metaphorical and material place for gay community as a legitimate community, and call upon the figures of people of color to authorize such legitimacy. For instance, Hawkes in one interview extract worries about the impact of unchecked police authority not only for the gay community but also for "other minority communities"; at a time when the understanding of gayness as a "minority" formation or attribute was highly controversial, such a deft rhetorical move retroactively naturalizes gay community as a minority alongside others. Such framings should be understood as both historically constrained by broader structures of legibility and politically problematic. On the other hand, the film simultaneously invests viewers' hopes in the promise of coalition across race and sexuality on potentially more complex, capacious terms. Testifying before the police commission, Hawkes places black and gay experience on parallel (if not intersecting) tracks vis-à-vis heavy-handed state authority and lack of accountability: "We've seen in the past, and the black community have seen in the past, that when we go to lay a complaint, what usually happens is that the complainant is charged with something, or their home is raided." Hawkes's ambivalent pronoun use here—"we" and "their"—toggles back and forth between (and among) permutations of blackness and gayness. Such framing simultaneously reproduces a putative divide between "black" and "gay" forms of collectivity and vulnerability, and alludes to possibilities for solidarity and knowledge exchange across shared alienated relations to state power.

The ambivalent framing of race—as grounds for analogy to sexual identity or perhaps something more complex, more intimately imbricated with sexuality—also suffuses the testimony of John Burt, a young gay man who was among the hundreds of "found-ins" arrested on the night of the bathhouse raids. Burt recounts in detail the mix of malice and grim, "just doing my job" passivity with which police entered the bathhouse, explained their presence, and broke open and searched lockers as shocked men stood naked before them, reduced to nothing. Burt, who makes note of his Jewish background, explains it was the humiliation and outrage of Operation Soap that enabled him, harrowingly, to better understand the experiences of his parents, who had survived the Holocaust: "I was very aware of this imagery that I was facing that night, and it just seemed too reminiscent for me. It was that night that I realized what my parents must have been going through when they had to stand naked in a concentration camp. And it's very hard to understand that sometimes, because intellectually you can understand it, but emotionally you don't understand it. And that night I understood it, and it was quite horrifying." Franklin Bialystok (2000) writes of the affective and temporal lag in Jewish Canadian communities in grappling with the Holocaust. Although some forty thousand Holocaust survivors immigrated to Canada in the 1940s, Bialystok describes a culture of shame and silence that did not break until the 1960s, when ongoing anti-Semitism forced survivors and their children to confront the ghosts that haunted the promise of a better life in Canada. As a second-generation Jewish Canadian, Burt speaks in a moment when official forms of memorialization outpaced an affective grappling with trauma—when factual and intellectual discussion of the Holocaust became more open in Jewish communities "but emotionally you don't understand it."

Dina Georgis (2013) writes of queerness as a "trace," an affective epistemology that enables us to turn back toward the political and affective losses that form us as subjects, to grieve those losses, and to reinvigorate desire for alternative ways of being intimate and collective. Here, Burt's queerness—his experience of dehumanizing trauma by police at the baths—opens him up to understanding the trauma of the Holocaust and to grieving those "quite horrifying" losses. But this queer trace takes Burt even further, to a gleeful description of the formation of alliances and kinship with a range of communities afflicted by police brutality:

> We've [gay organizers have] been very instrumental in helping to set up CIRPA, which is a Civilian Independent Review of Police Action, which is a citizen's group of many ethnic groups and many other minorities in conjunction with the gay community. That's the most exciting thing about what's happening in the gay community, because we're now being accepted as a community by other minority communities. I go to meetings with the Sikhs, and I'm welcomed as a brother. I go to meetings with the blacks. I go to meetings with Chinese. With West Indians. And we suddenly realized that we have a common enemy.

Burt makes recourse to a tableau of coalition here that figures various communities as parallel or analogous and that abstracts race and ethnicity from sexuality. Yet, in marking himself as a queer Jew, Burt also points to alternative concepts of race, sexuality, family, and kinship—"I go to meetings with the Sikhs, and I'm welcomed as a brother." Such encounters hint at emergent desires for solidarity and intimacy, desires reinvigorated by grappling with the trauma of the raids. Queer injury becomes a departure point, both for working through the transgenerational trauma of the Holocaust and for exceeding gay or Jewish identity politics and pursuing solidarity with other Others who share a "common enemy" in state violence. In this sense, Burt speaks directly to the centrality of the work of affect to an improper queer urban citizenship.

But what about the film's subjects of color (or other subjects of color, depending on how Jewishness is framed)? Rather than a redemptive coalition story, or simply appropriative, *Track Two* is a text in which the figures of people of color refuse to be easily consumed. Racialized figures intervene *both* to legitimate normatively white gay claims on minority status that depend on race/sexuality analogy *and* to stand in for more complex and potentially robust aspirations to coalition in a city that is awakening to its sexual and ethnoracial heterogeneity.

For instance, the film begins and ends with excerpts from an interview with Pat Case and Fran Endicott, respectively the first black Canadian man and woman elected to the Toronto School Board. In this encounter between the two black politicians and the (mostly white gay male) filmmakers, notice the shifts in the ways that race, sexuality, and community are positioned:

Pat Case: My only contact—the only contact people in the black community, many people in the black community, have with gay people in the city—is the annual Halloween thing on Yonge Street. And I think that's as far as a lot of people want to take it, or are even conscious of the fact of a large gay community living in Toronto.

Fran Endicott: I think that we have to be very careful when we start talking about communities in terms of "gay community" or "black community." I mean, it's quite obvious that the gay community would also have a number of blacks [laughs] as part of that community as well.

In terms of my own experiences, I was thinking back, I guess it was triggered off by what Pat said about the Halloween parade. I remember coming to Toronto ten years ago and being told about this parade and standing on the street corner at Yonge and Alexander and really losing interest in the parade itself, because I was terrified by the crowd. I was terrified by the kind of excitement among a number of youths and the insults and that kind of stuff that were being hurled at people. And, of course, it was a parade and the gays were there in costume and all that kind of stuff. But I remember being very frightened by the crowd and having for the first time a sense of how easily a mob could be formed, and being able to imagine myself being the target of that group—and that was scary. And I think that was the first time I ever thought about anything of a gay community in Toronto.

Case provisionally adopts a framework about relations between putatively discrete entities called "the gay community" and "the black community," a framing that perhaps echoes the one introduced by the filmmakers in interview questions. Black queer critic Roderick Ferguson (2003) argues that it is precisely through the form of analogy—through what he calls "ideologies of discreteness" (4) that queer of color histories and socialities are effaced and their political demands eschewed by more identitarian practices of queer citizenship. It is also possible that Case's framing of blackness and gayness as discrete, and his apparent discomfort, responds to the uncomfortable nature of his encounter with the filmmakers—that Case, perhaps rightly, perceived the filmmakers' engagement with him as an instrumental use of blackness to legitimate gayness.

Yet, in response and by contrast, Endicott rapidly eschews this "gay versus black" framing, bemusedly schooling the black heterosexual man and white gay men in the room that "it's quite obvious that the gay community would also have a number of blacks as well." Drawing attention to the intersectional character of identity (Crenshaw 1991), Endicott also goes further by offering an affective and social geography of solidaristic identification (Puar 2007; King 2015). Sketching the city's annual gay Halloween parade, the intersection of Yonge Street and Alexander Street, a hateful mob, and her own terror, she recounts and grounds her inaugural experience of identification with gay people. Psychoanalytic scholar Diana Fuss (1995) describes identification as "opening up a space for the self to relate to itself as a self, a self that is perpetually other," as "the detour through the other that defines the self" (2). For Endicott, it is not the Halloween parade itself that provides an occasion for identification so much as the vulnerability of gays "in costume" as "the target of that group." Seeing gay people as the target of a violent mob enables Endicott to draw upon life experience and collective memory of organized and routinized violence against black people, and black women in particular, such that "gay community" becomes both "me" (the potential target of a hateful mob) and "not-me" (gay). In excess of the race/sexuality analogical frame that underpins much of the film, and even in excess of many appropriations of intersectionality theory, which privilege retrospectively applied representational categories over affective encounters and movement, Endicott provides a sophisticated affective account of identification as grounds for coalition.

As Case's discomfort perhaps suggests, it is possible that the makers of *Track Two* sought to interview black community leaders in order to consolidate gay claims on minority status—or to performatively call into being more evidence of coalitional solidarities across race and sexuality than actually existed at the time. Yet Endicott seems to perceive the scene of encounter—with Case and the filmmakers, however awkward—as an opportunity to ask everyone in the room, and the viewers, what meaningful solidarity across race and sexuality, in all its surprising and banal intersections, might look like. Toward the film's conclusion, we again hear from Endicott, who offers a complex analysis of the potential value of gay organizing *beyond* the "gay community":

> I think we have to keep making those links [within and across movements and communities]. I think it is very important. And what I see the gay community doing now in terms of its organization is that it is helping people to make those links. The community's talking, very articulately, very clearly, about the issues that are involved—that it's not really even a matter of sex, or protecting people's right to the sexual preference. It really is about human rights in a very fundamental level. It's saying to people that you cannot expect individuals to exist in some kind of half-free state. The only time I think anybody tried to do that very seriously were the Americans after the abolition of slavery, in which you had certain rights, and you didn't have other rights. [She shakes her head.] And it doesn't work. It's crazy!
>
> And what we have to do is to get not simply politicians, not simply school board people, but the entire society making that kind of analysis. And that for me is the importance of the organization of the gay community, because they are saying those things in very real terms, so that you have people who might have been frightened of even talking about homosexuality going beyond that and seeing the real issues involved and really making an attempt to deal with it.

At first, Endicott seems to traffic in a simple and vexed race/sexuality analogy: just as the Jim Crow laws that emerged in the United States during Reconstruction deprived black people of their full human rights, so too do antigay police brutality and the state's tacit assent to informal homophobic violence. Yet Endicott's description of gay pain is firmly enmeshed in an account of capacious affective politics and coalitional organizing—in her words, "making links," both conceptual and material. Whether people make those links and enact an improper queer citizenship is a matter of ongoing affective and political work. But Endicott senses in gay resistance to police violence a kind of potentiality, in excess of gay identity, and a kind of pedagogical value that goes beyond identity politics to make a robust and complex range of rights claims. In this respect, she simultaneously articulates the potential value of gay politics to nongay audiences concerned with human rights and challenges identitarian gay politics that might otherwise remain satisfied with a race/sexuality analogy and fail to commit to antiracism. She even indicates that it is through a capacious solidarity politics ("making those links") that people might work through the affective difficulty of their own homophobia (or, for white gay men, racism and sexism)—that "seeing the real issues involved" could facilitate "really making an attempt to deal with it." Thus, rather than allow her presence to be instrumentalized, Endicott uses it as an opportunity to challenge identitarian politics by offering a model of improper queer urban citizenship that exceeds it.

Track Two also features a powerful proclamation of solidarity at a protest after the raids by Lemona "Monica" Johnson, a black woman whose late husband, Albert Cecil Johnson, a Jamaican immigrant, was shot and killed by Toronto police in August 1979 after a summer of escalating police harassment. The previous fall, Lemona Johnson had endured the exasperating trial of William Inglis and Walter Cargnelli, the two constables charged with her husband's death. Commentators noted that the court proceedings focused more on the putative eccentricity, mental health, and moral character of the late Albert Johnson than on the conduct of Inglis and Cargnelli, who had kicked in Johnson's back door and clubbed him with a two-pound flashlight before shooting him. The egregious case was so infamous in Toronto's Jamaican communities in the early 1980s that, according to some commentators, "Johnson" became "verbed" into a colloquialism, a term for police brutality and murder, as in "Don't Johnson me" (Siggins 1981; see also Sewell 1985, 160). According to his widow, Albert Johnson had told officers, "Leave me alone. I can't walk the street because of you."

Lemona Johnson, who maintained that police had entered her home illegally, fought to testify at the trial, but the Crown attorney for the case refused. The two officers were ultimately acquitted of charges of manslaughter (Siggins 1981). Given the timing—the acquittal occurred in November 1980, shortly after Hislop's electoral defeat and not three months before the bathhouse raids—a grieving Lemona Johnson's appearance at the rally is

Lemona "Monica" Johnson, the widow of Albert Johnson, a black Jamaican immigrant killed by police in 1979, speaks in solidarity at an anti-police-brutality rally in 1981 in the wake of the infamous Toronto bathhouse raids. Tim McCaskell, a gay antiracist activist who emceed the rally, looks on. Daily Xtra! *file photograph from* Track Two, *directed by Harry Sutherland.*

especially remarkable. Speaking at a huge, spirited demonstration outside Police Division 52 headquarters, near Dundas Street West and University Avenue, Johnson issues a call for accountability to a cheering crowd: "The raid and arrests of members of the Toronto gay community is a further indication that the police force of this city is lacking in discipline and proper supervision. The police force in this city is being used as a political tool by politicians, such as the attorney general, Roy McMurtry, and Premier William Davis, to achieve their personal and political ends at the expense of the people of Ontario." Johnson invites listeners to scale up, both by coming together across discrete but linked forms of injury and by directing scrutiny to the provincial scale, where activists sought an official inquiry into police–minority relations.

Building on encounters with racialized interview subjects linking multiple forms of injury and vectors of power enables *Track Two* to consolidate an uplifting narrative about the power of coalition across difference. Such coalitional ethos is further buttressed by speeches from labor, feminist, francophone, and civil libertarian activists and public officials, but racial difference, which surfaces again in the film's conclusion, is its linchpin. After some encouraging words from former mayor Sewell about minority rights and the necessity of social movement, the film's final scene opens onto a sun-soaked day and a pier on Lake Ontario. A dancer, clad in a black tank top and black slacks and carrying a pink-triangle flag, leans out over the pier's edge, as though testing gravity, then deftly turns back onto surer footing and reaches up toward the sun, as if aspirational. Ostensibly non-white, the dancer is credited simply as "Lim." Further research confirmed the dancer's identity as Lim Pei-Hsien, a noted Malaysian Canadian poet, dancer, registered nurse, martial artist, graphic designer, activist, and porn star who lived in Toronto through the mid-1980s and later died of AIDS-related illness in Vancouver in 1992 (see Fung 1986). As the credits roll, superimposed over the beautiful day, Lim keeps silently strutting his stuff. *Track Two* concludes by placing its desires and hopes—for community that bonds through oppression but remains politicized and vigilant, for capacious coalitions across multiple forms of difference that work together to set limits on state power over life, for a city in which powerful people are forced to apprehend diverse and overlapping formations of "minority" and "community"—in the figure of an out and proud gay man of color.

Track Two for the Present

How, then, are contemporary queer scholars and activists to read, view, and feel our way through *Track Two* in the present—particularly in light of the film's gestures to radicality and coalition, objects of desire we may well share? Given its preoccupations with the politics of community formation, security, and coalition, *Track Two* resonates in the contemporary queer moment in Toronto for a host of reasons. When it was "rescued" and recirculated by Pink Triangle Press, in 2011, many astute commentators made links between the 1981 raids and the dramatic and abusive urban securitization during mass protests against the 2010 G20 Summit in Toronto (see Malleson and Wachsmuth 2011). Bathhouse owner and activist Peter Bochove (2011), for instance, argued that the bathhouse raids' invidious distinction as the worst violation of civil liberties since the War Measures Act of 1970 had "been eclipsed by the atrocity that was the G20." And indeed, contemporary audiences eager for the kind of coalitional police-accountability politics that *Track Two* (through all its contradictions) powerfully anticipates in its closing scenes are almost sure to be disappointed. While some queers provisionally enjoy increased access to ordinary, unproblematic circulation through urban space vis-à-vis police and informal harassment, many, particularly queer and trans people of color and working-class queers, do not (see Walcott 2014). The racialized practices of brutality and excessive use of force that figure prominently in *Track Two* as a departure point for coalitions across racial and sexual diversity persist (Rankin et al. 2014; Sankaran 2012). As I noted in chapter 1, in Toronto, as in far too many places, transgender people, particularly transgender people of color, comprise a routine target for police brutality and dispossession in the court system. Moreover, the reception of important interventions against antiblack racism and police brutality like those of BLMTO in normatively white LGBTQ publics has proven (distressingly but not surprisingly) mixed at best, despite the organization's remarkable victories in its work with Pride Toronto.

Indeed, in the contemporary moment, celebratory accounts of gains made in police relations—accounts shaped by normative whiteness and middle-class social location—often stand in for all LGBTQ perspectives, and indeed even for the perspectives of all "minorities," as in police chief Mark Saunders's claim at the beginning of this chapter about "lessons learned" from the city's "many communities." As I have demonstrated, MCCT's flock is a site of ambivalence, ideological heterogeneity, and critique with respect to the police. Yet the church risks complicity in the erasure of heterogeneous perspectives insofar as it speaks on matters of security through the pulpit in a single and affirmative voice that insists "it got better." From this contemporary vantage, even given the limitations of its analogical thinking, *Track Two* does seem to document a more critical and contestatory moment in the history of Toronto gay movements with respect to questions of race, class, and policing. The damning implication of this gap between past and present—one obviated by many reactions to BLMTO's brilliant 2016 interventions—is that white gay men, who once worked in solidarity with and as part of sexually and racially diverse communities against police violence, abandoned a more thoroughgoing critique of state violence once they themselves had achieved provisional ordinariness.

Yet the ostensible discrepancy between a radical past and a neoliberal present also needs to be unpacked with more care. Was the past really as radical as it seemed, or as cut off from the present as the romantic formulation of a "radical past" would suggest? Although the film depicts the Right to Privacy Committee as boldly bridging differences around race, sexuality, gender, and class to confront systemic police brutality and profiling, an interview I conducted with a leading organizer suggests a more murky history. Simultaneously hoping to have my desires for a romantic, radical, and coalitional past confirmed and, I suppose, to be disabused of them, I contacted Tim McCaskell. McCaskell was a member of the Right to Privacy Committee (RTPC) and *The Body Politic* collective, and his work as an activist and a thinker in Toronto has been dedicated to solidaristic and coalitional politics across race, class, gender, and sexuality since the 1970s (see McCaskell 2016). McCaskell cannot be taken to speak for all Toronto gay activists, but many would share his skepticism of MCCT's role in brokering controversy over police–minority relations, both in the present and in the late 1970s and early 1980s. Against the romance of community and coalition that frame *Track Two,* McCaskell described the history of community activism against police violence as far more fragmented and contingent.

I began by asking McCaskell about the meaning and conditions of Lemona Johnson's participation in the rally outside the headquarters of Police Division 52 that cold night in February 1981. Framing my question in light of the present, I asked him whether we could understand such alliances as "redemptive" signs of radical solidarity:

Johnson's participation at the rally was very logical for the RTPC. The two groups most under attack from the cops were the black community and gay men, so it was considered an important alliance. We also had contacts with the anticop people in the South Asian community. A few months after the raids, we managed to get CIRPA [Citizens' Independent Review of Police Activities] set up. The major elements were black community organizations, lefty lawyers, civil liberties types, and the RTPC.

I don't know if that makes it redemptive or not. All sides saw this as a practical alliance. By '83, we had won the bath-raids cases, and the cops—maybe out of fear of AIDS or because they got so bashed—began to let up on gay men. It didn't stop them continuing to shoot black ones, though. Since CIRPA was focused on the police and one of its major components found that contradiction less antagonistic, it finally faded away—'84 or so?

Far from forging a robust or sustained coalitional sensibility, the RTPC, CIRPA, and similar coalitional bodies, McCaskell intimates, served contingent purposes and lost momentum when some participants lost interest. He also shed light on ideological and strategic differences within normatively white gay activist circles, including the rather disparate roles of MCCT and *The Body Politic* (TBP) collective:

> The [city-commissioned] Bruner report [on police–gay relations] in the middle of '81 made a lot of suggestions about "improving relations." One of these was a gay–police liaison committee. People were suspicious of that, and TBP finally came out against it. MCC was supportive. But as the bath raids retreated into history, that kind of politics replaced the militancy of the post-bath period, but it also focused on police attitudes to gay people rather than police practices to discipline unruly communities who in their day-to-day practices resist their marginalization.

Here, McCaskell frames MCCT as positioned on the side of the historical victors, preferring the work of transforming police attitudes on the basis of liberal identity politics to the more challenging task of confronting systemic and diffuse practices of state violence. I asked him whether it made sense to understand the intervening thirty years in terms of betrayal on the part of gay white men. By way of reply, he reframed coalition less as a matter of choice, or even interest, than one of shifting affective dynamics:

> Betrayal as a concept assumes a rational process. I think to understand it, it is more useful to think of affective charges that are attached to particular concepts. Police had always been in the forefront of social brutality towards gay men and lesbians, first as enforcers of the law, then as enforcers of social attitudes looking for laws or other excuses to put people in their place. The bath raids was just the icing on the cake. . . . So, there is a really negative charge associated with the police, similar to the negative charge experienced by young black men derived from their experience. That's grounds for an alliance. When that charge is dissipated through changing experiences and things like the liaison committee, the negative charge slowly disappears from dominant [white]

gay men's consciousness. Alliances lose salience when there is no shared affective charge.

McCaskell's reflections are mediated by his own preoccupations and interpretive frames as a Marxist historian-practitioner in antiracist and LGBTQ movements in and beyond Toronto. Yet, at the very least, he helpfully demystifies notions of a radical past untarnished by neoliberalism or other barriers to robust coalition formation in racial and sexual politics. In a similar vein, geographer Catherine Jean Nash (2005) sheds further light on the limits of *Track Two*'s gestures to coalition, suggesting that links between white gay men and racialized community groups were tenuous, belated, somewhat instrumental, at times unwitting, and, in many cases, reluctant.

Such demystification dashed my hopes of discovering a "better," more radicalized church, pastor, or urban gay movement of the past. But it also left me with a new question, different from the questions that had propelled my initial turn back toward the fantasized radical past of the church and of queer politics in Toronto: What would it mean to let the Other that is the past remain different from, yet also uncomfortably continuous with, the present, rather than forcing it to exist in a relationship of superiority or inferiority, of banishment or foreclosure? As Georgis (2006) contends in her writing on diasporic affect, loss—in this case, the loss of a fantasized past, never experienced but longed for in its imagined absence—is also an occasion for the resuscitation of desire. If melancholia, as a fundamental element of the process of mourning, orients us toward loss, a more direct confrontation with loss—never graceful, but necessary—can inaugurate feelings of dissatisfaction and desire that find a locus in the world, in the future. If both the contemporary church and *Track Two* as a snapshot of historic pastoral activism are impure, compromised, frustrating, and disappointing, then acknowledging the loss of fantasies of political redemption could also be the grounds for what Klein might call a more affectively integrative relation to the church, and to Toronto queer politics, as whole objects across converging and disparate timelines.

Perhaps *Track Two*'s gesture toward future possibilities for community and coalition can be read as appropriative or naive, and simultaneously as proleptic—as orienting viewers toward modes of collectivity that have yet to exist, attempting to performatively instantiate the existence of new kinds of political community and alternative models of urban citizenship (see Butler 1999; Butler and Spivak 2007). Perhaps what is valuable about my encounter with the ultimately not-so-radical, not-so-redemptive past is not my shame at having naively hoped I might find something radical and redemptive but the *interest* that shame revealed. Elspeth Probyn (2005) argues for the potential ethical value of shame, suggesting that precisely because shame tends to describe repudiated or unreciprocated interest, our willingness to risk repudiation or nonreciprocity can teach us about what we most value. Upon further scrutiny, I found some pretty disappointing part objects in the past: a turn from coalitional calls for structural change to the liberal idiom of "police–gay relations," and a profusion of fraught race/sexuality analogies. But I also found some good fragments, potentially nourishing resources that could help us understand what continues to be missing in the city of Toronto and in the world: meaningful identifications and capacious political visions on the part of Lemona Johnson, John Burt, Fran Endicott, and Tim McCaskell, and Brent Hawkes's bold tethering of faith to a radical critique of state violence. Thus, rather than reading *Track Two*'s narratives of community, coalition, and a gay pastor as an authoritative (or simply inaccurate) rendition of "what really happened" or a glimpse of alternative possible futures as envisioned in 1982, perhaps the film can actually remind contemporary queers, critics, activists, and people of faith of what still frustrates us, what we still long for politically, and what political futures we might yet pursue—what worlds we might conjure into being. It is with this question of prolepsis in mind that I turn to a more contemporary instance of pastor–diva–citizenship.

Diva Citizenship on the National Stage

On Saturday, August 27, 2011, thousands of people lined up outside Roy Thomson Hall and in the adjacent David Pecaut Square in downtown Toronto, in the hopes of witnessing the state funeral of Official Opposition leader and New Democratic Party leader Jack Layton. The charismatic Toronto politician, who had scored major gains for the New Democrats in a federal election just months earlier, passed away on August 22, 2011, at sixty-one, after an eighteen-month battle with prostate cancer. His memorial drew mourners from across partisan identifications and included eulogies by Layton's children, Mike and Sarah, and by Stephen Lewis, a former Canadian ambassador to the United Nations and a former Ontario NDP leader. Because of their longtime friendship, Layton had asked Hawkes for MCCT to play a significant role in the service, which featured musical performances from the church choir and both a greeting and a poignant, celebrated benediction from Hawkes (see Peat 2011; Bradshaw 2011; Porter 2012).

It is important to situate the Layton funeral as at once a highly orchestrated, rehearsed, routinized ceremony—an ordered materialization of the "national stage"—and a chaotic assemblage of unruly and not fully aligned parts, open to constrained but potentially surprising acts of spontaneity and intervention. The very decision to give Layton a state funeral was not uncontroversial and was criticized by some of the more vitriolic commentators on the Canadian right as a crass, instrumental conceit precipitated largely by the New Democrats' unprecedented electoral gains just a few months earlier (see Blatchford 2011).[7] In another unusual move, the ceremony took place at Roy Thomson Hall, a secular, not-for-profit institution that usually serves as a concert hall, making it the first and only Canadian state funeral to date not held in a Christian church of some kind. Yet the venue is hardly unaccustomed to liturgical uses; Roy Thomson Hall also provides space for MCCT's annual Christmas Eve midnight service, a tradition that has led MCC founder the Reverend Troy Perry to refer to the space wryly as "the National Cathedral of Canada." Because of interest and attendance, organizers also included live video streams of the service for overflow viewers in David Pecaut Square, a public plaza adjacent to Roy Thomson Hall that also provides access to the PATH network of walking tunnels, the largest underground shopping center in the world. The funeral brought federal political leaders together, including Canadian then–prime minister Stephen Harper and his wife, Laureen, to Layton's beloved Toronto, a city with a fraught position in the Canadian national imaginaries commonly mobilized by major political figures. Although Harper was born in Toronto, his Conservative political brand relies heavily on exploiting western Canada's historic antipathy to Toronto; no member of Parliament from the greater Toronto area has served as prime minister since the 1920s. As an official federal state funeral—only the thirty-second such event in Canadian history, and the first for an Opposition leader—the service was broadcast live on the Canadian Broadcasting Corporation and is archived on its website (see Marz 2011; Fedio 2011). It is under this wily, idiosyncratic set of geographical and historical conditions that Hawkes officiated at Layton's state funeral—a role he was asked to play as Layton's friend, political ally, and pastor to Layton and his widow, then-member of Parliament Olivia Chow.

Much as he had done in his multifarious role in activist responses to the bathhouse raids, Hawkes wore many hats at the memorial, at once officiating, offering blessings, setting a tone, and taking up a bully pulpit. But in contrast to his appearances in *Track Two,* in which affects like righteous anger at homophobic violence provided a departure point for critical political engagement and the formation of communities and coalitions, Hawkes's participation in the Layton memorial was marked by a tone of celebration and progress resonant with contemporary queer liberal promises that "it gets better"—or, indeed, with the kind of gay-end-of-history conceit that "it" already has gotten better, at least in Canada. And the memorial service was indeed quite a performance and an accomplishment on Hawkes's part, putting MCCT on the national map in a new way and drawing in hundreds of online viewers, attendees, new members, and interlocutors to the church. Here again, it proves crucial to situate Hawkes's moment of national pastoral pedagogy within the more multifarious geographies of the "shadow establishment" (Martin 2000) of Christianity in Canada. While the UFMCC does not claim a wide familiarity or following among the Canadian public, a range of factors primed audiences to encounter Hawkes as a redemptive figure: Christianity's diffuse and tacit hegemony; MCCT's liturgically blended style; a highly teleological dominant narrative of Canadian national progress on LGBTQ rights (see McCaskell 2016); and Hawkes's idiosyncratic activist itinerary.

Yet it is important to read generously and for irony here, for Hawkes's benediction also harbors moments of impish and creative critique, more proleptic political gestures that critically conjure and perform better political futures that are not-yet-here (Muñoz 2009). In key moments, improper queer citizenship critically addresses the nation-state through Hawkes, demanding and boldly imagining more ethical relationships to the losses and exclusions that haunt the nation-state. Thus, while the address in many respects consolidates a liberal progress narrative, it simultaneously exposes some of the limits of that much-touted progress. As in my reading of *Track Two,* I find myself unable to recover a purely radical, redemptive, or unproblematic queer church in contemporary MCCT or its senior pastor; rather, I find a complex and contradictory constellation of spaces and figures, continuous in some respects with the church and pastor represented in *Track Two*.

Though Hawkes played numerous roles at the Layton memorial service, at the core of his appearance on the national stage were the eulogy and benediction he delivered, the final spoken words shared at the memorial. Hawkes began and ended his message with gestures toward intimacy. He joked that the nervousness he felt speaking at the memorial remained eclipsed by the first time he met the parents of his future husband, John Sproule. He recalled Layton's endearing habit of asking after his friends' partners—for instance, "Hey Brent, how's John doing?"—as evincing the Opposition leader's gay-friendly politics and human touch. After a ten-minute address considering Layton's legacy and the stakes and significance of his work, Hawkes concluded by returning to his introductory frame:

> Yes, bring your seriousness about serious issues, but also have fun—sing together and pick up a harmonica once in a while. It's [Honoring Layton's legacy is] about remembering, about remembering to say, "Hi Brent. How's John doing?" [Hawkes directs his gaze toward Prime Minister Stephen Harper in the audience] Hi, Canadian prime minister. How's Laureen doing? [He turns toward Layton's widow, then-member of Parliament Olivia Chow] It's about saying, "Hi, Olivia. How's Beatrice [Chow's granddaughter] doing?" It's about remembering each other and our love and our lives together.
>
> Over the next few years, we might not be able to say, "Hi, Jack. How's Olivia doing?" But you can say, "Hi, Jack. How are we doing?"

Just as Layton had asked after Hawkes's husband, Hawkes asked after Prime Minister Stephen Harper's wife, Laureen, and Olivia Chow's granddaughter, Beatrice. Finally, he positioned Layton as a kind of national Big Other and framed the leader's legacy as a locus for collective self-reflection.

Hawkes used the idiom of intimacy and family that framed his eulogy to posit an equivalence, normalizing his marriage to a same-sex partner and putting it on legal and habitual par with that of the Harpers or of Layton and Chow. Such an equivalence is open to a number of interpretations. It could be argued that the gesture seeks assimilation into mainstream

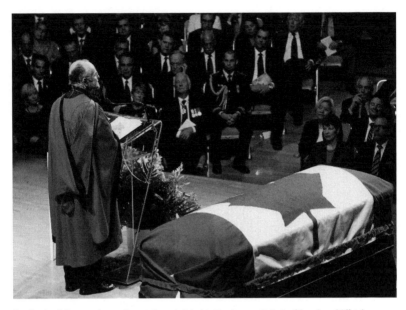

Rev. Hawkes delivers a eulogy at the state funeral of the late New Democratic Party of Canada and Official Opposition leader Jack Layton at Roy Thomson Hall in Toronto on August 27, 2011. Photograph by Frank Gunn; courtesy of the Canadian Press.

institutions of "national sexuality," positing liberal equivalence and deploying sentimentality to gloss over the potentially thorny or challenging dimensions of homosexuality (to say nothing of the challenges and possibilities of queer critique) that can prove threatening in still-heteronormative societies (Berlant 1997, 148). From this vantage, marriage is rightly critiqued as an inherently conservative project that drains resources and affective investments away from broader, more downwardly redistributive forms of political change (see, e.g., Duggan 2012; Spade and Willse 2013). Thus, it could be argued that Hawkes's preoccupation with it in his eulogy is not particularly surprising or subversive, merely a bad liberal object-choice. Performing gay normalcy and equivalence on the national stage, from this point of view, is hardly a radical act, particularly since same-sex marriage in Canada seems something of a fait accompli.

While my initial judgments were in this "anti-marriage" vein, I wonder whether this equivalence could also be read a bit more playfully, and with a bit more attention to historical and geographical context. Any consideration of same-sex marriage in Canada needs to embed it within specific histories of LGBTQ social movements (Smith 2007; Nicol 2006). Although the appropriateness of same-sex marriage as a political goal has been and remains a hotly debated question in Canadian LGBTQ politics and scholarship, many activists, including Hawkes, identified marriage as a key terrain of struggle in the late 1990s and early 2000s, for a fairly wide, chaotic, and contradictory range of reasons. In this pursuit of same-sex marriage rights, Hawkes was able to make provisional common cause with more radical activists who regarded marriage advocacy as a potential departure point for politicizing gays and lesbians and antagonizing the right wing, even if it also assimilated some gays and lesbians into dominant idioms for kinship (Smith 2014). In 2001, Hawkes conducted two same-sex weddings at MCCT, which were retroactively recognized as legal by the Ontario Court of Appeal—a moment the Toronto church now proudly claims makes it the site of the first legal same-sex wedding in the world (MCC Toronto 2014). Same-sex marriage then became legal in Canada at the federal level through changes to the Civil Marriage Act adopted under Paul Martin's Liberal government in 2005. Layton, a longtime supporter of legal same-sex marriage who advocated it with Chow at their own 1988 nuptials and in his first speech in the House of Commons, whipped the 2005 vote on same-sex marriage, ejecting from the party caucus the sole NDP member of Parliament who opposed the measure ("Jack Layton" 2011).

Yet, as Marci McDonald (2010) notes in her examination of conservative Christian activism in Canada, sustained opposition to same-sex marriage played a key role in the 2006 election that first brought Stephen Harper to power. Provincial appeals courts began recognizing same-sex marriages under the Canadian Charter of Rights and Freedoms in 2003, with Liberal then-prime minister Jean Chrétien vowing to introduce a same-sex marriage bill that same year. After the Liberals successfully amended the Civil Marriage Act to include same-sex marriage in 2005, Stephen Harper campaigned on a nebulous, carefully crafted promise to hold a free vote on reopening the marriage debate—a promise that some argue helped him win a minority government in 2006 (McDonald 2010). From 2003 through 2006, campaigns to prevent, and later reverse, federal legislation allowing same-sex marriage ushered in a massive influx of U.S. resources to support conservative Christian intellectual and political activity in Canada. Although marriage equality remained legal after a failed free vote on its rescindment in December 2006, the lengthy marriage battle and 2006 federal election galvanized cultural conservatives, leaving them more engaged, better resourced, and increasingly influential (though not indomitable) within the ruling Conservative Party of Canada (McDonald 2010). And although Harper declared the matter closed since the failed free vote, his government hardly smiled on same-sex marriage, particularly with respect to non-Canadian couples who travel to Canada to marry (Makin 2012). Finally, Harper had just won his only majority government in Parliament in May, meaning the Conservatives could pursue their agenda comparatively unimpeded for four years without much risk of a government falling.

Given this context, perhaps Hawkes's query to Harper—"Hi, Canadian prime minister. How's Laureen doing?"—cheekily trotted out a claim on equivalence that might still have felt somewhat vulnerable, particularly vis-à-vis a begrudging head of state who was not above fomenting and exploiting homophobia for his own political gain. Moreover, given the religious character of much of the opposition to same-sex marriage in Canada, that Hawkes, a man of the cloth, would ask such a question from the pulpit further attests to the power of the church's work in integrating the putatively contradictory passions of homosexuality and Christianity. Rather than regarding Hawkes as a straightforward advocate of normalization or assimilation, what would it mean to see his address as engaged in the work of prolepsis—imagining, calling into being, and performatively constituting a kind of ordinariness that does not exist quite yet, or that exists tenuously, subject to threat (Butler 1999; Butler and Spivak 2007)? If the relative ordinariness and liberal equivalence of many queers in the Canadian context remained "a complicated and unsettled trajectory" during the Harper years, then perhaps Hawkes was not simply celebrating a liberal reality that exists but insisting upon a queer one that could (Cowen 2010, 400).

There remains, however, a third, more playful reading of the improper, subjectless queer heft of Hawkes's gesture. It is worth noting that Hawkes did not simply equate his marriage with that of the prime minister. Rather, the pastor's eulogy spun a web of overlapping, intertwined, incommensurable yet, in his view, equally valuable intimacies—departed husband and grieving wife, husband and husband, grandmother and granddaughter joined in grief, prime minister and spouse, departed statesman and mourning nation. This set of pairings vastly exceeds and recasts the sexual,

Rev. Hawkes holds the hand of former member of Parliament Olivia Chow, Jack Layton's widow, as the casket is placed in the hearse following Layton's funeral. Photograph by Chris Young; courtesy of the Canadian Press.

racial, and affective norms for family and intimacy on the national stage, for intimate citizenship. Hawkes's list highlighted not only his own same-sex marriage but the intimate ties of Olivia Chow, a Chinese Canadian woman who was Layton's second wife and grandmother to Beatrice Layton, who is white. While Chow became a stepmother to Layton's children, her own marriage produced no children, making it a relationship of companionship in politics, parenting, and pleasure but not of heteronormative procreation. A distinguished urban and federal politician in her own right, Chow, who spent her teens in Toronto's low-income Saint James Town high-rise neighborhood after her family immigrated from Hong Kong, is often touted as a rags-to-riches model minority despite her robust, downwardly redistributive politics. Yet Chow's progressive views, professional acumen, and relationship to her late husband and granddaughter in fact flout racist, heteronormative stereotypes of white adoptive parents of East Asian children, bourgeois white children with Asian nannies, older white men with Asian trophy wives, and the trope of the model minority itself (see Khoo 2003). Linking queer and interracial intimacies across geographies and generations, Hawkes proleptically carved out a national space in which he and his husband, Chow and her white granddaughter, the late Layton and his Chinese Canadian wife might not be simply included in the national family but recognized as fundamentally comprising the body politic. This alternative national "we" (the one that asks, "Hi, Jack. How are we doing?") stands in marked contrast to the family normatively figured as the most national of them all, that of the white, heterosexual prime minister. By asking, "Hi, Canadian prime minister. How's Laureen doing?," Hawkes can also be understood as gesturing to the widely circulated rumors that the erotic life of the spouse of the prime minister away from the cameras did not accord with her stifled, blonde, monogamous, heteronormative public image. Without citing or explicitly recirculating such rumors, Hawkes subtly pointed to the *perversity* of normative understandings of intimate citizenship and proleptically proposed an "improper" alternative that gleefully embraces racial and sexual heterogeneity and forms of kinship in excess of white procreation as constitutive of rather than marginal to the national family.

Indeed, prolepsis rather aptly describes the tone of Hawkes's eulogy as a whole, which made an explicitly anticipatory series of turns back toward Layton's life as a resource for fantasizing about a wide range of possible political futures. If, following Georgis (2006), confronting loss is a crucial resource for the reinvigoration of desire, including political desire, then perhaps Hawkes's ostensibly liberal eulogy might have quietly staged such a confrontation. Referencing Layton's broad "goal to make life better and not to leave anyone behind," he listed diverse examples of what that goal might entail, "[from] ending homelessness or the rights of transgender people or getting HIV/AIDS medication to poor countries . . . [down to] helping your neighbor or picking up litter or turning off a light."

Intriguingly, and well before the vexed global visibility of figures like Caitlyn Jenner, Hawkes slipped the open and currently quite contentious question of transgender citizenship in Canada alongside seemingly anodyne practices of picking up litter. The eulogy located transgender citizenship—a matter that remained deliberately stalled in the federal legislative domain during the Harper government, and that continues to be violently struggled out in ordinary sites of citizenship at great cost—as relatively commensurable to staples of liberal pedagogies of good citizenship, freedom, and equality. It should be noted that overinvestment in the liberal, rights-bearing subject as the primary vehicle through which to deliver social justice is a danger, and a matter of critical debate within queer, trans, and a host of other social movements (Brown 2002, 2004; Spade 2011; Brandzel 2005). But here Hawkes's proposed to-do list read more as a cultural and political intervention than a straightforwardly juridical one—along the lines of how Judith Butler (1999) describes universality in terms of "holding out the possibility for a convergence of cultural horizons that have not yet met" (xvii–xviii). At work in the Layton memorial service was not the deeply outraged, self-professed radical Reverend Brent Hawkes of 1981—but nor was it a garden-variety, anodyne liberal. Indeed, it was precisely by operating within the idiom of the celebratory, big-tent pastor that Hawkes could impishly slip in a defiant reminder of liberal equality to one of its would-be foes; a profuse alternative vision of queer, interracial, and transgenerational kinship as the foundation of intimate citizenship; and urgent calls for transgender citizenship. Even when Hawkes's message seemed unreflexively sunny and progressive, in key moments improper queer citizenship spoke critically and defiantly to the nation-state through him—insisting on an ethical relation to the queer losses that progress disavows.

The Limits of Celebrity

Perhaps the angry Hawkes of 1981 and the celebratory Hawkes of 2011 share more than they appear to at first. Both fundamentally embrace the idiom of celebrity pastor–diva–citizen, assuming the complex, only provisionally coherent role of stand-in in a wide range of fantasies about religion, sexuality, rights claims, and LGBTQ community. Both seek to testify, to speak truth to power: relaying minoritized injuries, insisting on liberal equivalence, demanding recognition or performatively constituting and seizing that recognition when it is deferred or denied. In Berlant's (1997) formulation, the diva citizen is a figure that always leaves us wanting more, because the liberal machinery that absorbs her testimony—an individuating, depoliticizing "structure of sympathetic normativity" highly striated by race, gender, sexuality, class, and more—can never fully deliver the kind of collective and structural transformation the diva's individual trauma symptomatizes (Berlant 2000, 43). And indeed, whether the topic is the politics of security, marriage, or nondiscrimination policy, the promise of critical diva–pastor testimony, or that of any celebrity diva, to deliver broad social change—even in avenues where social movements have seen success—is extremely limited and highly geographically uneven.

At the time of this writing, Hawkes has yet to fully embrace the work (i.e., the tactics as well as message) of BLMTO and rise to the challenge of one of the most pressing social justice concerns of our time. When I spoke with Hawkes in November 2015, he indicated to me that addressing the deep fault lines around race and citizenship within the congregation was among his core priorities before retiring, that he didn't want to leave difficult conversations about race to the tenure of the next senior pastor. Hawkes's sermons in 2015 and 2016 contained some of the most pointed repudiations of racism and xenophobia within the congregation that I witnessed in my seven years of engagement with his work. In July 2016, shortly after BLMTO's intervention at Pride, Hawkes announced new antiracism adult-education programs designed to encourage white people to hold other whites accountable for racist biases and micro-aggressions, which had flared in reaction to the protest. Despite his tone of gratitude toward Toronto Police chief Mark Saunders, Hawkes has also voiced a cognizance from the pulpit of the harm that police continue to inflict—an awareness informed in part by his own recent experience.[8] In April 2016, Hawkes was charged with gross indecency and sexual assault in Nova Scotia, based on allegations made about incidents that occurred in the 1970s under laws widely and routinely used at the time to target gay men as an oppressed group (Canadian Press 2016). Two days after the charges were announced, a spontaneous Wednesday-evening prayer vigil drew more than two hundred people, and Hawkes's supporters continued to rally around him until January 2017, when he was ultimately acquitted of all charges (Support Brent 2016; Lalani 2017). That white gay men like Hawkes remain targets of state violence could be an occasion for a radical, coalitional, and intersectional critique of the state; but such a challenge has yet to fully surface, suggesting a kind of sustained split between acceptable (white) and unacceptable (black) challenges to state authority. It remains to be seen, however, whether Hawkes's contemporary remarks affirming the heterogeneity and excess of the national and congregational body politic, or encouraging individual congregants to rethink their racist attitudes, or expressing empathy with pain inflicted at the hands of police on a systemic basis will be paired with the kind of radical, religiously grounded critique of state violence he performed in 1981. For those of us who are supportive of BLMTO and also attached to MCCT, this impasse is an occasion for serious frustration.

But maybe that's part of the point. What if Brent Hawkes—the figure, not the man—were meant to frustrate us? I'm referring less to my ideological differences with Hawkes, or to those many congregants have with him on questions like police and Palestine (see chapter 3), than to frustration with the idiom of diva celebrity itself. Hawkes's activism is replete with lacunae and contradictions. Even as he led audiences in mourning Layton to powerful effect, there are still other queer losses that haunt the ministries and politics of MCCT. Yet, in my discussion of *Track Two,* I suggested that the film's gesture toward a radical, robustly coalitional past and future— even if not borne out by actual historical events or scrutiny—might prove ethically and politically productive in the contemporary moment, *precisely* in the frustration with the past and the present alike that the film might generate. Perhaps Hawkes's proleptic rhetoric in the Layton memorial service could have a similar effect.

Maybe the lesson from my frustrated turn to the past and return to the impure present, then, is that of defetishizing community, coalition, and celebrity, past and contemporary—of not externalizing political agency to a fantastical radical past or to an individual celebrity figure. (This lesson is certainly not lost on BLMTO, which has acted collectively and creatively in response to contemporary [though long-standing] concerns of the gravest moral urgency, and has intervened in ways that build on traditions of black queer resistance.) My profound frustration with the political limits of the contemporary MCCT—particularly Hawkes's reluctance to join other progressive faith leaders in criticizing the occupation of Palestine, and his support for former Toronto police chief Bill Blair and current chief Mark Saunders—led me to split the church in time, casting off its "bad" present in the hopes of redeeming a possible "good" past. I turned to the past in the hope of finding a more radical, redemptive, or pure church or pastor to which I could attach. Yet what I found were a messier, more complex pastor, church, and queer movement made up of disparate, contradictory good and bad fragments, and a more continuous relation between past and a present. What Klein (1975) calls integration—at once vigorously critiquing and finding value in such a complex admixture of good and bad fragments—is necessarily anxious, at times graceless, work. But living with that anxiety—as "an objective indication of the possibility of freedom" (Penney 2012, 50)—is precisely the affective relationship that an "impure," improper queer citizenship needs in order to act generously and politically in a messy world (West 2014). Indeed, at stake in living with anxiety and disappointment is the chance not to respond to the pain of de-idealization by finding a new object to idealize but to develop a more evenhanded and refined capacity to apprehend the possibilities for improper queer citizenship in the ongoing now. The loss of the fantasies of ideologically pure political community or radical redemptive past can prove devastating, but that loss proves crucial to the resuscitation of desire. The absence of a straightforwardly radical past or present, precisely because it is deeply unsatisfying, proves fundamental to a politics that constantly tarries with impurity—to freedom, as Wendy Brown puts it, as a project that is "sober, exhausting, and without parents" (Brown 1995, 72). Like many of my interview subjects throughout this book, I remain, in a Kleinian sense, lovingly attached to the church, to what it does and means in the world, and especially to what it could do and could mean—and I want far, far more. Thus, the fact that Hawkes and the church have not offered a vociferous endorsement of BLMTO is both an occasion for disappointment and an opportunity to de-oedipalize politics—an invitation to all of us to recognize celebrity for what it can and can't proffer, to do our own work to support BLMTO and a robust vision of social justice (Celikates and Jansen 2013). The task that remains is not simply to repudiate bad objects but to sustain a tensile relationship between love and the rage of disappointment, to stay frustrated, to do the messy, integrative affective work that accompanies and enables collective movement—as Berlant (1997) puts it, "to take up politically what even the strongest divas were unable, individually, to achieve" (246).

3

"Why Are You Doing This?"

Desiring Queer Global Citizenship

> *In writing close to the other of the other, I can only choose to maintain*
> *a self-reflexively critical relationship toward the material, a relationship*
> *that defines both the subject written and the writing subject, undoing the I*
> *while asking "what do I want wanting to* know *you or me?"*
>
> —Trinh T. Minh-ha, *Woman, Native, Other: Writing Postcoloniality*
> *and Feminism*

Against Sugar Daddy Missiology

At the time of this writing, the Universal Fellowship of Metropolitan Community Churches, at one year shy of fifty years old, lays claim to status as the largest membership-based LGBTQ organization in the world (Shore-Goss 2010, 202n1). As I noted in the Introduction, the denomination includes about two hundred congregations and fellowships in more than thirty nation-states. There are Metropolitan Community Churches (or affiliated fellowships) on every continent but Antarctica. When I attended the denomination's Twenty-Fifth General Conference in downtown Chicago in 2013, I was dazzled by the frequency of recourse, in speeches and in UFMCC literature, to historical and geographical timelines, mapping the institution's ups and downs, the many LGBTQ "firsts" it claims among its polity and communal achievements: the first church outside the United States, the first church outside the global North, the first denominational leader of color, and more. But such chronologies left unanswered questions about how and why the UFMCC went global, about the processes, relationships, and desires behind the church's precipitous growth at a global scale.

Intriguingly, one key leader in the denomination's international work whom I interviewed positioned the church's early move toward international ministry as a natural, politically progressive *successor* to "domestic" (i.e., U.S.-based) struggles over imperialism, racism, sexism, and homophobia. I asked Robb, a lauded denominational leader who had spent a decade providing support to MCC churches throughout the Asia-Pacific region, particularly in the Philippines, to reflect on how the denomination had changed since he first became involved in 1974. He explicitly linked the impulses of MCC with those of gay liberation, women's liberation, and the antiwar and civil rights movements. Robb positioned racism and sexism as significant but not necessarily constitutive domains of concern and agonism within the MCC movement:

> Our focus really was on the LGBT community, really on the community, and on those early issues of coming out and trying to get laws changed. Those were our focus, the initial objectives of the whole liberation movement, except we did it in a spiritual context.
>
> And then early on, I think, we began to realize that this was really bigger than that. It was bigger than we initially thought that it was. That we had an opportunity to be a new reformation in the church, to really change the church. So, we began taking on issues—I remember when we dealt with sexism and racism in this church. We had serious issues with racism in the early days of this church . . . people who came from very conservative, particularly southern areas. We had a lot of people who were just blatantly racist. We had a huge amount of misogyny and sexism in the church, people who did not want women to be clergy, we fought that fight. "No women clergy." So, we had to overcome those things.

Robb casts racism and sexism as challenges that the denomination has already successfully resolved. By some liberal measures of progress—a gender-inclusive approach to scripture and a population in which more than half of clergy identify as women—the MCC movement has seen major gains, particularly given accounts of misogyny and gender imbalance in its early years (see Perry and Swicegood 1990). However, as evinced in scenes of difficulty throughout this book, questions of race, gender, and nation remain quite central in struggles over citizenship within MCC churches, in ways that are obscured when racism and sexism are consigned to the "dustbin of history" (Eng 2010, x). On affective terms, figuring such relations of difference and power as external Others—discrete problems out in the world, back in the past—risks foreclosing more sustained and perhaps disappointing engagement with the Other(s) within. Yet it was a subsequent comment of Robb's that startled me most. Recalling the initial battles over explicit racism and sexism within the UFMCC, he went on to flag debates over whether the denomination should grow globally, adding, "And then we fought nationalism, and people who didn't want us to go outside the United States at all."

Given the contemporary convergences *between* empire, U.S. nationalism, and global LGBTQ politics (see Puar 2007; Alexander 2006), I hadn't expected *opposition* to global outreach to gay and lesbian Christians to be framed in terms of nationalism, xenophobia, or a kind of isolationism. When I asked Robb to elaborate, he recounted two strains of argument against church growth: an expressly racist argument, and a somewhat more polite scarcity argument:

> Robb: Some of it was—I'm trying to think if I remember any conversations that I think now were motivated by—that were justifiable. And I don't think I can think of any. The primary arguments, for the people who were against our becoming global—some of us were arguing for it from the beginning, but for the people who were arguing against it, their arguments were, number one, that people in other parts of the world were just using us, just using us to be the North American sugar daddy. It was that feeling of "Why should we take care of them? Let 'em take care of themselves." That was the crudest, the ugly face of this.
>
> There were other people arguing that—this sort of seemingly more civilized argument was we've got to build really, really, really strong churches here first, and then we can reach out and resource other people. But until we do it here first, we can't go other places, because we won't have the resources and it'll end up hurting us in the long run. That was kind of a scarcity argument: "There's not enough." And those of us on the other side were arguing the abundance argument: "There's always enough." A lot of it was racist. There's a lot of racism in it as well.
>
> *Did anyone [make] a sort of anticolonial argument, like "Oh, we just can't go over there"? Because it sounds like there's a really serious consideration of how not to repeat colonialism in the work that's*

undertaken [in the contemporary church]. . . . Were people on the
inside [in the 1970s] saying, "Oh, we shouldn't do that because
there's no way it could not be colonial for us to go abroad"?
Robb: Yes, there were people saying, "We've gotta figure this out
first. We've got to figure this out." And the rest of us were saying, "We can't figure this out. We've never done it right; what
makes you think we're gonna do it right now?" [I laugh.] So, we
were arguing, "Let's go build relationships with people in other
parts of the world and then ask them. Let's let them tell us for a
change."

For Robb, it is shrinking back from North–South relationality, rather than
risking it, that comprises a racist, nationalist orientation to the world. Later
in our conversation, Robb expounded on MCC's framework for engagement with churches outside the United States, particularly in its repudiation of colonial missiology. The express intention of MCC's global growth,
he told me, is to do better than (past and present) colonial missiological
iterations of Christianity's global circulation.[1]

Robb's aim—to "let them tell us for a change"—speaks to an overarch-
ing optimism, a faith that the historic imbrications of Christianity and colonialism are contingent rather than necessary and that better theologies
and better frameworks for ministry can make a meaningful difference.
Such an intention reverberates with the rise of oft-critiqued participatory
approaches to development, which also formally emphasize the inclusion
and agency of people in the global South. Moreover, a critique of isolationism in and of itself doesn't necessarily proffer much in the way of progressive politics, as isolationism routinely operates as a foil in imperial-
ist narratives. (Recall, for instance, U.S. president George W. Bush's 2006
State of the Union address: "Isolationism would not only tie our hands in
fighting enemies, it would keep us from helping our friends in desperate
need.") But although there is a great deal of literature on the constitutive
limitations of participatory approaches to development (Kapoor 2005),
including in religious and missionary contexts, there remains very little
social-scientific literature on the growth of the MCC movement outside of
the United States (for an exception, see Reid 2010).

It is not within the scope of this book to evaluate the "success" of an
avowedly noncolonial approach to MCC's global growth or to ascertain
people's reception of or critical engagement with MCC in specific global

South contexts, though such questions surely warrant further research. Yet Robb's framing of debates on global church growth can tell us something else of value, something about global North *desires* for global queer citizenship. The denominational "we" that Robb critiques in his narrative, a U.S.-based church, understands itself as possessing—and thus as positioned to either hoard or generously share—all manner of spiritual, material, and psychic resources. In the denominational debates on global growth, this "we" has different affective valences: paranoia about exploitation as a "sugar daddy," having its scarce resources appropriated; or a self-deprecating, generous abundance. But in each of these variations, the denominational "we" seems to hold many, if not all, of the agentic keys in an encounter with the "global" Other. As Mimi Thi Nguyen (2012) appositely observes, the privileged subject of the "gift" of freedom is ultimately the giver. This affective topography of the MCC global queer citizen left me curious and concerned about what MCC's global South engagements look and feel like on the ground for everyone involved—a matter I hope to investigate in future research. Such a world map of distributed psychic agency also left me wondering about alternatives. How might the sovereign North American denominational "we" work through and integrate good and bad elements of the world and in itself, such that it could be *affected by* transnational encounters, instead of seeing itself only as *affecting* "them"?

Feeling Global

Chapters 1 and 2 sought to open up desires *for* MCCT as a church—for church or its leadership to be more substantively antiracist and feminist, more critical, more radical, more prophetic. As Karen put it in her call for social justice as a kind of profusion in chapter 1, "I think we do good work. I just think we need to do more *of* it." Karen's primary geographical referent for such a thickening or broadening of social justice and spiritual ministries was the segregated, simultaneously colonial and postcolonial, and diasporic landscape of the greater Toronto area. This chapter maps different inflections of the desire to proliferate the ministries of the MCC movement, not only in and through Toronto but also, and in particular, "globally." Thus, the chapter stages an engagement with another kind of religious object that could be dismissed as a "bad attachment" by secular queer critics: not a normatively white church practicing Goldilocks diversity nor an avowedly "moderate" pastor, but the desire for global evangelism.

The rest of this book continues to map the potential and the limits of MCCT and the MCC movement as a space in which repairing a religious object might nurture an improper queer citizenship. It pursues this analysis through two closely related but also quite geographically distinctive figures of racialized alterity: the global queer church and the LGBTQ asylum seeker. Yet despite the ostensible shift toward more "outward-facing" or "international" ministries, the book's primary scale remains that of the intimate. Maintaining my emphasis on micropolitical, ethnographic, and affective approaches to the structural limitations of citizenship, this chapter begins by asking, What could it mean in terms of *citizenship* to desire a "global" queer community—in church? For indeed, despite decades of academic and activist critiques of the notion of global gay identity and community, images of universal, horizontal, global queer citizenship continue to proliferate in public cultures, social networks, and social movements. Much as Miranda Joseph (2002) writes of the discourse of community more broadly, the discourse of global queer citizenship has been both an object of "persistent critique" and a force with seemingly "relentless return" (vii).

In the past fifteen years, scholarship in feminist and queer cultural studies has built on critiques of cultural imperialism to map the highly variegated and power-laden circulations of global queer identities and discourses. In their pivotal, agenda-setting essay on the conceptual uses of transnationalism in the critical study of global sexual identities and movements, Inderpal Grewal and Caren Kaplan (2001) argue for greater attention to the roles of hierarchical political-economic conditions, geopolitical struggles, and diffuse neoliberal governmentalities in producing highly differentiated global sexual citizens and subjects. They challenge habits in academic thinking and writing that figure LGBTQ activism as always already subversive, insisting on scholarship that "will enable us to understand global identities at the present time and to examine complicities as well as resistances in order to create the possibility of critique and change" (675). Working in the idiom of transnational feminist cultural studies, both Jasbir K. Puar (2002) and M. Jacqui Alexander (2006) offer critical examinations of gay tourism, bringing critiques of capitalism, empire, racial formation, and neocolonialism to bear on queer global circulations and engagements. Such scholarship offers an important counterweight to the fantasies of horizontality and organic community that at times characterize narratives about globalization and queer citizenships, reinvigorating critical attention in queer studies to historically and geographically specific and uneven relations of difference and power.

The call to bring complex critiques of contingent, structural political dynamics into conversation with the study of global LGBTQ identities and practices has also resonated with ethnographic scholarship on globalization and sexuality. Much of this work has focused on the cultural politics of language, identity, and translation (Manalansan 2003; Wekker 2006; Boellstorff 2005). This diverse work critiques discourses of global queer citizenship, exploring the nuances of people's contextually specific and highly variegated practices of identification, practices that often bespeak an ambivalent relationship to the concept of global queer community, to say the least.

But what is it that people *want* when they want global queer citizenship? A promising line of contemporary ethnographic inquiry has sought to make questions of affect and desire more prominent in analyses of globalization, sexuality, and citizenship. Anthropologist Naisargi Dave (2012) draws on Michel Foucault's ([1984] 1990) work on pleasure and ascesis to understand the richly ethical dimensions of queer activism in Delhi and to highlight queer women's ethical self-fashioning as a crucial terrain of politics. While she follows Foucault's studied evasion of the putative truth of *individuated* desire, Dave also charts relationships between competing social and collective desires (e.g., for recognition) and the emergence of alternative forms of freedom. And in her important ethnography of gender, class, and sexuality in public cultures in postsocialist China, Lisa Rofel (2007) innovates an understanding of neoliberalism as productive of new forms of both subjectivity and desire. Reading everything from Chinese soap operas that in the 1990s began to feature gay characters, to court cases over intellectual property rights, Rofel carefully demonstrates the linkages between uneven neoliberalization in China and changing understandings of the meanings of citizenship and subjectivity. Rofel critically engages earlier work (Altman 1997) that theorized the nascence of a global gay culture and presented Western idioms as that global culture's universal telos. Part of what makes Rofel's scholarship particularly generative is her shuttling between the work of Michel Foucault and Gilles Deleuze and Félix Guattari to insist on an understanding of desire that is simultaneously social, productive, open, and nonessential (Rofel 2007, 211–213n43).

This chapter builds on Rofel's insights to argue that scholarship on affect, in both its psychoanalytic and Deleuzian-Guattarian variants, can help scholars to better understand the heterogeneity of desires for global LGBTQ citizenship in complex relation to the political-economic and geopolitical conditions that generate them. Chapters 1 and 2 explored MCCT as a site where people both impose and contest barriers to belonging based on race and gender, where the contradictory and exclusive norms of congregational citizenship are subject to creative disruption by racialized churchgoers seeking "a house of prayer for all," and where pasts riven with good and bad fragments haunt equally but differently incoherent presents. Here, I turn to the diverse promises of global queer citizenship that reverberate in and through the church and that are mobilized to both consolidate and disturb normative citizenship in the nation, the city, and the church. MCCT and the global Metropolitan Community Church movement are sites where people go to belong, and to sustain a desire for belonging, in queer and faith polities that are simultaneously global and local. Indeed, the promise of global queer citizenship figures centrally among the contradictory and multiplicitous objects that many people in the MCC movement yearn for, particularly as the denomination has come to frame itself less as "the gay church" than as "the human rights church." While a turn to "human rights" might comprise a progressive move in its dethroning of an identitarian rendition of "sexual orientation" as monopolizing the ethical horizon for MCCT, it remains important to ask what genealogies and substantive figurations of the human (white, European, Christian) haunt or inform the "human" in the UFMCC's vision of "human rights." Indeed, maintaining an ambivalent orientation toward the discourse of human rights proves especially important as a so-called international turn in contemporary Toronto and Canadian LGBTQ activism has made the city and MCCT particularly dense and prolific sites of desire for global queer citizenship (see, e.g., McDirmid 2014; Easton 2015). Such a turn draws on longer-standing national fantasies of a sterling and salvific global reputation for tolerance and human rights (Razack 2004), one that the Liberal federal government elected in 2015 seems keen to revive (Trudeau 2016). I focus largely on the insights, experiences, and desires of participants in the MCC movement from within the global North, many of whom are in positions of leadership within the Toronto church or the MCC denomination. This focus speaks to the limits of the scope of my current project, but it also enables me to explore the fault lines within, and the heterogeneity of, global North desires for queer global citizenship.

This chapter thus follows anthropologists like Eva Mackey (2002) and Scott Morgensen (2011), whose ethnographic gaze focuses not on the colonial Other but on the Western or Northern desire to relate to that Other (and to "the West's" alterity to itself) in an unevenly transnational world. Again recalling Wendy Brown (1995, 62) here, this chapter asks, Given the uneven geographies and (neo)colonial histories that form them, given the theological, economic, and political logics that infuse them, what do MCC desires for queer global citizenship *want*?

To answer this question, I engage interviews and participant-observation at MCC Toronto and in the broader MCC denomination to map four distinct but at times overlapping affective inflections of and orientations toward "the global" within this queer faith movement: (1) the global as a target of entrepreneurial-evangelical enthusiasm for expansion, (2) the global as the object of liberal humanitarian benevolence and fantasies of saving the world, (3) the global as inductor of ambivalence and critical hesitation regarding a perceived turn away from critiques of inequality within the global North, and (4) the global as an object of minor, revolutionary yearnings, a stand-in for an end to racism, nationalism, economic inequality, and U.S. hegemony within and beyond the church. These desires for global queer citizenship share an optimistic affective structure, directing attention toward the possibility of repair, amelioration, better forms of relationality. Yet whether affective relations to "the global" necessarily prove "cruel-optimistic" remains an open question (Berlant 2011a).

Distinguishing among these modes of desire, I link the first two inflections to an ego ideal that compels subjects to *save the world,* while the second two resonate with a more integrative form of identification that seeks to *save the self*—including from the self. This self–world tension resonates with the competing preoccupations of North American liberal and evangelical Christians, respectively, who are often located on opposite sides of the polarity; yet psychoanalytic perspectives are helpful in pointing out the relative continuities as well as differences between both affective investments.[2] In "On Narcissism" ([1914] 1957), Freud famously argues that self-love should be viewed as a quite literally vital facet of the subject and the socius, rather than a vice or a stage to be outgrown. While the organization and distribution of self-love—its geography within the psyche—shift over the course of one's development (from the ego to the ego ideal in the superego), Freud insists that self-love remains present in one's affective relations throughout one's life. "Saving the world," then, describes a desire for global queer citizenship structured by an ego ideal of a benevolent, noble, agentic, and altruistic self, one that elides the role of self-love in all relationality. This ego-ideal image excludes any elements of the self's vulnerability to or need for the Other, or the self's capacity to do harm. "Saving the world" proves dangerous, because it can see in its love objects—its would-be fellow global queer citizens—only what it wants and aspires to see about itself. Indeed, as I will further demonstrate in the case of queer asylum seekers in chapter 4, saving the "global" queer Other eludes the fact that the savior needs the Other to be "really" gay, to act in a particular way, to be grateful, in ways that can gravely endanger and profoundly constrain that Other. Saving the world disavows the subject's dependence and need—her own alterity—and thus her capacity to be affected by the Other.

By contrast, "saving the self" describes a process of working to live with the difficulty and the narcissism that always accompany relationality (and haunt it when disavowed). Following Klein's (1975) account of the depressive position as a state that repairs the splitting of the ego and the world, saving the self entails integrating bifurcated and contradictory fragments of the ego and its objects. To save the self is not to retreat into the ego or to relinquish psychic agency but to live with, rather than paper over, the anxiety that inexorably accompanies self-recognition of one's vulnerability, need for the Other, and capacity to do harm, alongside one's more noble or beneficent aspirations or capacities. Living with such anxiety departs from the territory of the guilt of the privileged, the drama of injured self-love that ensues when one briefly glimpses one's distance from an ego ideal of unproblematic benevolent normalcy and feels compelled to seek evidence of one's restored goodness in relationships to others. What might the forms of solidarity that global queer citizenship seems to promise feel like if would-be citizens in the global North began by doing their *own* affective work (Pratt 1984)—if they began by saving themselves? I argue that eventual integration of such "bad" fragments of the ego with more redemptive, "good," world-saving aspirations and ideals might enable a more ethical alternative to the salvific desire to "save the world" and the violence that inheres within it. Thus, while the chapter maps desires for global queer citizenship in the church as chaotic and heterogeneous, I also draw on psychoanalysis to highlight the potentially generative or emancipatory qualities of improper queer global citizenship projects that save the self. It is my hope that this chapter helps contribute to the ongoing formulation of "good-enough" global projects for the denomination and MCCT, and of better forms of relationality therein (Winnicott 1953). I want to begin, however, with a little consideration of the kind of engagement with desires for global queer citizenship that Deleuze and Guattari's "minor" desire enables.

Mapping Desire

What would it mean to approach desire as something *more social* than an individual, private force irrevocably shaped by inaugural familial trauma, yet more idiosyncratic than a superstructural derivative of political-economic organization? As something more complex than either structuralist Marxism or classical psychoanalysis could entertain? While such questions have animated a host of social thinkers (Williams 1978; Oliver 2004; Berlant 2011a), the work of Gilles Deleuze and Félix Guattari innovated an approach that radically reconceptualized desire by "mapping" it. In *Kafka: Toward a Minor Literature* ([1975] 1986), Deleuze and Guattari refuse most of the conventions characterizing classical psychoanalytic and Marxist interpretations of Franz Kafka's writing, which they regard as ultimately eschewing his oeuvre's true, "minor" political heft. In this passage, the two embark on this intellectual project with characteristic boldness, even flippancy:

We won't try to find archetypes that would represent Kafka's imaginary, his dynamic, or his bestiary (the archetype works by assimilation, homogenization, and thematics, whereas our method works only where a rupturing and heterogeneous line appears). . . . We aren't even trying to interpret, to say this meets that. . . . We believe only in one or more Kafka *machines* that are neither structure nor phantasm. We believe only in a Kafka *experimentation* that is without interpretation or significance and rests only on tests of experience . . . .

To enter or leave the machine, to be in the machine, to walk around it, to approach it—these are all still components of the machine itself: they are state of desire, free of all interpretation. The line of escape is part of the machine. Inside or outside, the animal is part of the burrow-machine. The problem is not that of being free but of finding a way out, or even a way in, another side, a hallway, an adjacency. . . . Desire evidently passes through these positions and states, or, rather, through all these lines. Desire is not a form, but a procedure, a process. (7–8 [emphasis original])

Instead of simply finding the "properly political" in the literary or locating the oedipal in every intimate drama—moves that both operate by means of analogy—Deleuze and Guattari map a proliferation of diverse, at times overlapping, and inassimilable desiring relations in Kafka's universe. This approach, like object relations, also proves particularly useful for the study of religion, because it displaces oedipal readings in which relation to religious space and religious authority are always already transferential, repeating past conflicts with paternal (and in some cases maternal) authority. By mapping desire in religious space rather than interpreting it with alacrity as belying religion's airtight alignment with paternal law, we start to see how the religious object is itself chaotic and contradictory, and perhaps open to structural transformation.

Indeed, in their reading of Kafka, Deleuze and Guattari position Kafka's work as revolutionary only and precisely in its "minority." "A minor literature doesn't come from a minor language," they explain. "It is rather that which a minority constructs within a minor language" (16). Minor literature is marked by three characteristics: "language affected with a high coefficient of deterritorialization," requiring displaced subjects to negotiate linguistic disenfranchisement; the convergence of individual concerns and the social milieu on a single, immanently political plane; and the social, more-than-individual character of the writing such that "there are only collective assemblages of enunciation" (16–17). In her cheeky, important essay "'68, or Something" (1994), Lauren Berlant explains that "Deleuze and Guattari emphasize the need to imagine the impossible—an exoteric freedom, without the old legitimations that made the nation and its identities possible. Remaining foreign to a hegemonic imaginary—with its dreams of a linguistic ethnoutopia, the privilege of uncontested generalizing and control over reference—requires remaining outside of the dream of enforcing a new master tongue, for eating or writing, or singing" (136). Rather than inventing a new master language (an ironically oedipal move), minor literature works within a dominant paradigm of intelligibility but works to remain illegible to it—an escape from within.[3]

While Berlant and Deleuze and Guattari are directly concerned with literary and aesthetic works, their formulations of the "minor" and attention to the lines of flight and escape immanent to hegemonic political and linguistic projects prove generative for my concern with the desire for the global. How might it feel to desire a *subjectless,* improper global queer citizenship? What would it mean to refrain from rejecting the global in order to prop up a new, better, more redemptive language, one ultimately likely to make the same slide toward co-optation? How might we attend to lines of flight, forms of virtuality and potentiality, within some desires for the global in the MCC movement and other transnational LGBTQ polities? And how might such lines of flight open up Marxist and psychoanalytic interpretations of religion that can reduce it to an essentially conservative and oppressive patriarchal or capitalist function?

Importantly, the Deleuzian-Guattarian concept of lines of flight or lines of escape—the virtual edges of a social assemblage that both carry it away and recompose it somewhere else—guarantees not political redemption but only the immanence of potential for alternatives (Deleuze and Guattari [1975] 1986, 88–89). Deleuze and Guattari and many of their interlocutors indicate clearly that lines of flight do not necessarily eventuate in alternatives commensurable to progressive-left visions of good, equitable life. In a dazzling ethnography of normative whiteness in the psychedelic and trance scene in Goa, India, geographer Arun Saldanha (2006) demonstrates how lines of flight that could take Goa sociality in other directions often end up closing, crystallizing, and forming deadening closed circuits. "It's true that hippies transform themselves into freaks of whiteness by challenging the holding together of white modernity," Saldanha writes. "But, as Deleuze and Guattari warn over and over again in *A Thousand Plateaus,* lines of flight all too often close in on themselves while being actualized, becoming 'microfascistic,' paranoid, regressive, suicidal" (53–54; Deleuze and Guattari [1980] 1987). Likewise, geographer Ben Anderson (2006) writes against the tendency in some currents of affect scholarship to regard the concept of virtuality as a "gift" in and of itself. While the excess that characterizes virtuality can indeed condition hope, for Anderson, this excess is not simply a surplus of potentially fortuitous events. Rather, "becoming hopeful takes place from within specific encounters that diminish or destroy" (748). It is from within encounters with violence and diminishment that a hopeful orientation toward the not-yet becomes possible, but even then, there are no guarantees.

Thus, I build in this chapter on Deleuze and Guattari because their engagement with desire as a positive, productive, and multiplicitous relation allows for a slightly different approach to debates on sexuality, globalization, and religion. I cannot promise to refrain from the project of interpretation and representation of the sociospatial world. I can, however, endeavor to carefully map a complex proliferation of desires without rushing to either assimilate them to preexisting, critical categories oriented toward the persistence of hierarchy or simply describe and validate liberal fantasies of horizontal or universal global gay community. Carefully tracing desire as bound up with geopolitical projects, racial formations, and forms of neoliberal rationality, and also as productive in its own right, enables an approach to desire that isn't quite as quick to simply subsume it under political-economic or geopolitical conditions. Likewise, approaching religion and religious polities as chaotic assemblage, in Deleuzian-Guattarian terms, or an untidy "whole" object for Klein, might open up new readings that help us attend to the radical or progressive political force of some "minor" instantiations and inhabitations of religious polity. Indeed, I am interested in what a more sustained engagement with desire in its heterogeneity might provide for queer critics, even if the results are largely unlikely to prove redemptive. As we will see, several of the desiring orientations toward the global within the MCC movement that I encountered—particularly enthusiasm for expansion and liberal humanitarianism—reflect oppressive ego ideals of saving the world, whereby our passionate attachment to recognition leads us to ruthlessly "devour the others we wish to be" (Rose 2007, 63). But sustained engagement with the heterogeneous inflections of the global in the movement also occasionally points to integrative, "minor" desires, alternative inflections of the global that yearn for and experiment with other, more emancipatory forms of relationality.

Evangelical Enthusiasm for Expansion

It is impossible to talk about the Metropolitan Community Church movement without talking about the project of growth. Formal and informal histories of the denomination routinely cite UFMCC's trajectory from a (propitiously populated) twelve-person service in founder the Reverend Troy Perry's Los Angeles living room one Sunday in October 1968 to a global movement. In celebratory accounts of the denomination, growth proffers evidence of progress; growth demonstrates the denomination's foresight and attunement to the zeitgeist; growth both addresses and performatively attests to the continued need for LGBTQ-affirming Christian spaces.

Critical social theorists, meanwhile, have demonstrated that growth is also an unyielding imperative for capitalism and evangelical Christianity alike. Broadly speaking, capital is notorious for its relentless need to grow itself across space and time (Harvey 2007), while evangelicalism is likewise dogged in pursuit of investments not fully realized in the ephemeral, secular world (O'Neill 2009). For both capitalism and evangelism, whether in sync or at odds, growth is also a profoundly geographical project. Neil Smith ([1984] 2008) famously demonstrates how geographical variegations in capitalist development stem in large part from the logics of capitalism itself, while recent scholarship on Christian evangelical movements finds a marked and concerted effort to grow in the global South (Han 2010).

But how do the two imperatives—to grow profits and to grow God's flock—encounter each other? I find great utility in theoretical formulations such as Wendy Brown's (2003) account of neoliberalism as "the extension of economic rationality to all aspects of thought and activity" and Miranda Joseph's (2002, xxxii) work on community as a "supplement" that both "displaces and supports" a voracious capitalism. These scholars direct critical attention to the ways in which domains ostensibly "external" to capitalism might find themselves both constitutively and increasingly infiltrated by market logics, and might help to reproduce capitalist niche markets, all while still ideologically rendered innocent sites of love in a loveless world. Others, meanwhile, have demonstrated the profound complicity and conviviality between the church and capitalism. Janet Jakobsen (2002), for instance, disputes the imagined abstraction of the church from the market, arguing that conservative "family values" grounded in religious faith can serve to naturalize the exploitation and inequality endemic to capitalism (see Han 2010; Moreton 2010).

But where might MCC fit in a literature largely focused on capitalist growth and *conservative* evangelicalisms? On the one hand, MCC's "liberal" theology of openness—open Communion and sex positivity—and the denomination's history as a "revolving door" suggest that members are not expected to stay, and that conservative logics of growth and evangelism do not neatly apply to the denomination in the same way. On the other hand, scholars of the MCC movement have long demonstrated its openly and unapologetically entrepreneurial and evangelical provenance and valences. In his important study of the church, sociologist of religion R. Stephen Warner (2005) positions UFMCC founder the Reverend Troy Perry as a gay twist within a tradition of charismatic U.S. "religious entrepreneur" preachers such as George Whitefield, Charles Grandison Finney, and Oral Roberts (186). As we will see in my conversations in this section, the entrepreneurial character of the movement is hardly lost on MCCers, however critically some would regard neoliberal public policies. Thus, rather than frame MCC's orientation toward growth as colonized by or supplementary to capitalism, I want to explore how evangelism and entrepreneurialism converge to condition desire for global growth. Particularly insightful here is William E. Connolly's (2008) work on evangelical-capitalist affective "resonance machines." Like the scholars I have just reviewed, Connolly theorizes the relationship between capitalism and its putatively external domains, in this case evangelism, beyond the terms of causality, functionalism, or discrete ideology. But, for Connolly, the relationship between capitalism and evangelism also requires affective resonance between linked but incommensurable and irreducible elements. I find the model of the resonance machine helpful in thinking relations between Christianity and capitalism not through causality but through "energized complexities of mutual imbrication and interinvolvement, in which heretofore unconnected or loosely associated elements fold, bend, blend, emulsify and resolve incompletely into each other, forging a qualitative assemblage resistant to classical models of explanation" (39–40). As a historically entrepreneurial institution that is also theologically progressive, MCC's orientation toward growth is not simply a matter of the church's infection by diffuse market logic, much less by heteronormative logics of reproduction. And while church communities exist in supplementary relation to capitalism, this supplementarity can be more precisely understood through an analysis of its affective dynamics. In this section, I situate MCC's global growth in terms of a broader structure of desire for growth as an end in and of itself. Through conversations about the growth of the denomination—in congregations, neighborhoods, globally, and on the Internet—I demonstrate how global growth is shaped in part by an affective orientation I call "enthusiasm for expansion." This affective orientation, in which entrepreneurialism and evangelism resonate and converge, is a key condition of the desire within UFMCC for global citizenship.

The MCC movement has been growing outside the United States, chartering new fellowships and congregations, almost immediately since its founding, in 1968. In 1972, MCC movement founder the Reverend Troy Perry visited the United Kingdom at the invitation of a group of British gay rights activists and, intriguingly, curators at the British Museum.

Following the visit, a group of gay men founded a small fellowship that in 1973 became chartered as the Metropolitan Community Church of London (Perry 1990). That same year, MCC minister the Reverend Bob Wolfe left a pastorate at MCC Sacramento and moved to Toronto, responding to correspondence from Toronto gay Christians and citing a call from God to help pastor the church in Canada. Two years later, Wolfe gave the inaugural sermon at the newly formed Église communautaire Montréal, or Montreal Community Church (McLeod 1996). With congregations in the United Kingdom and Canada, the denomination began to grow in Australia, Africa, and Latin America. In Perry's (1990) narrative, the longer the denomination existed and the more widely word of its ministry circulated, the more prolific the correspondence and lecture invitations MCC leaders received.

The denomination's leaders concede that the church's experiments in growth have yielded mixed results, but they say they remain optimistic. The vast majority of MCC congregations count fewer than one hundred members. The denomination's presence in Canada, which in the 1980s stretched from Vancouver to Halifax, is now concentrated in three congregations in southern Ontario: Toronto, London, and Windsor. Several larger U.S. congregations have disaffiliated from UFMCC, citing reasons ranging from alleged financial corruption to theological differences on both the right and the left. The most notable departure was by the massive Cathedral of Hope in Dallas, which split from UFMCC in 2003, taking with it 4,200 members, approximately 9 percent of the denomination's population at the time (Caldwell 2003). Contemporary victories for mainstream LGBTQ movements in U.S. and Canadian public policy and Protestant churches have positioned the UFMCC as a "revolving door" rather than a permanent home, and have led to questions in those places about the continued necessity or utility of a "gay church" (Zoll 2013). Meanwhile, however, UFMCC continues to see growth in much of the U.S. Bible Belt and Midwest, but it has proven especially successful outside anglophone North America, particularly in Latin America and Asia.

For many leaders of both MCC Toronto and the larger UFMCC, church growth, particularly the global scale of such growth, comprises unqualified goods. Heather White (2015) notes that by 1977, the UFMCC was the largest gay and lesbian grassroots organization in the United States. From the very beginning, she writes, "in many ways, the UFMCC was not at all an exception to the prevailing logic of church growth" among U.S.

evangelicals (157). Clearly, this zeal for expansion was not limited to U.S. boundaries. Indeed, in his second memoir (1990), which chronicles the history of the MCC movement, Rev. Perry describes the desire animating church growth in terms of ethical response to articulated need: "Globally, the expanding outreach is based on a desire to found evangelical centers of worship from which our compassionate Christian gospel can be spread to many, including heterosexuals. People around the world reveal their needs to us and we respond, undaunted by the enormity of the task" (206). A storyteller above all, Perry fleshes out this need/response narrative with vignettes from church outreach in locations including Mexico, Canada, Nigeria, and Australia. Offering his own rendition of reports from UFMCC missionaries, Perry paints a picture of a global church in which different people relate to MCC in a chaotic, variegated, and surprising range of ways. For instance, while the denomination's Australian contacts wrote on behalf of "a lot of gay people who are really hungry for a Protestant denomination," the church's predominantly heterosexual congregations in Nigeria turned to UFMCC for "the ecumenical vision inherent in Metropolitan Community Church, with successful unification of people from all Christian churches" (218, 216). Interestingly, Perry never seems to regard the prospect of predominantly heterosexual MCC congregations as problematic, provided the church does good work in "the Third World, where frequent shifts of politics and starving multicultural peoples are continuing facts of life" (216). In short, whatever good people might find in MCC as a multivalent object is good, in part because growth is good.

When I had the opportunity to follow up with Perry about his writings in person, I came to realize that the denomination's global growth is bound up with a more comprehensive evangelical-entrepreneurial orientation toward expansion at multiple scales, including those of the individual congregation and the neighborhood. During an interview with Perry at his home in Los Angeles in 2013, I asked him about the potential difficulties or dilemmas associated with church growth. Though I had never met anyone who opposed church growth per se, I had heard numerous allusions in conversations with other denominational leaders to opposition to the paradigm of church growth in the past. Not knowing whether that opposition had once been concrete and was then invisibilized by growth's hegemony, or whether antigrowth was a kind of rhetorical foil to the project of expansion, I asked Perry about possible downsides to church growth. Perry responded to me with a vigorous defense of the denomination's investment in entrepreneurial idioms such as strategic planning and property.

> *I'm interested in the work around strategic growth. I'm interested in both why that's important to people and also, I know that not everyone in the denomination agrees about strategic growth. How would you describe that?*
>
> Troy: Usually those are people who know they're not gonna ever pastor a large church—I'm sorry, but . . . those who don't believe in strategic growth, they're folks who are a little frightened that they're gonna be judged. And I try to explain, "No, no, no, no, no, we understand. You may have 30 people in that local Metropolitan Community Church in West Texas, but honey, that's 30 more than any other organization the town has."
>
> Now, it's very rough when we have it, but we have learned that if we can have from 30 to 50 people, we can afford a pastor. Those 30 to 50 people contribute and make it possible for us to buy property and to pay pastors, and to pay for Sunday School material and everything churches do. We do it. But strategically, if you want a church to grow, you have to be strategic about it and say, "How are we gonna do this better? How do we get beyond 100? How do we get beyond 250? How do we get beyond 500 in church? How do we get beyond 1000 in church?"

I distinctly remember my eyes growing wide as Perry spoke of growing numbers. On the one hand, Perry is a dynamic, often jocular preacher and storyteller. Though he sometimes interrupts himself to speak in the voice of another character in a story or to address that character, his intonations usually make this multiplicity of voices quite easy to follow, in person if not in writing. Perry's rendering of many different actors in a scene has a way of making a vignette he recounts feel atmospheric, if also clearly framed through his perspective. I found it hard not to be charmed by his miraculous account of the promise of church growth as I relay it here.

On the other hand, I wondered what such a push for growth might feel like for different MCC congregants. Having grown up in and bounced around mainline and liberal Protestant churches in the United States and

Canada my entire life, I had been part of faith communities of a range of sizes, and the biggest among them felt a bit impersonal, indifferent, antiseptic, and a little too self-assured. I could imagine disadvantages to large churches that didn't show up in this story about growth. Meanwhile, Perry continued:

> Troy: We really do believe in church growth. . . . We talk about it. It's not wrong. It's not a sin. We want to see churches grow. And we thank God that we do have churches that continue to grow and continue to do well. . . .
>
> I'm a strong believer. I always said, I usually can tell how healthy the MCC is by the way they keep up their property— meaning I believe in keeping up property, that you don't let it, you know what I mean, you keep working on it to make sure it's attractive. So we buy property. We owned—the L.A. church was the first piece of property owned by a GLBT organization in American history. Our first property. There was no one who owned property before us. Not any of the gay groups in this country or anything. They owned bars. But most of them were owned by the Mafia. They were straight-owned, most of 'em.
>
> *Because that's what we could get, yeah.*
>
> Troy: That's what we could get to let us go in. It wasn't that we wanted anything to do with the Mafia, but that's the best we could do.
>
> And so, Toronto, when I look at the Toronto church, and I go there, and I see that building fill up, and there's just not parking around there, I am just amazed, I mean just amazed. But it proves if you're strategic about it, you can grow. You keep looking forward, not backwards. I remember the past, but I live in today. I plan for tomorrow. That's what strategic growth is about. We may be here today. But we want a bigger building. We have to do it. Whether we build it from the ground up or whether we buy an existing property, we have to do it. People are trying to get in here. And once you fill a building 80 percent, people quit coming. It gets too crowded then for people. So, you've got to have room for people in a building.

Perry's rendition of the desire for growth aligns a heterogeneous cast of means and ends: property ownership, futurity, the evangelical project of spreading the good news, and gay liberation. Property ownership enables LGBTQ community formation, relative autonomy, and disaffiliation from organized crime. Property ownership simultaneously indexes the "health" of a given congregation, a metaphor that links the congregational body, its embodiment in property, and an ethic of self-care. Growth is good, and a strategic approach to growth enables a congregation to sustain alignment between the size of its membership and the capacity of its physical space.

This enthusiastic orientation toward growth resonated in my other conversations with denomination and MCCT leaders, but each conversation revealed specific ways in which people related affectively to the notion of growth and its global scale. For instance, James, a luminary within the denomination who came out of retirement to work on questions of demographic development and engagement at MCCT, described his perspective and ministry as shaped by a "bias toward growth." In a series of conversations, this reserved but quite generous man described to me the connections between ordinary practices and events—such as registering church attendance and keeping electronic records, or a Sunday service that's more than 80 percent full—and competing models and theories of what spurs or deters church growth. Very careful to cite the ideas that nurtured his thinking, James provided a lengthy booklist and rationale. He stitched together a fascinating, highly variegated mix of scholarly and lay perspectives on how to effectively engage churchgoers and foster church growth: organizational sociology, anthropology, entrepreneurial writing, theology, and insights on church growth from evangelical leaders and intellectuals. James was just as quick to cite anthropologist Edward T. Hall's (1963) work on "proxemics" and the cross-cultural norms of personal space as he was to borrow from evangelicals like *Hour of Power* founder and positive-thinking exponent the Reverend Robert H. Schuller, or South Korean Pentecostal pastor the Reverend David Yonggi Cho, founder of Seoul's million-member Yoido Full Gospel Church. Countering the claim (and my own anxiety) that church growth is necessarily an impersonal affair, James described how Cho's congregation grew dramatically by bringing together individual cells of ten congregants each for weekly prayer and group bonding. When I asked James about the potential limits to growth, he provided me with a reflection on the forces and conditions that he thought contributed to his predilection for church growth. He cited a number of factors, such as his evangelical upbringing and his professional formation in corporate America, as orienting his desire toward church growth.

My conversations with Troy Perry and James demonstrated how multiscalar and wide-ranging the imperative to grow is for denominational leaders. But most of the examples the two men used focus on church growth at the congregational and denominational scales within the United States. What does the evangelical-entrepreneurial desire to grow on a *global* scale feel like?

As with Perry, my conversations with the Reverend Dr. Brent Hawkes were marked by his case for candor, directness, and vision in fund-raising and church growth, as well an eye toward global outreach to LGBTQ people of faith. Since December 2008, MCCT has produced a webcast of its 11 a.m. Sunday church service, making it available for live streaming or download from an archive on the Internet. In early 2017, the church began broadcasting using Facebook's Live video-streaming service. At the time of this writing, the webcast has reached viewers in 120 countries, with hundreds, and in some cases thousands, watching a given Sunday service online over the course of a week, alongside six hundred in-person worshippers across three services (MCC Toronto 2017). In one of our interviews, I asked Hawkes what had precipitated the genesis of the webcast, what had made it happen. He described to me a moment of convergence between the imperative to reach vulnerable people looking for spiritual guidance and a fiscal contingency requiring an innovative, entrepreneurial approach. The vision that Hawkes ultimately proposed and successfully raised funds to support included the webcast as a central feature. Hawkes frames the origin of the webcast as one of propitious convergence. He explained to me that the webcast stemmed from a broader vision for expanding the church's ministries logistically, financially, and geographically. On the one hand, he told me that he and many in the congregation had long yearned for the opportunity to do more global and Internet outreach, in part because of the distressing dearth of progressive and LGBTQ-friendly religious resources for youth online. On the other hand, he described a moment when the church's structural deficit precipitated some creative action on his part, including seeking and acting on the advice of a prominent local conservative businessman, John Tory, who in 2014 became Toronto's mayor. In my view, the convergence Hawkes describes here points to a more complex orientation toward growth than a simple instrumentalization of Christianity by capitalism. To be sure, the desire to share and circulate alternative, progressive faith perspectives does not transcend capitalism, but it is marked by its own logics—and affects. Melani McAlister (2008) describes the centrality of religious affect—what she calls "enchanted internationalism"—in global evangelical engagements that take on a surprising range of political valences. Here, Hawkes recounted how affective tugs—anger and disgust at a conservative monopoly on representations of Christianity—bind with a market-based solution, suggesting a complex resonance between faith-based global outreach and fund-raising to fuel growth.

Thus, although MCCT and the MCC movement take on entrepreneurial approaches to fund-raising, growth, and global church outreach, the relation between capitalism and religion is not a straightforward one. My conversations with MCC leaders point to a liberal evangelical enthusiasm for expansion that traffics in the idioms of entrepreneurialism, fund-raising, and organizational growth but understands itself as instrumentalizing those idioms in the service of the global dissemination of an antihomophobic "compassionate Christian gospel" and of LGBTQ movement more broadly (Perry 1990, 206). The MCCT global webcast, among the church's most significant outreach efforts and one of a handful of webcasts to LGBTQ Christians in the denomination, must be read as bound up with a zeal for growth that is in a sense both evangelical and entrepreneurial but also more than either of those elements on its own. A litany of imperatives—around "vision," global solidarity with LGBTQ people, effective fund-raising practices—converge in rendering growth an end in and of itself. The point here is not to assign a prime place to market logic, LGBTQ activism, or religious conviction but precisely to map their momentary ontological convergence and resonance in a global church-growth assemblage.

Saving the World

Alongside, and often profoundly intertwined with, evangelical enthusiasm, people involved with MCCT's global outreach articulated aspirations and desires for the global in terms of a kind of pleasure in liberal humanitarianism. This humanitarianism routinely converges with evangelical enthusiasm for expansion, but its affective structure has an analytically distinct economy. Rather than a desiring orientation toward growth (economic, demographic, or spreading the good news) in and of itself, the liberal humanitarian orientation's primary object is nothing less than saving the world.

The salvific orientations of Christian missiology and Western feminist and LGBTQ politics have been subject to diverse, productive, and wide-ranging critique (e.g., Abu-Lughod 2002; Mahmood 2004; Ahmed 2009; Burton 1994; Puar 2007; Brock and Parker 2008). Gayatri Chakravorty Spivak (1988) famously identified colonial preoccupations with the status of colonized women—concern for "saving brown women from brown men"—as crucial in legitimating oppressive colonial power relations (92). Spivak's claim about the colonial scene resounds in figurations of gender and sexuality in postcolonial development politics and geopolitical entanglements. In a study of U.S. imperial narratives of the Vietnam War and Vietnamese diaspora, Mimi Thi Nguyen (2012) tracks how liberal empire discursively renders freedom as a gift beneficently presented to empire's Others, a gift that in turn affords the giver "a power over" the Other, a power that endures over time (7–8). In his controversial book *Desiring Arabs* (2007), Joseph Massad critiques the rise of a "gay international," whose putatively benevolent or salvific interventions in Arab contexts impose Western understandings of sexual practices and identities, at times to the detriment of practitioners of same-sex sexuality in those contexts.

Yet of particular interest to me are the affective and ethical dimensions of the desire to save the Other, and the (non)relation it stages. Anne Mc-Clintock (1995) fleshes out colonial encounter in all its simmering, tremulous detail, using erotics as a means of highlighting the simultaneous vulnerability and sovereignty of the colonizer in the face of the Other. In a feminist recasting of Edward Said's *Orientalism* (1978), Meyda Yeğenoğlu (1999) draws on psychoanalytic theory to argue that colonial *fantasy*, in tandem with colonial discourse, renders the body of the colonized Muslim woman—her sexuality, her veiling or unveiling—a key terrain in the making of the male Western self. Yeğenoğlu's work is helpful, because it directs attention to desire and fantasy as themselves productive of colonial subjectivities. As we will see, the liberal humanitarian desire to save the world proves powerfully productive of MCC's denominational self-concept and the subjectivity of individual MCCT congregants. Indeed, the desire to save the world as a way of engaging in global queer citizenship is particularly pronounced in the global/local context of Toronto.

In the wake of the legalization of same-sex marriage a decade ago, Canadian and especially Torontonian LGBTQ institutions and actors have engaged in a pronounced "international turn." Such actors have argued that the city's tolerant and enlightened status obligates local queers to support their less fortunate queer peers, and pointed to Toronto's centrality in many diasporic networks as evidence of its suitability for affecting global antihomophobic change. MCCT is key among these local actors, whose efforts have sought to renew the mandate of local LGBTQ institutions, brand Toronto as queer-friendly, and help secure the city as the site of the World Pride celebration in 2014. It proves invaluable to bring a fresh and critical reading to claims generated in this "international turn," for, as Rinaldo Walcott (2009) asserts in his important affective and historical mapping of the city, Toronto must be apprehended as a simultaneously colonial and postcolonial city. Walcott's point is not only that Canada is a settler colony or that legacies of empire have impelled diasporic populations to settle there but that colonial epistemes persist with a vengeance in ordinary urban scenes of labor, domesticity, intimacy, and policing. Given the imperial and colonial freight that any conversation about Toronto or its transnational ties inherits, what does it mean for some of the city's LGBTQ activists to hail a turn to the "international" (Easton 2015)?

The MCCT webcast introduced in the preceding section proves an instructive case study in the affective and aspirational dimensions of salvific orientations toward global queer citizenship. Routinely cited in worship services and interviews during elaborations of the congregation's global scope, stakes, and desires, the webcast is a crucial vector of community formation, both for viewers and within the localized MCCT congregation. Because at the time of this writing the church collects little qualitative information about webcast viewers, not much is known about people's global experiences of viewing the webcast outside of what people elect to write in e-mails to Rev. Hawkes or the webcast ministry and what Hawkes and the webcast volunteers in turn elect to share. But the impact of the webcast on the live event of MCCT services, from my vantage as an empirical researcher, has been palpable. Gestures to the webcast—to "our friends watching around the world"—have become a fixture in prayers, sermons, and announcements. Integrating webcast technology has added additional layers of performativity and discipline to Sunday services: choir members have been advised to be more vigilant about their microphones during anointing for healing and Communion when people stand in line to receive a blessing, and those who remain seated are likely to lapse into friendly banter that is now audible to webcast listeners.

On affective terms, the webcast comprises a form of relation with the potential to save the world or save the self. It enables the circulation of some key facets of MCCT services and allows people within MCCT to understand the generosity, altruism, and significance of their institution as global in scale. In Sunday services and at fund-raising events, I have noticed that statistics about the webcast often punctuate larger claims about the world's need for MCCT, providing quantitative evidence of the extent of the church's work alongside powerful anecdotes about experiences of persecution, expulsion, courage, and love. At the same time, the webcast serves as a proxy for a more diffuse and complex range of desires on the part of viewers both regular and occasional. People may attach first and foremost to the very premise of a gay church, making the webcast a "good-enough" object, whatever its limitations in terms of content, format, or linguistic accessibility (Winnicott 1953). Indeed, reconciling nonnormative sexuality and gender with Christianity is, for many, an act of Kleinian integration, a process of threading together two passions that can make, or threaten to cleave apart, a world. Yet such a process takes a wide range of forms, the iterations of which cannot be fully predicted in advance. Indeed, the webcast ministry has reported that some viewers deploy the webcast in various other processes of community formation, tethering the broadcast to their own social, spiritual, political, erotic, and cultural ends. And these integrative possibilities are not lost on those who plan and implement the webcast—in fact, they become the object of further speculation and fantasy on the part of MCCT congregants about the ministry's limitations and potentiality.

Take my conversation with Rudy, for instance. I met Rudy, the webcast-ministry team leader, for coffee after he finished a day of work at a hospital in downtown Toronto. Rudy was brimming with fascinating statistical information on the webcast and analysis of the geography of its reception. Though most online viewers tune in from anglophone countries, he told me, the fourth-highest number of viewers watch from Poland. He described to me aspirations to dub or subtitle the service in Polish, and eventually in Russian. He also recounted to me the layered itinerary of the webcast's growth, from serving vacationing parishioners in Ontario cottage country to increasing transnational circulation. Rudy cited two singular (yet, in a way, ongoing) events—a shout-out from the Los Angeles gay YouTube personality Davey Wavey in March 2012, and Rev. Hawkes's eulogy at New Democratic Party and Official Opposition leader Jack Layton's August 2011 state funeral—that drew the most significant number of unique and repeat visits and ultimately increased the webcast's weekly viewership. Amid an enlightening and wide-ranging discussion of the geography of the circulation of the webcast, his technological wish list for improving the ministry, the need for better metadata to increase visibility, and the intellectual-property restrictions shaping the dissemination of church hymns, Rudy turned briefly to his own motivations for playing a leadership role in the ministry:

> It's really rewarding to—a couple of months ago, we had our first visitor from Uganda, and another visitor from Kenya. So, knowing that in areas where LGBT people are being persecuted, particularly that this is an opportunity for someone there, if they have a PC, to connect and to hear about the good news about God's unconditional love, that they may not otherwise have access to. The ministry itself is actually quite fulfilling in the sense of the fact that it does reach out and provide that outreach to people who wouldn't otherwise hear good news.

For Rudy, love is a universal message, but one that requires labor to circulate under geographically, politically, culturally, and technologically uneven conditions. Simultaneously, the very work of circulating this message—a ministry he finds "quite fulfilling"—marks a vector for love.

But what kind of love is this? As MCCT leaders and webcast volunteers are all too aware, a one-way webcast remains a limited medium, particularly with respect to democratic forms of participation and more reciprocal, mutually vulnerable forms of exchange. In this respect, the webcast stages a return to "older" forms of core–periphery media circulation, which position the colonial or imperial metropole (*Metropolitan* Community Church) as the privileged, active site of information that other locales inertly receive. This model has been complicated, however, by viewers' engagement with the webcast, as Hawkes and his husband, John, recounted to me:

> John: The other major challenge with the Internet presentation is we've been asked by [people in] Ukraine, Romania, and Russia

to have the services subtitled in Russian, because that is a common language that would reach all of those areas, and it would present a community of faith with a different point of view from what is currently influencing Russia and its antigay laws. The problems with that [are], first of all, finding somebody who can do the subtitling into Russian, but as soon as you do that, you begin to need pastoral support in Russian.

Brent: Yup. So, there's a whole kind of thing that we have to think about, how we build. But to me it's just an amazing opportunity. Here are Russian activists saying, "We love MCC Toronto service because of the traditional"—because Russian Orthodox is the main [religious community]—so they want some kind of tradition, they don't want to just see informality. They want to see some kind of tradition so there's some feeling of familiarity. And so, when you think about it, here's this church in Toronto that may be the main spiritual resource for the GLBT community in Russia. It's just amazing. Amazing opportunity.

The exchange of gazes and identifications that Hawkes and Sproule recount here situates the desire to go global as exemplary of both saving the world and saving the self. On the one hand, Russian activists see something that reflects their experience in the MCCT webcast, and Hawkes takes pleasure and hope in being the Other's object of identification. The experience of being looked to—for guidance, for a message of inspiration that cuts across cultural contexts—confers a forceful sense of agency, the capacity to affect others, and the universal salience and applicability of what one has to say. This experience can reinforce a subject's sense of wholeness, identity, integrity, and sovereignty—and also foreclose self-reflexivity, openness to revising judgment. On the other hand, the encounter can be read as staging queer, integrative affective work. Russian activists find something of "the traditional," some resonance with Russian Orthodoxy, in the webcast that helps them synthetically fashion the church as a "good-enough" object (Winnicott 1953). And providing pastoral care in Russian harbors the potential (though no sure-footed assurance) of a more dialogical encounter between MCCT's ministries and the world. A webcast iteratively projects a single message—a message that could be affected by correspondence with web viewers, but on a much longer feedback loop. By contrast, linguistically appropriate and accessible pastoral care (counseling via Skype or e-mail) creates room for both parties to a conversation to be affected by the Other, in ways that *might* productively unsettle the sense of wholeness and solidity of each. The webcast is thus a potentially ambivalent site of a range of forms of identification and global queer community formation; how this goes down remains to be seen.

Affective slippages between saving the world and saving the self echoed in conversations I had with several lawyers involved in refugee and human rights work connected to the congregation. One of the most strikingly geographical accounts of global LGBTQ activism came from Hugh, a prominent Toronto LGBTQ human rights lawyer who has been another central actor in the "international turn" in contemporary Toronto and Canadian LGBTQ activism. Like Hawkes, Hugh identified eastern Europe, Africa, and the Caribbean as pivotal zones in the emergent geographies of contested homophobia. For him, gains in LGBTQ human rights in some locales had played a causal role in the exacerbation and retrenchment of homophobia elsewhere. Thus, Hugh regarded Canadian nationals, among others, as saddled with an especial obligation to address the shifting geographies of religious fundamentalism and homophobia:

> I really do think that a shift to focusing on the plight of members of the LGBT community in other countries is appropriate for us and necessary and an obligation, actually, because I think the backlash that's happening in other countries against the LGBT community—in Russia, in Nigeria, in Uganda—I think it's directly related to the rights that we have achieved, and it's an attempt for the governments there, the power holders there, to make sure that what we have here doesn't happen there.
>
> If you look at the measures that are being taken, they're not just criminalizing the act, the homosexual act. They're criminalizing homosexual relationships. They're criminalizing participation in LGBT organizations. They're criminalizing LGBT advocacy, as they have done in Russia. And that, to me, speaks to the fact that they don't want—they want to cut off the movements [like the ones] that happen[ed] here that [legalized] same-sex marriage—they want to cut them off right at the inception, at the beginning.
>
> And so, I think that we have a responsibility, given the fact that

members of the LGBT community in other countries are suffering because of what we've managed to achieve here, I think that puts a bit of a responsibility on us to respond and step up to the plate and do some real advocacy on their behalf. So, I do think that focusing on international issues is where we have to go. I do have that optimistic, human rights feeling that all ships rise with the tide, and that the rights that we gain here do eventually have a ripple effect and affect people in other countries. But I don't think it's a uniform process, I think it's a process that can entail backlash, and that's what's happening, I think, in other countries.

Strikingly, Hugh locates key causal factors behind homophobia in Africa, the Caribbean, eastern Europe, and the Middle East in a live and ongoing relationship to events in the global North. Hawkes, likewise, has spoken of the role of northern actors, particularly conservative evangelicals, in the production of southern homophobias (CBC News 2014). This geographical imaginary does not center practices of colonialism, empire, and capitalism in its consideration of what conditions the politics of sexuality, and in an odd way, it rehearses the narcissistic post-9/11 U.S. claim that "they" hate, fear, and/or envy "our" freedom (Alexander 2006; Grewal and Kaplan 2001). Hugh's claims also echo the neoliberal rhetoric of former Citizenship, Immigration, and Multiculturalism minister Jason Kenney, who advocated and implemented the devolution of responsibility for refugees to civil society by calling on LGBTQ and immigrant communities to "step up to the plate" (Kenney 2010). However, Hugh's account does helpfully counter culturalist explanations of homophobia and sexism that tend to cast the Other as perpetually mired in regressive tradition (Puar 2007; Mamdani 2005; Razack 2008). Here, an awareness of Western complicity in ongoing scenes of homophobic and transphobic violence—rather than a celebration of Western enlightenment—forms the basis for ethical obligation and for the desire to go global.

At the same time, Hugh's account points to the affective limitations of saving the world. My purpose here is not to weigh in with my own opinion on Hugh's analysis of the shifting global geographies of homophobia. Nor is it to criticize his activist or legal work, which is to be admired in many respects. Rather, I aim to consider the affective dimensions of the kind of subjectivity he imagines as appropriate for Canadian LGBTQ citizens at the current historical juncture. For Hugh, LGBTQ Canadians are achievers

of significant gains. For some unspecified reason or mix of reasons—
perhaps to do with right-wing North American evangelicals—these lofty
accomplishments, in turn, become the objects of resentment. Others fear
and dislike what we have achieved, and so they redouble their efforts to
harm other Others—other Others with whom we also share at least a vector of identity. In this view, "we" cannot rest on our laurels, nor may we remain complacent about our complicity in the suffering of others. We must
act.

The kind of subject Hugh envisions is complicit in the suffering of others and must confront that complicity, but that complicity seems principally coextensive with inaction. We must become aware of our capacity
to do harm to others by doing nothing. The prospect of harming others,
or ourselves, by doing *something* does not appear to arise. As an achiever
and a respondent to the vulnerability of others, this subject answers to an
ego ideal that is outward-looking. The subject wants to save the world.
The subject sees and derives a sense of self-worth from evidence of having agency in the world, even when that evidence comes in the form of
a negative reaction. But the subject and the world never fully interpen-
etrate. The fantasy Canadian LGBTQ subject seems to suffer no vulnerability, no internal divisions or conflicts, no wounds, no queer damage, no
nonsovereignty—and no anxiety about a capacity to do harm. It's only the
world that needs saving.

Awkwardly, I tried to follow up with Hugh, bringing up criticisms of
the impulse toward the global that had come up in interviews with MCCT
congregants and friends (I will detail this ambivalence in the following
section). Hoping to seem politically relevant and respectful of the urgency
of Hugh's work, I framed my question less in terms of the affectivity and
potential dangers of wanting to save the world than in terms of the types
of political lacunae such an orientation might risk.

> One of the arguments that's come up, interestingly, in some of my in-
> terviews with congregants, actually about the refugee program at
> MCC Toronto in particular, is this sense that if the LGBT move-
> ment's focus is too international—not that that's not a good thing,
> I mean, there's pretty universal respect for that work—but that it
> might have the effect of blunting certain kinds of political criti-
> cism of inequality or the persistence of homophobia or transpho-
> bia within Canada. . . . I don't know how you, as someone whose

work is predominantly international, respond to those kinds of concerns. . . .

Hugh: How is the concern . . . Just develop the concern a little bit more for my own understanding.

Sure—just that, like, "We have all of this freedom now, we have good relationships with police," despite all of the concerns around the G20, around racial profiling, around the treatment of trans people at the hands of the police, right? And it's more convenient for us to go help the Other over there than to look at how we might still be implicated in inequality in our own backyard.

Hugh: I don't think it's an either/or, really. I think we can certainly do both at the same time. I think if people feared that the push for same-sex marriage would somehow blunt our advocacy in other areas, I don't know that it did. But I still think that when you look at what we've achieved here, and when you look at what's going on in other countries, there's a huge imbalance there, and I think that imbalance needs to be addressed, given our implication in the imbalance itself.

And you know, I find that really resonates with people. I find my advocacy, my involvement with [the LGBTQ asylum-support organization] Rainbow Railroad, everyone I speak to about it just seems to think that the time has come for an organization like this, that's actually focused on helping people in a really tangible way to get to a place of safety. It's amazing. There's nobody who feels like there isn't a need for this, or worries about the implications of establishing an organization like this. There's huge support for it.

In retrospect, I realized that I had asked Hugh the wrong question but that I was likely not in a position to ask him the right one. The defusion of criticism of injustice "at home" is certainly a potential effect of an orientation toward saving the world, and a routine and deleterious one. But more fundamentally at stake here is a politics of affect, which might ask, among other things, "Where are you in all of this?" Without a more comprehensive realization of one's own need for relationality and one's capacity to do harm—one's partiality, likelihood of blundering into things, propensity for harsh judgments, vanity, aggression—integrative forms of global identification and community formation are foreclosed. If we respond to the needs of others but without the capacity to be vulnerable, to be undone, to hear and learn from critique, we respond out of an unacknowledged narcissistic orientation toward the Other that focuses on the tremulous maintenance of one's own sovereignty. As Sara Ahmed (2009) contends, the point of critical attention to the affective dynamics of global LGBTQ rights work is "not to withdraw from a commitment to freedoms, but it must mean acquiring a certain caution about turning our commitments into our own attributes or even ego ideals (as if we as activists know in advance what is good or right for ourselves or for others)" (n.p.).

I am not interested here in leveling a blanket critique of liberal humanitarian politics as narcissistic—as if narcissism were a bad thing *tout court*, or a thing it was possible to divest from through conscious disavowal. After all, as Freud ([1914] 1957) would have it, sociality itself would not be possible without a measure of narcissism, and the case of the MCCT global webcast demonstrates how the desire to save the world might give way to a heterogeneous proliferation of lines of flight, both narcissistic and integrative forms of community and subject formation. Rather, my conversation with Hugh directs our attention to the tensions between saving the world and saving the self—tensions that revolve in part around our capacities to avow our own narcissism rather than seek to banish it in subservience to altruistic ego ideals. I turn now to a third, more expressly ambivalent affective orientation toward global queer citizenship, in which such tensions and convergences come expressly to the fore.

Global Zeal, Critical Hesitation

Enthusiasm for the project of growth and a liberal humanitarian desire to save the world comprise two key orientations toward global queer citizenship within the MCC movement; neither necessarily nurtures the kind of improper queer citizenship that compels me in this book. Yet my conversations with friends and members of the church suggest that such desires are far from universal and that the permutations of their articulation are far from universally vociferous. Many people I spoke with at MCCT worried explicitly about the political and geographical analysis undergirding the church's global ministries. What makes these concerns significant for my purposes in this chapter is both the proliferation of alternative political analyses that my subjects offered and especially the affective dynamics and implications of such analyses. If desiring relations to growth and saving the Other share an orientation that prioritizes saving the world, the affective orientation I am calling critical ambivalence toward global queer citizenship attends more directly to the inseparable project of saving ourselves. At work in saving the self is not a reification of scalar hierarchy (Isin 2007) that pits the self and the world or the global and the local as discrete domains. If we can agree that the subject and the socius are coconstitutive (Oliver 2004), then critical ambivalence toward global queer citizenship does not prescribe a turn toward solipsism or isolationism; rather, it attends to localized materializations of ordinary and traumatic global power relations, including the self, in the hope of moving through the world in a more integrative and relational way. Critical ambivalence toward global queer citizenship doesn't simply offer a political analysis; it wonders, and worries, What gets lost when "we" rush too rapidly to save the big, sexy, exotic, romantic world "out there" without attending to our own vulnerability, queer damage, implication in global relations of difference and power as those relations play out locally, and capacity to do harm and be harmed across multiple scales? While the church offers messages in sermons, pastoral care, and support groups that speak to people in intimate and socially organized experiences of trauma and anxiety, this critical ambivalence asks what it would mean for the church to incorporate that engagement with nonsovereignty into its more activist, more expressly "global" political engagements as well (Berlant and Edelman 2013).

Here, it proves helpful to consider my conversation with Jeremy, a thoughtful young queer activist who turned to MCCT in a moment of major life transformation and a deep yearning for community as he worked through trauma. Jeremy recounted to me a process of trying to form an integrative relationship with MCCT, struggling to determine its possible status for him as a religious and political object only potentially worthy of repair, sifting through the parts of it he could relate to, worrying about the persistence of the parts he couldn't, and trying to live with the mix. Given the similitudes between our political worldviews, I was curious about how he felt his way through an attachment to the congregation, and I sought Jeremy out for an interview. At a café near his home in the historically working-class but rapidly gentrifying Parkdale neighborhood on the city's west end, I asked Jeremy what his relationship to the church was like.

Because I know you're also involved in the sort of queer, radical, progressive, whatever-you-want-to-call-it side of the political spectrum, how did the church feel for you in terms of your political values?

Jeremy: There were parts that I connected to, but there were large chunks of it I didn't. One of the more telling moments about the difference between my views and the church's views was during Public—what was it?—[Emergency] Services Appreciation Day with Bill Blair, the police chief. It felt like a very middle-of-the-road, safe, middle-class view of the world, where activism and social justice were what we exported to other countries, versus talking about any real critical looks at what's going on in our own country. I mean, the church has picked its issues to work on. Those are refugee issues. There were issues, I think, around poverty, et cetera, but it seemed to be very focused on the world, and queer rights abroad, and that came across as a little bit privileged to me, like, "We've got it made in Canada, so let's go."

My opinion is there was a little bit of evangelism to it. Maybe not outright, but there was a bit of evangelical work in that it was very focused on issues outside of Canada. I think I would have had an easier time with it had there been a more critical look at the work the church could have done within its immediate community as well. Refugee work is incredibly important, and I'm not saying I diminish that in any way, but there was no talk about HIV criminalization, about poverty. Everything was kind of incredibly middle-of-the-road, rah-rah Pride, we're in the Pride parade, we have the biggest rainbow flag in the world, kind of "We have it so great in Canada." And issues of social justice in Canada weren't as forefront, and I didn't connect with that. I felt the church had a role to play in some of the more immediate issues in Toronto, and they weren't playing it.

Jeremy feels haunted by, and accountable to, the queer damage that gets left behind in an approach to LGBTQ politics he apprehends as "evangelical," "privileged," "safe, middle-class," and "rah-rah." Without giving short shrift to refugee-support work, Jeremy wonders how a global solidarity agenda that decries forms of state and informal violence can be concretized to address related but more localized injustices. While it is worth noting that the church's Social Justice Network has organized events to raise awareness around several of the issues Jeremy named, particularly HIV criminalization and police brutality, his skeptical characterization of an affective structure organized primarily around the pleasure of "going global" resonates with my own experiences of participant observation at Sunday services. Indeed, while the small but dedicated and feisty group populating the Social Justice Network warrants precisely the kind of shout-out I sought to offer in chapter 1, insofar as most people vote with their feet, far more people at MCCT seem to be moved by pleasure in feeling global, whatever "global" might mean to them. By the time of our interview, Jeremy had left the congregation. He told me that he remains grateful for the time he spent at MCCT but that he grew wary of the feelings of incongruity between his own ethical and political attachments and his perception of the institutional orientation of MCCT.

Jeremy is not alone in his ambivalence toward and curiosity about the increasingly global orientation of MCCT's ministries, including among people who have sustained attachments to MCCT. A social worker and community activist who was married at the church, Darius described to me a complex process of identification with both MCCT and the idea of a global gay rights movement, one that at times left him wanting more accountability to politics and history.

> Darius: The refugee work is awesome. That's actually something I really like, and that attracts me to [the church]. . . . I fully support that stuff and I think it's great. I do kind of wonder, what are the other social justice pieces that they're doing, and that's where it gets tricky, because in the past, the social justice movement was just the gay rights movement. That was about gay equality. But now that we have a lot of gay equality, in terms of legal and the traditional rights of marriage and all that, what are the social justice issues that the church is working on? This is where it gets really tricky, because what are their perspectives on economic inequality? What are their perspectives on global inequality?
>
> It's tricky, right? Because that's the same thing that led my parents to leave the United Church in the '80s, a church that took a real strong political viewpoint about American

imperialism. Would MCC do something like that? I don't know. What does it mean to be a social justice church, in this time, post–gay marriage? It's kind of a bigger question for the whole gay community. The politics are so broad. . . .

I think you're identifying some really important parallels between the postmarriage LGBT community and the church. Like, what is the common cause? Is it a charismatic leader? Is it a particularly robust vision of global social justice?

Darius: Or does it become a homonationalist kind of endeavor which is so connected to the Canadian state and connected to a history of colonialism and imperialism? I'm very much a centrist in a lot of ways, but sometimes I can kind of lean toward the left on this stuff, because I just think about what's happening globally. When you think about the refugee issue, there is sometimes a—how do I put this? Christianity has an awful history of colonialism and genocide and destruction. I mean, we know that. [He laughs.] Residential schools in our country, and there's a lot of awful, awful stuff. And you have to be cognizant of that kind of evangelical, that missionary, that proselytizing, that stuff's really rubbing me the wrong way.

And I worry sometimes that in the gay rights movement— I do believe there is a global gay rights community, a global social justice–connected movement happening. But I kind of worry that groups like MCC could easily become, in the post-gay-marriage world, quite conservative and quite right-wing and quite racist in the way they think about the rest of the world. I'm not saying they are now. But there's that risk that they could become that kind of, "We have to save the world, we have to save those black and brown people, they're uncivilized." And I see that sometimes on Facebook, people I know that make comments about what's going on in Uganda and Jamaica, and it's tricky. I'm also involved in these issues, and I also want to help. It's not so cut and dry, right? But I do kind of worry sometimes.

Like everyone I spoke with at and beyond MCCT—indeed, like even the church's sharpest critics—Darius is quick to commend the refugee-support work, giving some confirmation to Hugh's contention in the previous section that such work is widely admired. But Darius insists on an approach to global queer citizenship that is more fully oriented toward the difficulty that such work inherits and necessarily involves, and he worries about the foreclosure of such an approach by MCCT's orientation toward saving the world. Explicitly referencing the work of Jasbir Puar (2007) on "homonationalism," he fears the consolidation of nationalist and neocolonial forms of identitarian queer citizenship. For Darius, there is no easy resolution to this difficulty. On the one hand, he sustains an attachment to a vision of queer global citizenship: "I do believe there is a global gay rights community, a global social justice–connected movement happening." On the other hand, Darius feels enmeshed in practices and norms that inherit and reproduce violent colonial tropes and relations and remain uncritically oriented toward saving the world: "People I know . . . make comments about what's going on in Uganda and Jamaica, and it's tricky." These contradictions leave him uneasy about the church's global work.

Ambivalence about the desire for global queer citizenship and the complicities of that desire with colonial power relations also suffused my conversation with Darius about the occupation of Palestine. In one recent Toronto Pride parade, Darius recalled, Rev. Hawkes waved an Israeli flag in solidarity with a contingent of LGBTQ Jews supportive of the state of Israel. Such a display, in Darius's view (and mine), exhibited a profoundly homonationalist orientation toward Israel that mobilizes the image of Israel as gay-friendly in ways that naturalize and legitimate colonial occupation (Puar 2007). Dismayed, Darius followed up with the pastor, indicating his concern about such a display for Israel in the context of its relationship to Palestine. Hawkes indicated that the feedback he received from MCCT congregants was divided between those supportive of the Israeli state, those critical of the occupation of Palestine, and those who wanted Hawkes to have no part of such debates, preferring a putatively neutral approach. While Hawkes discontinued his visible support for the Israeli government, he later served as chair of a 2010 Pride Toronto committee that decided on the right of Queers against Israeli Apartheid (QuAIA) to participate in the city's Pride celebrations. Under pressure from the City of Toronto, a significant financial backer, Pride Toronto had initially banned the organization from participating, a decision that triggered outrage among LGBTQ activists over censorship and colonial complicity. The panel Hawkes chaired reversed that unpopular decision but also sought to maintain the "neutrality" of Pride and LGBTQ politics with respect to the question of Palestine (Creelman 2010). In 2011, when the city made the same threat to defund Pride Toronto and QuAIA opted not to participate in the Parade, Hawkes praised the group, saying that while he did not support QuAIA, the organization "did the right thing" to protect other, apparently nonpartisan LGBTQ institutions (Beauvais 2011). This curious and unfortunate posture of neutrality comes at a time when other progressive and mainstream faith communities, such as the United Church of Canada, have denounced the Israeli state's colonial actions and responded to Palestinian calls to boycott Israel until a more just constellation of relations between Israelis and Palestinians can be forged (Tapper 2012). Such a history left Darius feeling uneasy about the limited critical potential of Hawkes's ministry—an unease that I share.

Given his serious hesitations about homonationalism in MCCT's approach to the project of global queer citizenship, what kept Darius engaged in the church and other identitarian LGBTQ institutions? Later in our conversation, Darius expounded on his own activist praxis, tracing an integrative process of remaining within mainstream LGBTQ contexts to help forge connections across movements ideologically rendered discrete:

How do you look at the bigger picture? Like, I don't want my gay rights to be, I don't want the fact that I have rights to be used as a—I mean, I care about more than just gay rights. I care about indigenous people, I care about poverty, I care about a whole range of different things. So just because you are protecting gay rights doesn't make you, as a politician or as a leader, progressive, especially in this day and age. We have to talk about what are the problems we still have as a society, and where are we going?

I like the idea—and this is why I'm still involved in things like World Pride and Rainbow Railroad—where I have to sometimes suck it up a little bit, like I kind of have to deal with what I call the homonationalist kind of thinking . . . because [I care] about education and helping. If people come to learn about the broader refugee issue, if they come to learn about indigenous rights, through the gay stuff, then that's a good thing. . . . We can learn about—and I think that as gay people who have a history of oppression, and many have personally felt it and understand—I think we have an obligation (and I think this makes me more left-wing than right-wing) to understand other people's suffering and other people's issues.

Darius maintains a tremulous, unsure, somewhat self-conscious relationship to large, "big-tent" LGBTQ institutions, including the refugee-support organization Rainbow Railroad, Toronto Pride, and MCCT, because he is keen to help create opportunities for people to access knowledge about a more capacious web of political and ethical obligations and attachments than world-saving liberal identity politics can countenance. Implicitly addressing the white gay men and lesbians who make up the majority of MCCT (for whom sexuality, and in many cases gender, have likely been the primary vectors for marginalization and the "proper objects" of politics), he invites empathy and engagement with "other people's issues." (The formulation of refugee and indigenous concerns as "other people's issues" reifies a disjuncture between those terms and "queer." However, I suspect it should be understood here as offering a contextually specific intervention in a normatively white context, in which such discreteness is often reified as a matter of course.) Sustaining a multifarious relationship with institutions that one finds politically problematic and also admires can be a key element in practices of improper queer citizenship. Such a praxis is not necessarily comfortable; in my interview, Darius interrupted himself frequently, vacillating, as if issuing partial corrections. But, as Klein (1975) would point out, integrative forms of identification rarely prove comfortable; her alternative to the paranoid-schizoid position—an alternative offering insights that make life habitable—is simply "depressive." At stake here is no less than a queer citizenship that can work through and integrate good and bad elements in itself and its objects in order to embrace a capacious politics without identitarian referent (Eng, Halberstam, and Muñoz 2005).

Perspectives like those of Darius and Jeremy thus speak to the ethical and political value of ambivalence for an improper queer citizenship. In a context where accountability to salvific ego ideals can lead to dangerous forms of nonrelationality—complicity in and even overt support for colonial regimes in the name of global queer citizenship—critical hesitation is a crucial first step in a different direction, an important precondition but not a guarantee of transformative change. Still, making room for ambivalence enables a more sustained recognition and working through of good and bad fragments of the self and the world, and enables more serious consideration of one's own capacity to do harm, to disappoint, as well as to do good. Further, such ambivalence helps us understand institutions like MCCT not as sovereign states, with the word of Rev. Hawkes standing in for that of the sovereign, but as chaotic assemblages. Often, those assemblages are given over to lines of flight that crystallize and reconsolidate hegemonic power relations, as in the case of Hawkes's stance on Palestine or in a salvific approach to work with asylum seekers. But the critical ambivalence that others within the congregation articulate points to the church's enmeshment in other constellations of faith, citizenship, and political praxis—other lines of flight. Desires for global queer citizenship at MCCT and in the denomination often lapse back into identitarian idioms—but sometimes they don't. Both Darius and Jeremy shed light on the agonistic and pluralistic character of the differences within the congregation, differences that help map the heterogeneity of what the church, growth, or globality stands in for as an object of desire. If involvement with MCC both helps produce and enables people to stage a desire for global gay citizen subjectivity, people articulate desires for the global for a lot of chaotic and contradictory reasons. Many articulate a desire for the church to grow out of a bias toward growth, or to help save their LGBTQ brethren overseas, desires that often resonate with the affective orientations of liberal identity politics and capitalist development, and Western Christianity's long-standing orientation toward saving the world. Yet this is where attending to the affective politics in a religious community, rather than reading only for the endless reiteration of patriarchal and imperial complicity, has something to gain from mapping desire. For some also want a church and a queer world-making project that connects the dots, that challenges structural violence in seemingly discrete but connected locales, and that refuses to obscure "localized" violence or reify "national" enlightenment in favor of more "global" engagements. As we will see, these latter articulations of global citizenship entail not simply saving the world but relational and social work of the self on the self.

From Saving the World to Saving Ourselves

How does critical ambivalence about global queer citizenship inflect, temper, and recast the growth-happy and salvific dimensions of MCC's work? What linked yet discrete desiring orientations toward global queer citizenship might this critical ambivalence make possible? This final section considers how differently positioned MCC leaders respond to concerns about the potential affective, ethical, and political pitfalls of global engagement. By the time I attended the UFMCC's global General Conference in Chicago in July 2013, I had conducted enough interviews and been in church long enough to wonder how transnational growth efforts might navigate the heavy prospect of reiterating colonial and imperial relations of power, but I also knew that I was not entirely alone in worrying along these lines. I wondered about both (re)imposition of Western Christian theology and gay identity logics in transcultural contexts with connected yet distinctive theological and cultural constellations of meanings, affects, and bodies (Rofel 2007; Dave 2012). Given Western Christianity's grave and ongoing imbrications with projects of colonialism and empire, and contemporary critiques of the imperialism of many strands of Western LGBTQ movements (Puar 2007; Ahmed 2009), I was curious about how a queer Christian denomination that understood itself as simultaneously entrepreneurial, evangelical, and progressive would approach transnational outreach.

My conversation with the Reverend Elder Darlene Garner offered a generative take on what an alternative affective orientation toward global queer citizenship might feel like. Garner shares in Robb's professed wariness (which began this chapter) of approaching the global in accordance with old colonial missiological patterns, and in his optimism about the prospect of the church breaking with colonial and imperial forms of relationality. Yet she emphasizes that breaking such a mold is not only a matter of better organizational structure or formal guarantees (offering "values" rather than imposing "culture," asking "them" for a change). Rather, for Garner, real change is simultaneously a matter of affective transformation, vulnerability, and integrative work on the self.

I first met Garner at the General Conference, shortly after she'd given an electrifying sermon meditating on the forty-fifth anniversary of the denomination's founding, on how it could remain, in her words, "relevant" as it moved into "middle age." The sermon offered a playful but rigorous challenge to the denomination to work to avoid a grim possible future as a "country club for middle-class, middle-aged, cisgender, able-bodied, white, U.S. American gay men and lesbians." When I later interviewed her and asked my standard questions about how she became involved with MCC, she described to me a layered process of integration—both (and simultaneously) in the political sense of racial integration and in the

Kleinian sense of sustaining a "loving" relation with a complex and contradictory object. As a young single parent in the 1970s and a black lesbian, Garner wanted to maintain a relationship to Christianity for herself and her children, but she also required a church that "would really embrace me without condition." Moving from her hometown of Baltimore to Washington, D.C., Garner described her first experience at MCCDC in 1976 as "a strange mix of feeling as though I had come home and that home was a foreign land." Key dimensions of "being in church and around church people" felt familiar, but the normative whiteness of MCCDC didn't resonate with Garner's background in black churches. "And at the same time," she told me, "I felt that I was very quickly welcomed and was very quickly put to work—I mean like [we both laugh], *very* quickly put to work. So, from the very beginning, I felt that there either was or could be room for me in MCC." Garner's insight—"that there either was or could be room" in the MCC movement—resounds with those of church leaders of color in chapter 1 who describe an immanent, palpable, yet "not-yet-here" queerness in the space of the church (Muñoz 2009). Alongside her extensive secular organizing work in black LGBTQ communities, Garner became a delegate to the MCC General Conference, treasurer of the church, and, eventually, an ordained minister. In 1993, she became the first black person elected to UFMCC's Council of Elders.[4] At first, much of the work Garner felt compelled to do in the denomination centered issues of race, "because it [MCC] was not a place that was easy for people of African descent to make their home." Over time, however, she "began to get a much clearer sense that MCC really did struggle around issues of inclusivity, and it was not only around issues that were defined by race."

In her work as an elder, Garner has traveled internationally to support and cultivate relationships with MCC congregations outside the United States. She lived for two years in Cape Town, South Africa, to work with and for African MCCs, and for five years in Mexico to work with churches in Latin America. Her ministry outside the United States, she told me, was an education in the geographically contingent and relational character of subjectivity, and in the need for a church that is relevant and mutual in context-specific ways. As she traveled between the United States and South Africa, she narrated a particularly pronounced moment of horror and shame at ugly American racism and imperialism abroad. Hearing and watching Americans speak disparagingly to and about the South African flight attendants and passengers they met on the plane, Garner "experienced their brashness, their relative arrogance and sense of entitlement, so much that it was embarrassing to me." In response, Garner spent the rest of her flight in silence, hoping, somewhat desperately, to pass as South African "and not be associated in that particular instance as being American at all." Garner's attempted disavowal of her nationality spurred critical reflection on the privileges afforded her by U.S. citizenship and imperialism. After decades of working for expansive gender, class, and racial enfranchisement within normatively white, bourgeois, and male LGBTQ institutions in the United States, Garner engaged in ethical deliberation in which she could not immunize herself against criticism or shame, in which her blackness, womanhood, and queerness were not "wounded attachments" or grounds for sovereignty but "rifted grounds" for empathy with differently marginalized and exploited people (Brown 1995; Butler 1994, 21). If colonized and postcolonial elites (Fanon [1952] 2008; see also Benedicto 2014) experience the horrifying revelation of their positioning as "locally" privileged and "globally" marginal when visiting the colonial metropole, Garner traces a North-to-South itinerary that muddles "local" (i.e., U.S.) marginality with a (still racialized and sexualized) "global" privilege—but that also points to such a crossing as an occasion for ethical responsibility.

In her current role, Garner heads the denomination's curiously titled Office of Emerging Ministries, an office she described as "charged with new church development everywhere in the world, including in the U.S. and Canada." Expounding on the spirit of the office, Garner gestured to a "responsibility of creating ways for MCC to say 'yes' to ministry opportunities that are unexpected, to expand our capacity to do cross-cultural ministry in a way that honors cultural diversity and has integrity and is seen as having integrity by others." Much as in my conversations with Robb and with other UFMCC leaders, Garner does not regard the potential ethical and political dangers that haunt transnational LGBTQ and Christian engagements—the risk of extending or reiterating colonial or imperial relationships—as a reason to shrink back from global solidarity and growth: "I can no longer just accept that this is hard work, therefore it ought not to be done," she told me. "Rather, I accept that this is hard work and *must* be done in order for MCC to continue to be relevant to people around the world and in the twenty-first century. It's my passion. It's my heart pulse." Garner refuses to stop at simply heeding critique and receding from the risks of transnational relationality. Instead, she positions such criticisms as an ongoing invitation to accountability. Providing global support to anti-homophobic faith voices, Garner suggests, is simply too important a project to give up. As an alternative, she describes a framework for relationship that welcomes critique—a frame within which critiques helpfully provoke more experimentation with less hierarchical relationships among churches in the North and the South, and the valorization of a more heterogeneous range of knowledges and capacities for relationality.

As should be clear by now, Garner is a magnificent orator and a gifted rhetorician. During our conversation, she had a habit of pausing, revising herself, as though drafting a manuscript for a beautiful sermon. Given my admiration for her activism, and especially for such evocative writing and speaking, I had to push myself to challenge her in our interview. Much as in my conversation with Robb, I told Garner that I wondered whether I could get a clearer, more specific sense of what a better form of relationality between congregations and between queers in the global North and the global South might look like. She responded by telling me a story. But rather than give me an ethnographic vignette of an encounter with "an Other" church, she told me a story about desiring orientations toward global queer citizenship within the global North—about a dialogue regarding failures to dialogue:

> I was very recently approached by a U.S.-based church that has been really excited about and wanting to do more with regard to providing financial support to emerging churches outside of the U.S. And there came a moment in that conversation, and this person was in touch with me, because the church that they had been supporting or to which they had been providing financial support, for whatever reason, that church decided that they didn't want to continue that relationship but wanted to try somebody new. The way the questions were framed about who else they might be able to help—the questions were all about some poor person somewhere.
>
> There was no acknowledgment, no recognition at all, of a desire to be in mutual relationship or to recognize that churches outside of the U.S. have much to teach in the U.S. There was no recognition, and even resistance. I got a little bit of resistance when I suggested that it would not be appropriate for them to give their gift, because it met their need to give without consideration of what the

needs of the recipients might be. Saying, "We wanna do this once a year, and we want them to tell us on an ongoing basis what they're doing with our money."

And it's like, "Wait a minute, why are you doing this? Why are you entering, why are you saying you want to be in relationship, if the relationship is only about meeting your needs? If that is your primary driver, and you are unable or unwilling to open yourselves up to the possibility of being in mutual relationship with people who are not like you, then you ought not to do this."

They were rather taken aback. "What do you mean? We have money. Why can't we do it?"

"Well, because this is not about money. This is about relationship. This is about mutuality, not about you as a donor being able to determine what someone else has to do for you because you have given them a gift. It's a different kind of relationship. It's not about picking and choosing among poor people all around the world 'cause that's what Christians do—the old model of missionary, 'We know better, we know what is good for you better than you yourself.' It's a horrible, horrible model that we've inherited for a cross-cultural ministry, regardless of whether we're talking about crossing national borders or just crossing attitudinal borders, cultural borders."

For me, we must enter into our sharing with one another from a place of humility, from a place of really recognizing that those with financial means have as much of a need for relationship as those without financial means. It's not about us abusing our privilege but about having integrity in our relationships with one another. And I think it's especially important in the context of MCC, where we are intentionally a global church, which implies "mutual." We are in mutual ministry with people around the world. And the issue for those from—I'll just call it the global North—the reality is that there's not a whole lot, at least in the American context, there are not a lot of opportunities for us to experience what it is to be in mutual relationship with people around the world. Far too often, the attitude or the expectation has been that we are and should be those who protect the world but not being part of that world, not being in need of protection ourselves—usually from ourselves.

Garner confronts an orientation toward the global that comports with the much-feared "sugar daddy missiology" model of relationship that Robb described. Some in early MCC debates on global growth feared that becoming a "North American sugar daddy" would lead to economic exploitation by congregations in the global South—pseudochurches interested only in money (not unlike the specter of the "fake refugee," which we will encounter in chapter 4). Here, however, Garner castigates a North American sugar daddy who terminates relationships "for whatever reason" and moves cavalierly from beneficiary to beneficiary, confident in the capacity of his wealth and goodwill to attract another southern lover and hopefully one more cooperative, more pliant. "Why are you doing this?" she counters. "Why are you entering, why are you saying you want to be in relationship, if the relationship is only about meeting your needs?"

It is not incidental, I would maintain, that Garner critically interrogates the impulse to go global, to relate globally, in the domain of desire. Garner begins from an understanding that class, racial, and geopolitical hierarchies condition, striate, and constrain efforts at transnational LGBTQ and Christian solidarity. But she refuses the presumption that structural distributions of privilege necessarily overdetermine people's capacity for relationality, calling instead for a recognition "that those with financial means have as much of a need for relationship as those without financial means." By bringing the affective and spiritual dimensions of relationality to the fore in an intervention already shaped by a critical recognition of the global politics of difference, she accesses the vulnerability at the heart of a salvific, sovereign affective orientation toward global queer citizenship, one that seeks to "protect the world" without "being part of that world, not being in need of protection ourselves—usually from ourselves." As Eric Santner (2001) might advocate, such a shift in emphasis from "external" to "internal" forms of difference and out-of-jointness marks "the point at which we truly enter the midst of life, that is, when we truly inhabit the proximity to our neighbor, assume responsibility for the claims his or her singular and uncanny presence makes on us not only in extreme circumstances but *every day*" (6, emphasis original).

It may be asked what is to be gained ethically and politically from a focus on the affective vulnerability of comparatively privileged, global North queer subjects. Indeed, engagement with one's own vulnerability—one's own need of protection, including (and usually) from oneself—can play out on microfascistic terms that authorize one to act without account-ability because one sees oneself as a victim. Yet, as the psychoanalytic and literary scholar Jacqueline Rose (2007) helpfully distinguishes, "Suffering is not the same thing as victimhood" (54). Regarding oneself as a benefi-cent actor in the world with a greater capacity to affect others than to be affected by them (as in the case of the sugar daddy congregation) reiterates a violence both on the "external" Other and, vitally, on the subject's alterity to herself. Rose writes, "We need to ask, when we refuse the other psychic right of entry, even *in extremis,* what we are doing, not only to them, but to ourselves" (12). Whether engendered by habit, conditioning, a sense of insurmountable difficulty, altruistic ego ideals, or choice, an eschewal of the need to save and work on oneself, Rose argues, is precisely the affec-tive orientation that makes us likely to carry out acts of banal evil in the Arendtian sense (Arendt [1963] 2006). In an insight rather in sync with that of Rose, Garner is asking what it might mean for differently situated LGBTQ Christians everywhere to engage *with their own suffering* and that of others—including suffering bound up with the capacity to do harm—while remaining aware of their propensity to let that suffering ossify into obdurate savior/victim identifications, into identitarian global queer citizenship.

It would be incorrect, I think, to position Garner's approach to her global ministry as fundamentally departing from the entrepreneurial-evangelical enthusiasm for expansion or the liberal humanitarian desire to save the world. Zeal for MCC—its theology, its project—suffused my interview with her as much as it did my time with Hawkes or Perry. Like Hawkes, Perry, and the MCCT leaders of color whose perspectives take center stage in chapter 1, Garner is simultaneously a critic and an institu-tion builder, and MCC is her brand.

Still, I want to suggest that critical moments in Garner's engagement with desires for global queer citizenship might point us to other, minor in-flections of a hegemonic, salvific and identitarian narrative of global queer citizenship. The line of flight Garner might proffer is immanent to, works within, the MCC evangelical-entrepreneurial-salvific global growth-resonance machine rather than transcending it. Garner repairs the church as an object, organizing her relationship to it on terms that feel "good enough," in order to dream up possibilities for a global queer citizenship that interrupts rather than repeats missiological dynamics. "Remaining outside the dream of enforcing a new master tongue," Garner does not eschew the project of global queer citizenship even as she is highly cognizant and critical of the power relations that crosscut it (Berlant 1994, 136). Rather, she works through that fraught project, living with its contradictory mix of progressive and microfascistic elements, interrogating its ethical and psychic dynamics. Garner's ministry thus resonates, in some ways harmoniously, with the call from Grewal and Kaplan (2001) "to examine complicities as well as resistances [in the circulation of global LGBTQ identities] in order to create the possibility of critique and change" (675). But Garner's approach to critique and change directly engages a politics of affect in general and desire in particular, asking, "Why are you doing this?" If Garner feels she cannot afford *not* to engage transnationally (Spivak 1990), she also indicates that such work cannot take place on emancipatory terms without ongoing self-transformation.

Whether attachments to queer global citizenship ultimately prove "cruel-optimistic"—whether the terms that organize such attachments are inimical to the flourishing of some or many people who articulate them—remains to be seen, in part because those attachments are so variegated and geographically diffuse (Berlant 2011a). People in MCC want church growth as an end in itself, and they want to save the world; some are ambivalent about such projects, but even critical ambivalence can be heard and incorporated in ways that seem to reiterate a sovereign, world-saving, or evangelical-entrepreneurial subject. But given the "relentless return" (Joseph 2002) of queer global citizenship narratives and desires, perhaps attending a bit more immediately to the self, in its nonsovereignty and capacity to do harm, might offer a modest line of flight, a "minor" inflection of the desire for the global. At stake in such integrative affective work is not anything like a clean break or an alternative, radical, redemptive paradigm with pretensions of saving the world from world-saving projects. Like Darius's work within mainstream LGBTQ institutions or with institutions of whatever kind, it entails "sucking it up a little bit," and "it's tricky." But critical engagement with the self, its vulnerability and desires, might make the global queer citizenship to come one that is marked by a little more "give," humility, mutuality, and forbearance—precisely the affects that an improper queer citizenship at any geographical scale demands. The project of mapping heterogeneous desires for queer global citizenship is thus necessarily incomplete, because it is necessarily iterative. For Christians, for queers, for "*everyone* [to] live as a minority among minorities," perhaps it is to desire that we must continue to return (Asad 2003, 180 [emphasis original]). In the following, final chapter, I turn to another figure central to the desire for global queer citizenship in church—a figure that variously elicits anxiety, paranoia, hesitation, scrutiny, sympathy, salvific desire, and, in key moments, solidarity: the queer asylum seeker, or not-yet-refugee.

4

From Identity to Precarity

Asylum, State Violence, and Alternative Horizons for Improper Citizenship

As I observed, and participated in, these debates, I wonder how differently
they might sound if our abiding image of who we are was based less
on autonomy and self-sufficiency, less even on the responsibility of
the "privileged" for the "less fortunate," but rather on a fundamental
conviction of shared vulnerability, mutual laceration, ubiquitous
fragmentation that cannot be overcome—only denied.

—Kent L. Brintnall, *Ecce Homo: The Male-Body-in-Pain as Redemptive Figure*

The Waiting Room

Perhaps the most remarkable thing about the waiting room in the Canadian Immigration and Refugee Board (IRB) office at 74 Victoria Street in downtown Toronto is its unremarkability. In its rows of drab chairs, people sit, stretch, look at their phones, make small talk, yawn, check their watches, review documents. They may tense up. They may appear bored, blasé. Some haven't slept the night before their hearings. Some haven't slept well for maybe days, months, years. Some come dressed in what might be their finest clothing. Others look more business casual. The most formally dressed in the room, accompanied by rolling briefcases and large file folders, are the immigration lawyers.

Any two people in this room could share a geopolitical conflict that indelibly touched both their lives, a relationship to empire, a last name, a religious faith, or a favorite color—or next to nothing. Incommensurable histories, differences, trajectories cross, collide, and combine in unpredictable but still decidedly stratified permutations. Perhaps the only thing these people most certainly share is that they must wait.

People sit in families, in couples, in groups. Babies scream. To the ear of this Anglophone-Francophone, people seem to be chattering in Farsi, Jamaican patois, Russian, Somali. They could be talking about something urgent or rehearsing the most salient, straightforward renditions of their stories in their heads—or not. In any case, talking passes the time, something the asylum seekers I've interviewed described experiencing as both a dearth and a surplus.

Too much time: asylum hearings endlessly deferred for already backlogged adjudicators who've fallen ill or gone on summer vacation; endless time in the waiting room, at the whim of the banal rhythm of one little corner of the Canadian nation-state immigration machine; formidable commutes from suburban and exurban rooming houses to downtown lawyer's offices and most LGBTQ institutions—expensive journeys straddling two or even three regional-transit systems; long gaps between appointments, church services, job interviews downtown, with few options for places to pass the in-between time safely, cheaply, warmly.

Not enough time: sped-up hearings; work permits threatening to expire; just sixty days to acquire all the requisite documents from impenetrable and often hostile bureaucracies back home; late warnings at second- and third-shift jobs after those lengthy, unpredictable commutes; working all the time but not making enough to pay for rent, transit fare, remittances, groceries.

The waiting room is a site where these distorted timelines, at once stretched out and compressed, "too much" and "not enough," converge. Anodyne as it might seem at first glance, the waiting room spatializes the liberal fetish of state neutrality. Concealing the nation-state agendas and economic and geopolitical contingencies that structure people's experience of migration, the waiting room disingenuously posits a horizontal relationship among equal applicants, all of whom must wait their "equal" turn.

I first came to the waiting room at the IRB in September 2013 to support Paige, a friend and interview subject I had met in the refugee peer-support group at MCCT. Paige had agreed to call me as soon as she got her hearing date, and she did. Paige, who volunteered at church as a candle bearer, enthusiastically made a beeline for me after I came to the support group looking for interview volunteers. A few weeks later, she and I met up and chatted at a mall near her home, in Toronto's Jane and Finch neighborhood, then began routinely catching up after church services. After getting to know her for a few months, I nervously but unhesitatingly wrote a letter of support for her request for asylum from the homophobic persecution she described experiencing in Saint Vincent.[1]

I initially showed up for Paige's hearing wondering whether I could secure permission to attend it as a silent observer, as she had requested. I had seen hearings on refugee-status claims only in aesthetic representations, such as the acclaimed Canadian film *Monsieur Lazhar* (Falardeau 2012), and was eager to observe an actual hearing. As fate or bureaucratic norms would have it, I ultimately wasn't able to get on the list to attend Paige's asylum-claim hearing. But this spatial constraint serendipitously gave me greater insight on a less remarked-upon, yet in my view equally significant space in the everyday geographies of asylum seekers and of nation-state immigration management (Mountz 2011): the waiting room. Sitting in the waiting room also gave me the chance to chat with Paige's girlfriend, Edie, who was, like Paige, an asylum seeker from the eastern Caribbean. Because their relationship had begun quite recently, Paige's lawyer thought it better for Edie to wait outside than to testify and risk incurring suspicion about the authenticity of the relationship—and thus of Paige's sexuality, a key component in her claim on refugee status.

So there Edie and I sat for over three hours one September afternoon, apprehensive yet numbed by the gray of the room and the almost inaudible but relentless hum of charmless fluorescent lights. The hearing both began and ended much later than expected. There was only one break, at which time a tense and uncharacteristically taciturn Paige came out for water. To pass the time, Edie and I chatted intermittently, texted friends about the hearing's imagined progress, and took turns going to the washroom and getting paper cups of water.

In my conversations with both Paige and Edie, they described complex lives and immigration cases. Both had children back home from previous relationships with men. But both could point to well-documented legal and extralegal hostility to same-sex sexuality among women in their island nations of origin, much of it influenced by U.S.-backed evangelical groups. Both described experiences of beatings and death threats. The two met in a social group for black women who love women organized by an ethno-specific AIDS service organization in downtown Toronto. On Wednesday nights, Edie told me, the two would attend LGBTQ asylum-seeker support group meetings at a secular community center, and then stop at a bar in the city's gay village that charged no cover and boasted a comparatively decent-sized cadre of black drag performers. For the most part, though, the two lived and worked far from downtown.

Paige finally got out of the hearing. She told us the immigration judge had offered a few reassuring words and said she should hear back about the decision on her claim by mail in about a month.

Waiting Room as Queer Space

Debates on queer space-time and queer "subjectless critique" have generated more politically and analytically capacious understandings of queerness, adding such figures as the welfare queen, the indigenous child, the unmarried migrant worker, and the terrorist to a heterogeneous litany of queer subjects (Edelman 2004; Muñoz 2009; Halberstam 2004; Oswin 2010; Puar 2007). Such scholarship has argued for an understanding of queerness based not on the "truth" of one's sex but on heterogeneous but shared estranged relationships to processes of normalization (Foucault [1976] 1978). As I argued in the Introduction to this book, at stake for subjectless queer critique is not simply an interesting, expansive *analytical* understanding of queerness but also the prospect of coalitional *politics*—the hope of directing scholarly and activist attention and care to surprising ethical and political affinities, encounters, and solidarities among differently marginalized people. With dreams of surprising affinity and political change in mind, then, this chapter proposes the asylum seeker as a queer figure, and a crucial figure for improper queer citizenship. As many destination countries, including Canada under the Conservative federal government in power from 2006 to 2015, embrace increasingly paranoid and austere approaches to refugee policy, nation-state actors use narratives of (in)authentic sexual-minority identity to undermine people's requests for asylum based on a "well-founded fear of being persecuted" for being LGBTQ (U.N. High Commissioner for Refugees [1951] 2011, 14).[2] Working against the tactical ossification of LGBTQ identity in the service of state violence, this chapter investigates how asylum seekers' structured, vulnerable, and ordinary experiences of space-time—especially in *waiting rooms,* both literal and figural—position them as "queer," regardless of sexual orientation or gender identity. I go on to trace the complex figurations of subjectivity and solidarity at play in MCCT's ethicopolitical response to asylum seekers in the church's refugee-support programs.

My argument for the asylum seeker as queer takes its cues both from recent debates on queer temporality and queer subjectless critique, and from postcolonial criticism. In an incisive critique of Eurocentrism in liberal narratives of historical and political change, postcolonial theorist Dipesh Chakrabarty (2000) critiques a persistent spatiotemporal imaginary that positions western Europe as the primary and original seat of modernity. Such historicism at times explicitly and at times more tacitly consigns all other, "rude" spaces—Africa, Asia, the precolonial Americas, and Australia—to what Chakrabarty calls the "waiting-room of history" (8). He elaborates that "historicism—and even the modern, European idea of history—one might say, came to non-European peoples in the nineteenth century as somebody's way of saying '*not yet*' to somebody else" (8 [emphasis added]). In the imaginary of Eurocentric historicism, the modernization of the "rude" rest of the world—the process by which people become historical actors—is hopelessly ancillary, derivative, and, above all, deferred. Queer critic David L. Eng (2010) extends Chakrabarty's critique of modernization narratives to the domains of sexuality and sexual politics, sketching a "queer liberal" imaginary that figures racialized queernesses as illegible, closeted, not-yet-modern, underdeveloped. In Eng's account, queer liberalism imagines queers in the global South and diasporic queers as mired in conservative cultures, and figures the closet as the waiting room of history from which such queers must emerge to become modern (see also Brown 2000).[3]

This chapter grounds Chakrabarty's metaphor of the waiting room of history in empirical engagement with the everyday geographies of asylum seekers. Drawing from interviews with asylum seekers about their everyday geographies, I contend that Canadian federal immigration policy and diffuse, everyday xenophobia position asylum seekers as infantile, chronically liminal subjects. I trace the physical and sociosymbolic spaces through which asylum seekers' deferred relationships to modernity are experienced. I take cues not only from asylum seekers' experiences in literal waiting rooms, like the one I sat in with Edie, waiting for Paige, but also from other quotidian and psychic spaces through which asylum seekers move: substandard housing, lengthy commutes, and even the church itself. Asylum seekers' ordinary geographies are crucial to understanding the structurally imposed temporal lag that organizes their relationships to hegemonic conceptions of intelligible personhood, political subjectivity, and historical agency. Whatever claimants' "true" sexual orientation or gender identity, claimants are, in many cases, made materially and affectively precarious by virtue of their deferred status as asylum seekers.

In the chapter's second half, I sketch the church's refugee peer-support group as a site of solidarity between refugees and nonrefugees on more-than-identitarian grounds, and of improper queer citizenship. The refugee program's formal mandate and rhetoric can easily be read as reiterating the trope of authentic, universal LGBTQ identity and the fantasy of a white savior that suffuse Canadian refugee law and much of international human rights discourse (Hage 1998; Razack 2004; Nguyen 2012). Moreover, the xenophobic suspicion of "fake" refugees articulated and performatively produced by agents of the Canadian nation-state also infuses the atmosphere of the congregation, to chilling effect (see Lidstone 2006; Gill 2010). At the same time, however, interviews and participant observation with asylum seekers and refugee-program leaders also position the project as a more ambivalent, and at times critically queer, faith-based response to federal immigration policy and to racism and xenophobia within the congregation. Significantly, the program refuses the Canadian nation-state imperative to police the sexual and gender identities and religious affiliations of participants, and harbors no expectation that people involved in the program become formal members of the congregation. Answering to conceptions of citizenship beyond the nation-state (Isin 2012), such practices stem from a queer and faith-based recognition that asylum seekers demand an ethical response not simply on the basis of identity (as "proof" of vulnerability) but because of their structured, precarious experiences of space-time, their repudiated desire to survive (Butler 2004; Hondagneu-Sotelo 2008; Yukich 2013).

I have just outlined what this chapter is about: an argument for asylum seekers as figurally queer, regardless of sexual orientation or gender identity, and an exploration of ethicopolitical practices at MCCT that model a more capacious queer citizenship. Before continuing, however, it seems crucial to briefly clarify what this chapter is *not* concerned with. This chapter is not an apologia for the refugee program at MCCT. As I demonstrate in this chapter, the program is an object of at times fractious debate within the congregation and beyond it. Official representations of the refugee program within the congregation risk shoring up a geographical imaginary in which Canada figures as an enlightened, welcoming, tolerant, and salvific exemplar within the global North vis-à-vis the ignorance, hostility, intolerance, and danger of the global South, a figuration that tends to conceal the ongoing neoliberal and neocolonial processes that condition the uneven geographies of homophobia and transphobia (see Grewal and Kaplan 2001). Moreover, alongside the refugee program's official rhetoric, the congregation itself is a space of atmospheric xenophobia and racism, within which asylum seekers face scrutiny from some white Canadian citizens who fear claimants are simply "using" the church. Such informal skepticism inflects everyday acts of inclusion and exclusion in the church, and positions the church as partially continuous with the paranoia and austerity circulated in nation-state discourses on "fake" refugees.

Yet crucially, participants and leaders in the refugee program anticipated and vigorously contested both of these vexing tendencies. On the one hand, the worrisome prospect of complicity in politically unsavory civilizational discourse was not lost on many of the participants I interviewed—asylum seekers and others who remained both hesitant about certain dimensions of a refugee humanitarian project and committed to the refugee program's capacity to generate more and better possibility and survival for more people. On the other hand, program leaders and participants directly confronted the trope of the "fake" refugee, from the pulpit and in everyday sociality, challenging violent, provincial, and identitarian forms of national and LGBTQ citizenship that long for a "proper" object or subject. Amid practices of complicity with racist, xenophobic, and civilizational power, I stumbled upon moments in fieldwork that surprised me (Sedgwick [1997] 2003) and insights that I think might pleasantly surprise readers who are critical of unevenly proliferating restrictions on transnational human mobility and citizenship in much of the contemporary world. It is the expansive capacity for ethical responsiveness on more-than-identitarian grounds that I argue makes the church refugee program surprisingly exemplary of improper queer citizenship. Such an ethical and political response—not quite a choice—answers to the structural precaritization and thus the queerness of the asylum seeker as such, and to queer desires for more expansive, improper modes of collectivity and affinity (Puar et al. 2012).

Asylum Seeker as Queer

What might it mean for politics to think of asylum seekers as *figurally* rather than literally queer? Over the past two decades, a proliferation of scholarship on sexuality and migration has shed light on the complex negotiations made by LGBTQ migrants, migrant sex workers, and subjects whose gender and sexual nonnormativity cannot be adequately articulated through normative Western sexual identity categories. Such writing includes some excellent and illuminating scholarship about the Canadian context, where refugee claims on the basis of persecuted lesbian, gay, bisexual, and transgender identity have gained traction in the courts since 1992 (e.g., LaViolette 2013, 2009; Rehaag 2008; Murray 2014). Drawing on important interview-based research with LGBTQ refugees in Montreal, Canadian social work scholars Edward Ou Jin Lee and Shari Brotman (2011) indict a federal immigration system fraught with essentialism, normative whiteness, heteronormativity, and cisnormativity (see Luibhéid and Cantú 2005). The paradigms for evaluating the experiences of LGBTQ asylum seekers, Lee and Brotman contend, draw narrowly from scholarship on sexual identity formation that suffers from overrepresentation of the experiences of cisgender white gay men and a dearth of ethnic, racial, gender, and cultural diversity. Other critics have noted that refugee law's approach to sexuality and gender consolidates nonnormative sexual and gender identities as essential, fixed, discernible, and epistemologically transparent forms of difference (see also Fortier 2013.) Such essentialism can have particularly deleterious effects, because it tends to render non-Western sexual idioms and practices as sad, underdeveloped, "backward" (Giametta 2014) formations, mired in the closet as a "waiting room of history" (Eng 2010). The normative framing of refugee-claims processes tends toward a homonationalist (Puar 2007; Dryden and Lenon 2015), "liberationist narrative" in which Canada appears as a "generous," benevolent nation-state offering safe haven to precarious subjects with nowhere else to turn (see Murray 2014; Luibhéid and Cantú 2005). Such salvific framing obscures the complex and contingent economic and geopolitical conditions, particularly neoliberalism and imperialism, that shape LGBTQ and all migration, and simultaneously effaces the layered and chaotic itineraries, desires, and agency of individual asylum seekers and those of their would-be saviors (Grewal and Kaplan 2001). Thus, far from conducting a straightforward evaluation of the validity of asylum seekers' requests for asylum based on well-founded fears of persecution, the Canadian IRB makes some claimants legible as persecuted LGBTQ subjects and "legitimate" refugees, and deems other lives too chaotic, contradictory, unintelligible to warrant reprieve from the waiting room of history.

Much like Eng's (2010) trenchant take on queer liberalism, LGBTQ and queer asylum scholarship offers a compelling critique of the limits and violence of fetishistic nation-state grammars for intelligible LGBTQ identity and acceptable, legitimately vulnerable refugeeness. My project in this chapter, however, is slightly to the side of such important critical endeavors. I am not interested here in exposing how nation-state efforts to make queerness legible necessarily fail and wrongly mistake good, intelligible, futurity-worthy LGBTQ people for bad, futureless queers and "fake" claimants. Nor am I arguing that more ethnographic attention to the empirical complexity of asylum seekers' lives or experiences of gender or sexual diversity can help develop less hypocritical, Eurocentric refugee policy or less complicit strategies for politicized asylum advocacy. Nor, finally, am I concerned with shedding fuller light on how asylum seekers tactically make recourse to liberal idioms of "universal" gay identity for complex, shifting, and opaque reasons. All of these are worthy and highly instructive intellectual projects that continue to inform and inspire my own thinking. Building on such work, this chapter focuses instead on how attention to asylum seekers' everyday geographies—the structured impact of nation-state and informal paranoia and xenophobia on their lives, including in church—establishes claimants' figural queerness *precisely as asylum seekers,* regardless of "true" sexual orientation or gender identity. This queerness in turn elicits an ethicopolitical response, not only in the form of better policy but from civil-society actors—in this case, queer people of faith.

By reading the asylum seeker as a precarious queer figure and a figure that demands accountability from and through improper queer citizenship, this chapter engages the ongoing work of "subjectless critique" in queer studies, work without "proper object" (Eng, Halberstam, and Muñoz 2005, Butler 1994). While such scholarship is vast and continues to proliferate, it is crucial to note that questions of space-time have figured centrally in more expansive, capacious understandings of queerness. Judith Halberstam (2005) calls for greater attention to "queer"—but by no means necessarily LGBTQ—spaces, times, and lives that play out in excess of sanctioned everyday geographies and life courses endorsed by heteronormative capitalist "repro-time." Engaging Halberstam from within human geography, Natalie Oswin (2010) has further fleshed out subjectless critique's salience in social and spatial analysis, exploring how teleological, heteronormative assumptions about the proper life course shape legal eligibility for coveted housing in postcolonial Singapore. Simultaneously moral, sexual, spatiotemporal, and juridical, such norms not only exalt heteronormativities but work to the detriment of people who are not necessarily LGBTQ, such as migrant workers, whose lives are effectively rendered queer by virtue of their nonnormative, nondomestic life courses and geographical itineraries. Oswin's work models how attention to the spatialization of exclusive norms can help us track the queerness of subjects rarely framed as such.

Scholarship on queer space-times has also approached diaspora as a queer site, a site of privileged access to the *psychic* space of expulsion. Taking up the essays and fiction of renowned Trinidadian Canadian writer Dionne Brand, Dina Georgis (2006) sketches affective resonances and affinities between queerness and diaspora. Both queerness and diaspora, she contends, entail a loss of home, an often irrevocably severed (and thus all the more desired) attachment to nation, family, home, belonging. While Georgis's archive lays plain that such expulsion often proves all the more acute for queer diasporic subjects, her analysis boldly argues for a queerness inherent to diaspora itself. "I suggest that diasporic space is a queer space, or a space that opens us to Eros," Georgis writes, "not only because people with non-normative sexualities and diasporic subjects share the experience of expulsion from home, but because expulsion from home is a return to the fundamental trauma of relationality and renounced desire" (6). Where Lee Edelman's (2004) engagement with psychoanalysis focuses on the death drive's "no" to futurity, Georgis argues the queerness of diaspora, by virtue of its return to the psychic space of inaugural repudiation and loss. Such a reckoning with repudiated desire seems particularly urgent in the case of the politics of asylum, in which state agents purport to discern with (impossible) transparency the relative "purity" and "authenticity" of the motivations of asylum seekers—to biopolitically sort out "good," "legitimately" vulnerable sexual desires from "bad," despised economic ones, to devastating and deadly effect. Grappling with the queerness of diaspora might precipitate a turn back toward loss, a "yes" to loss, that could engender more emotionally honest forms of political solidarity that begin with rather than repudiate our primary, and politically structured, vulnerabilities (Butler 2004).

As I argued in this book's Introduction, and as the works of Halberstam, Oswin, and Georgis suggest, at stake in subjectless queer critique is not simply a more expansive or interesting analytic understanding of queerness. Approaching queerness as figural enables critics and activists to recast our visions, to notice queerness's heterogeneous proliferation of groundless grounds, precisely in order to nurture a capacious, improper queer citizenship. Taking cues from subjectless queer scholarship helps open up new approaches to LGBTQ migration studies that impishly sidestep questions of identity and practice and trace looser affinities and solidarities that hinge on vulnerability. Understanding the asylum seeker as queer, then, derives not from the "true" sexual orientation or gender identity of an individual claimant, nor even from an understanding of an individual's identities or practices that might flout or exceed current prevailing Western conceptions of LGBTQ identity. Rather, the queerness of the claimant takes groundless ground in the spatial, temporal, and psychic vulnerability that "limbo life" induces. Nation-state and extrajuridical practices of expulsion, exclusion, and the deferral of meaningful subjectivity shape the organization of asylum seekers' daily geographies and configure many everyday spaces as literal waiting rooms of history—including the space of the church itself. Yet the MCCT refugee program, understood in part as a critical response to the production of such precarity, enacts a queer politics of solidarity that is not neatly reducible to liberal or nationalist identity politics.

It is crucial to be clear about the political and conceptual stakes of "reading" asylum seekers as figurally queer. Certainly, one might contend, a solid argument for the figural queerness of asylum seekers could be made easily enough. But isn't it all "merely" academic? Indeed, what does calling one more object of analysis "queer" do for the lives of actually existing asylum seekers? And is it really necessary or productive to go around throwing that queer "proprietary loop" (Dinshaw et al. 2007, 186) around every fractured, marginalized subjectivity or vulnerable organization of space-time? Why can't asylum seekers just be asylum seekers?

Taking for granted that refugeeness is a political-geographic discursive construction, never neutral, self-same, homogeneous, or divorced from ideology (see Buff 2008; Mountz 2011; Nguyen 2012), two key points advance a conceptualization of asylum seekers as queer. First, a reconsideration of asylum seekers as queer further extends the ethical and *political* promise of queer subjectless critique, of what I am calling improper queer citizenship. As Judith Butler (1994) makes clear, at issue for "improper" or subjectless queer critique is not merely a more expansive or innovative way of reading or analyzing figurations of difference in social and cultural life but a more capacious, robust, dexterous, contestatory, and playful orientation toward the political (for resonances, see Connolly 1991; Brown 1995; Cohen 1997). Upending universal, essential sexual identity as the basis for political solidarity and making room for a more nebulous sense of affinity and obligation based on precarity generates alternative ways of being collective—divergent possibilities for lateral, transformative encounters among differently situated and differently marginalized people.

Second, that a more capacious queer politics could be modeled by an organization typically understood by scholars as a "gay church" and a paragon of essentialist identity politics (see Warner 2005) constitutes a good surprise worthy of careful attention (Sedgwick [1997] 2003). Where a paranoid reading could quite rapidly (and indeed, not altogether wrongly) dismiss MCCT's refugee program as a "homonationalist" liberal project (Puar 2007; Dryden and Lenon 2015), offering more "sanctuary" for white guilt and pride in putative Canadian enlightenment than meaningful, downwardly redistributive solidarity, my fieldwork pushes such an account to sustain openness to revising judgment upon encounter with good surprise. At play in this chapter are both the queer Foucauldian impetus to denaturalize sexual identity categories (Foucault [1976] 1978) and the queer reparative impulse, an impulse that often works belatedly in taking the creative means by which people cultivate nourishment in fraught environments (Sedgwick [1997] 2003). What if this "gay church" is never quite just a "gay church"? What if it's simultaneously bound up in vexed national imagery, *and* articulating a critique of nation-state power over life, answering to improper queer concepts of citizenship? With these questions in mind, I turn to the MCCT refugee program and my ethnographic engagement with some of its participants and leaders.

MCCT's Refugee Program

Formed in 2007, the refugee program at MCCT consists of several core initiatives: direct sponsorship (including fund-raising and the solicitation of donations of funds, food, clothing, and furniture) of so-called Convention refugees, who are recognized by the United Nations High Commission on Refugees and the Canadian government; the organization of donor groups to sponsor additional Convention refugees; and a monthly peer-support group for asylum seekers who have claimed Convention-refugee status since arriving in Canada. When MCCT received a one-million-dollar gift from Margaret and the late Wallace McCain, the heads of a prominent and conservative New Brunswick entrepreneurial political family, in 2010, the refugee program was listed among the key beneficiaries of the funding (Goddard 2011). In 2013, MCCT received approval from Citizenship and Immigration Canada (CIC) to become an independent "sponsorship agreement holder," meaning it can directly marshal funds and coordinate with CIC to sponsor Convention refugees. Intriguingly, the program's supporters and organizational partners range from conservative families like the McCains and state agencies like CIC, to advocacy organizations like the Canadian Council for Refugees. The program has also engaged more loosely (cosponsoring events and lending space) with No One Is Illegal, a radical migrants' rights group with strong ties in indigenous and queer communities.

While it is difficult to fully quantify the impact of the refugee program's work, its effects have been both intensive and extensive. At the time of this writing, the church has sponsored thirteen Convention refugees from Iran, the Democratic Republic of Congo, and elsewhere in Africa and the Middle East, providing core material resources such as shelter, clothing, food, and access to job training. By contrast, the peer-support group for so-called in-land refugee claimants has reached more than fifteen hundred individuals at the time of this writing and registers an attendance at its monthly meetings of sixty to one hundred people. Meeting in the sanctuary after the popular 11 a.m. worship service, the group shares testimonials and tips from successful refugee claimants on negotiating the legal and logistical hurdles of the immigration process, organizes presentations from local immigrant social service and LGBTQ organizations, and offers participants the opportunity to collect documentation from the church to help advance their refugee claims. As of 2014, church officials had written letters of support for more than two hundred individual participants in the refugee program.

As is the case with many LGBTQ organizations providing documentation and support for asylum seekers, the process of assembling such information is a rigorous and complex one. New participants undergo intake interviews conducted by trained volunteers regarding their personal histories and interests in the church. Participants are not required to become members of MCCT, and program leaders officially emphasize the non-proselytizing character of their work. However, participants must attend a minimum number of church services and peer-support-group meetings to receive a letter of support. Thus, participants in the refugee peer-support program authenticate their relationship to LGBTQ community and identity not through claims on LGBTQ identity itself but through compiling portfolios attesting to their engagement with LGBTQ institutions. People amass such documentation through tiny but concerted quotidian actions: filling in blue "connection cards" each Sunday, signing the attendance sheet at the monthly refugee peer-support-group meeting, working as church volunteers (often at the information desk in the social hall), and taking photographs with clergy in front of a rainbow flag. Such dossiers are configured to meet the requirements of the state to authenticate LGBTQ identity, a crucial element in claims based on a well-founded fear of persecution in one's country of nationality.

The MCCT refugee program enables asylum seekers to accrue paper trails that performatively consolidate their queerness, strengthening their asylum claims. But that people must "prove" their queerness at all speaks to long-standing contradictions in the Canadian nation-state apparatus that have produced intensified effects during the Conservative government in power from 2006 to 2015—effects that have yet to be adequately addressed by the Conservatives' successors. Canada is routinely framed in nationalist and liberal multiculturalist discourses as "very generous" with respect to immigration and refugee status. Yet, although Canada has historically been touted as progressive in relation to the draconian policies of Australia, with which it is often favorably compared, more careful study (e.g., Mountz 2010) positions Canadian refugee policy as growing more and more continuous with a broader global trend against refugee claims: "In an increasingly securitized global environment, governments prefer to select refugees from abroad for resettlement and to decrease the number of those who arrive on sovereign territory of their own accord to make an asylum claim" (Mountz 2011, 382). Under the 2006–2015 Conservative regime, the federal government granted itself the authority to indefinitely detain asylum seekers deemed "irregular arrivals"; implemented deep funding and eligibility cuts to basic health care for refugees and asylum seekers; expedited hearing times for all asylum seekers to sixty days to impede claimants from developing well-supported cases; sped up hearing times even more dramatically (thirty to forty-five days) for claimants from putatively safe countries; cut the number of publicly sponsored Convention refugees; further devolved responsibility for refugee support to civil society; dramatically reduced access to health care for asylum seekers; authorized the collection of biometric data for asylum seekers from twenty-nine countries in Africa, Asia, and the Caribbean to share with the Royal Canadian Mounted Police; and, in the midst of all these funding cuts, called on LGBTQ and ethnic civil society to "step up to the plate" (Black and Keung 2012; Canadian Council for Refugees 2013; Keung 2012, 2013; Kenney 2010; Marshall 2014). While the biopolitical character of the Canadian nation-state immigration apparatus has long and insidious roots (Bannerji 2000; Mongia 1999), migrant justice activists (see, e.g., No One Is Illegal Toronto 2010) and even liberal immigration experts (Cohen 2013) have characterized the period of 2006 to 2015 as marked by mounting paranoia and austerity.

Under such conditions, amassing the right kind of portfolio—of one's identity, relationships, and fears of persecution—becomes a matter of life and death. To be sure, "proving" one's LGBTQ identity is not the only element required of claimants for presenting a successful case. Destination countries, including Canada, are notorious for using spurious generalizations about the relative homophobia of refugees' countries of nationality to decide whose fears of persecution are truly "well founded" (Ling 2012). But for LGBTQ asylum seekers, a bevy of cases—some of them high-profile, but most of them under the radar—attest to the costs of assembling an inadequate personal case history of LGBTQ identity. It was after one such instance of "failure"—when an LGBTQ asylum seeker compiled the wrong kind of dossier in the eyes of an agent of the nation-state—that I first became aware of MCCT's political advocacy on the question of asylum. In spring 2011, Alvaro Orozco, a young Nicaraguan-born man with strong ties in the Toronto's queer and arts scenes who had been refused Convention refugee status under rather unusual circumstances (a video webcam interview with an IRB adjudicator who decided he didn't look "gay enough"), was picked up by city police, turned over to immigration authorities, and slated for deportation (Mills 2011a). In part because of his strong social ties and the moral outrage associated with the injustice of his idiosyncratic case, Orozco saw a groundswell of support in migrant justice, queer, New Democratic Party (NDP), feminist, and media communities that ultimately led to a reversal of the decision and his approval for permanent residence in Canada. As a participant in community meetings and rallies of the "Let Alvaro Stay" campaign that spring, I noticed that MCCT members and affiliated activists were routinely at the table in rallies and planning meetings, along with NDP organizers, a range of queer activists, and members of No One Is Illegal. Moreover, I noticed how MCCT members made a point of mentioning their affiliation with MCCT front and center in introductions at meetings and in formulating advocacy tactics, like having Rev. Hawkes speak at a press conference in support of Orozco at Buddies in Bad Times Theatre, a local queer institution. As will become clear, I have come to understand over the course of this ethnography that the invocation of faith in the context of such advocacy is not simply a matter of rhetorical or moral authority (expedient and/or earnest) but part of the critical difference MCCT's approach to refugee support makes.

Although the Orozco case eventuated in a successful outcome for queer and migrant justice advocates, MCCT has also been a player in support for subjects whose narratives of refugeeness prove far less legible, far less sympathetic. In October 2013, the church hosted a screening of Paul Émile d'Entremont's gripping National Film Board of Canada documentary *Last Chance* (2012), which follows five LGBTQ asylum seekers as they await news from the IRB that will decide the course of the rest of their lives. The screening was organized by migrant justice group No One Is Illegal as a fund-raiser for Augustas Dennie, a middle-aged man who was deported back to Saint Vincent and the Grenadines in April 2013 after his request for refugee status was denied. Even from the account of himself that he made public, Dennie had had a messy life, a life riddled with the kinds of complexities that can keep one on the outside of legibility to nation-state litmus tests of authentic gayness, and thus refugeeness. Dennie recounted experiencing severe homophobic persecution in Saint Vincent, including one beating so severe it affected his brain and capacity to use one of his arms. Attempting to pass as heterosexual, he formed relationships with women and became a father to one son. These relationships, Dennie conceded, were far from happy, and he had spent time in jail and on probation based on domestic-violence charges during his time living in the United States.

I first met Dennie in the fall of 2012, while I was writing as a journalist about emerging social services for LGBTQ migrants on Toronto's historically working-class east side. I readily connected him with the Toronto LGBTQ publication *Xtra!,* which helped publicize his case. I felt motivated to do so in large part because I doubted that Dennie's far-from-cookie-cutter narrative would elicit the same kind of sympathy from the IRB, and from identity-based LGBTQ groups, that Orozco's had. Yet, fortuitously, *Xtra!* followed up and publicized Dennie's case. A petition drive supported by No One Is Illegal ultimately gathered seven hundred signatures against deportation and for Convention refugee status for Dennie, and then–member of Parliament Olivia Chow publicly inquired on his behalf. Whenever I ran into Dennie episodically in the social hall after church, we chatted, ate cookies, and drank bad church coffee from Styrofoam cups. A self-described regular in Toronto's gay village, he told me it was precisely the forms of sociality he enjoyed—a mix of friends, lovers, and acquaintances but no singular bourgeois romance to trot out before an immigration judge—that made his queerness so hard to authenticate in the eyes of the IRB. Since his deportation, Dennie's dispatches to contacts in Canada have described his effective social death: socially determined unemployability and routine death threats against his life and that of his son. Fund-raising efforts by Toronto-based migrant justice and black queer community networks continue to support Dennie as he constructs his own home (for more information, see Cromwell 2015).

These two very different cases illustrate the variable consequences of the increasingly obdurate imperative to authenticate one's LGBTQ-ness in the context of a federal crackdown on "fake" refugees (Rennie 2012). While the refugee claims of Alvaro Orozco and Augustas Dennie diverged in their levels of legibility and their outcomes, together they attest to the drama and danger of failure, of failed refugeeness. Both cases, which enjoyed relatively high levels of visibility in queer and migrant justice publics, point to the urgency of looming deportation as the pivotal, singular event it surely comprises in many people's lives. My ethnographic engagement with participants in the church's refugee program, by contrast, provides glimmers of insight into the ordinary, "stretched-out present" temporalities and spatialities through which people negotiate that threat of being deemed inauthentic, of having failed as asylum seekers (Berlant 2011a; Shakhsari 2014). It is with people's ordinary experience of living with the menacing, future-anterior figure of failure—one whose claim will have failed—in mind that I want to turn to some revelatory moments from my fieldwork that elucidate the precarious space-time of asylum that I am calling queer.

"Limbo Life": (In)authenticity, Opacity, Precarity

Nation-state violence creates the spatial and temporal conditions that render asylum seekers vulnerable, nonsovereign, queer. But as a long tradition of critical social and political theory contends, nation-state violence goes beyond formal nation-state actors. Indeed, scrutiny of asylum seekers' authenticity, modeled by practices of some agents of the nation-state, reverberates discursively and atmospherically, infusing perceptions and practices beyond the formal ambit of the public sphere as it is normatively conceived in liberal societies (Hage 1998). The imperative to authenticate one's LGBTQ identity as a key part of the basis for one's "legitimate" precarity is a demand that haunts asylum seekers not only in their performance of subjectivity in the eyes of the law but in everyday life—including congregational life. Over the course of my fieldwork, several informants—both within the congregation and in closely connected LGBTQ organizing circles—voiced skepticism about whether all the asylum seekers involved in the church's refugee program were "really gay." Indeed, anxiety about refugee authenticity was productively and critically addressed in the interviews I conducted with the officials responsible for the refugee program, to say nothing of my interviews with asylum seekers themselves. But it is crucial to first demonstrate the key affective effects of an increasingly stringent refugee regime that polices authentic refugeeness and especially authentic LGBTQ-ness: the proliferation of everyday dramas of (in)authenticity. These dramas help to position both the church itself and the psyches of asylum seekers as waiting rooms, spaces in which nation-state violence and informal xenophobia must be lived through on an everyday basis. It is precisely such vulnerability, rather than the "truth" of putatively transparent motivations, that makes asylum seekers queer.

The figure of the inauthentic, not "really gay," "fake" refugee consistently occupied an ambivalent space in the conversations I had with participants in the refugee peer-support group. In my more formally structured interviews, I made a point of asking people's opinions about the increasingly austere and paranoid reforms to the refugee system enacted by the government at the time—reforms I had regarded, somewhat simplistically, as overblown, self-evidently motivated by and (re)productive of xenophobic anxieties about poor brown hordes going "gay for a day" to secure comfortable futures off the largesse of the Great White North. Yet, in contrast to my armchair-lefty understanding of refugee policy, every claimant I asked about refugee policy gestured to what they viewed as the *necessity* of such reforms, regarding those who would falsify their sexuality and experience of persecution with great scorn. Although initially puzzled by this response—how could an asylum seeker, "authentic" or otherwise, support a new, breathtakingly short timeline for gathering documents to support her refugee claim?—I saw that the recurrence of this trope pointed to a more generalized and structured orientation toward falsity. What Bridget Anderson, Nandita Sharma, and Cynthia Wright (2009) write of the "foreign national prisoner" in Canadian immigration law could easily be said of the "fake" refugee as well: it makes for "an important (spectacular) figure in the justification of enforcement policy and practice, a rallying point whose deportation can be universally agreed upon" (14). What might this "rallying point," this foil, this absent center portend for the psychic lives of those most vulnerable to the imputation of falsity, that is, asylum seekers? If the figure of the "fake" LGBTQ refugee looms so large in the implementation of current refugee policy and public discourse, then it would only make sense that such a figure would occupy a primary and abject position within any narrative of authentic refugeeness.

Over time, I came to wonder whether asylum seekers' antipathy to the figural "fake refugee" might index the exhausting infinitude of the performativity of refugeeness—the extent to which the imperative to authenticate LGBTQ-ness is a task so endless that it renders one constitutively and chronically inadequate in relation to the state and oneself; as Eric Santner (2011) might put it, mere creaturely "flesh" that takes on an especial vulnerability at the very moment when it fails to resuture itself to biopolitical intelligibility as it traverses forms of life. For instance, two young men, both asylum seekers, whom I interviewed at a Starbucks in Toronto's gay village described their frustration with the prevailing grids of intelligibility used by federal bureaucrats to ascertain gayness. Fernando and Craig bemoaned the spuriousness of such standards, which they said simplistically conflated gender nonconformity with homosexuality and gender normativity with heterosexuality. Fernando described how the pitch of his voice marked him as effeminate, and how he had habitually remained silent on public transportation in Jamaica to avoid incurring scrutiny. Craig, by contrast, told me he had a hard time convincing both white Canadians *and* Jamaican diasporics in Toronto of his sexuality, because of his masculine gender performance, which he aligned with the trope of the "roughneck man." Thus, the assumption of correspondence between gender nonnormativity and homosexuality notoriously at work in many IRB hearings posed a problem of a particular kind for Craig.

Fernando and Craig were among the youngest people I interviewed in my research. At times, our closeness in age and their jocular bearing toward me seemed to engender a certain frivolity and fun in our conversation.

Yet, as in many of my conversations with asylum seekers, I simultaneously wondered whether I was read as just another agent of the church, a social service agency, or the state—another privileged white gay boy in the village, a white do-gooder with agendas of his own (characterizations that are not without truth). Without hoping to eliminate the structural awkwardness, the "misapprehension," inexorably at play in such encounters, I consistently sought in interviews to establish my critical distance from both the church and the nation-state—an effort that had varied degrees of success (Brand 2005, 5). Hoping to elicit a spark of something more intimate, more erratic, something that would keep the interview from being a dry run for a refugee hearing, I asked both men how they coped with the anxiety they faced before a refugee hearing that made no guarantees. Craig responded that he usually sought out a man on the Internet for sex, just to relieve stress. We all laughed, and then he added a mirthful, not entirely unserious thought: "The thing I have to do to make my case solid is—I go to the extreme level, because there's no way they're gonna tell me I'm not gay. So, I go to the extreme level. I would video myself doing what I'm doing. So, if that day comes and they say they have doubts, I would say, 'Is this enough proof?' [We all laugh.] So, I'm not taking no chances with that process, I ain't going back to that country." Together, my interviewees' repeated disavowals of the figure of the fake refugee, coupled with Craig's incisive joke about the putative juridical heft of a homemade sex tape, offer an important clue into the affective dynamics of refugeeness—dynamics that feel emotionally specific and singular in the course of a given day but that share a more diffuse and dynamic, yet palpable, "structure of feeling" (Williams 1978). Even though Craig avowed his gayness throughout our conversation, in this singular moment I think he simultaneously satirized the fantasy of revelation and transparent difference that undergirds the imperative to authenticate one's sexuality enmeshed in federal refugee policy—and, as Michel Foucault ([1976] 1978) would remind us, the "act to identity *telos*" that characterizes the modern history of Western notions of homosexuality more broadly. Haunted by the figure of the fake refugee, a ghost that one cannot *not* disavow (Spivak 1990), the asylum seeker can simultaneously *never* offer "enough proof" (Lewis 2014). Craig gets naked in his joke to show that it is the Canadian nation-state, with its spurious standards for the performativity of refugeeness, that is in fact naked, the arrogant emperor who has no clothes.

If anxiety and drama about (in)authenticity play out in the intimate negotiations and self-fashionings of asylum seekers, this complex, diffuse structure of feeling also implicates the ordinary life of the MCCT congregation. While I was episodically asked about the putatively dubious LGBTQ-ness and potentially nefarious motivations of asylum seekers throughout my fieldwork, one of the times I encountered this question most pointedly was on a Sunday in June 2013 over dim sum with a large group of men I had met at a church men's retreat the previous month. One congregant, an engaging middle-aged man with a family in the western Toronto suburbs who had come out later in life, asked me what my research on the church had found so far. As I did in many conversations about my research, I focused on the refugee program, because of its tangibility and widely legible significance for people within and outside the congregation. Eager to tackle head-on what I saw as a politically noxious myth about "fake" refugees in the program, I replied that my conversations with asylum seekers pointed to people's religious backgrounds, particularly in the theologically polyglot Caribbean, as the basis for their *genuine* attachments to the church's (and the denomination's) similarly eclectic liturgy and theology (see White 2015, 154).

"Really?" my friendly acquaintance replied. He told me that asylum seekers seemed to "disappear" after they received refugee status, suggesting that the relationship of claimants to the church was a less authentic, more instrumental one. "It seems like they only come on the one Sunday [per month] when they have the refugee group, they come late and are all done up—it doesn't seem like they're participating. I know I'm bad for saying this, but I sometimes wonder if all of them are really gay." Positioning himself as both contained by and transgressing political correctness or Canadian politeness—"I know I'm bad for saying this"—this man expressed anxiety about the veracity of asylum seekers' claims on belonging—in the nation-state, in LGBTQ community, and in the church itself. Even asylum seekers' aesthetic and sartorial choices, which could be read as deeply reverent—wearing their "Sunday best," a practice not emphasized at MCCT but common in Christian communities in the Caribbean diaspora and elsewhere—incurred suspicion and contempt. Such conversations continue to trouble me, because they evince the more polite manifestations of atmospheric racism and xenophobia in the congregation that can have far more pronounced, deleterious effect for racialized people. In the heat of the moment, though, frustrated by such a racist dismissal of asylum seekers as "the worst kind of beggars" (Isin 2002, 272), I simply balked, insisting that claimants' motivations in fact struck me as quite authentic—a retort I have come to regard as ethically and politically unsatisfactory and inadequate.

Alongside such banal, anxious, xenophobic conversation, the dramas of refugee (in)authenticity manifested in struggles over church spaces that were simultaneously ordinary and exceptional, particularly those of the sanctuary and social hall. In an especially revealing and haunting conversation, Karen, a longtime lay leader at MCCT who identifies as black and whom we first encountered in chapter 1, recalled a particular incident that she said had a chilling effect on asylum seekers' sense of citizenship, of being in place within the congregation (Cresswell 1996). One February, Karen, who has a professional background in arts-based approaches to social services, had worked with a group of asylum seekers of African descent to put together a program for Black History Month. The team prepared a series of testimonial performance pieces for the church's four-service series celebrating black queerness and black liberation struggles. While the production of these aesthetic works required participants to confront difficult histories of expulsion, torture, exile, malevolent pursuit, nonrecognition, and atmospheric racism, Karen said, the process of producing such work had contributed to a growing sense of recognition and ample leadership capacity among many participants. However, one act of exclusion revealed that this sense of power was in fact quite fragile:

[The asylum seekers who created the Black History Month services] were really becoming prominent in the church, which was good. I'm really proud of them. One of them started to sing in the evening [service].

Then one thing happened that I think really, really squashed their spirits, where I think had this person known what black culture is like, they would have approached it differently. So, what happened is, because they [asylum seekers] all live very, very far [from the church], they all live in these rooming houses where they can't tell people that they're gay. So, again, they're living in that situation that they came from, right? Because that's the only place they can afford to live.

So, what they'd do is they'd come for the morning [11 a.m. worship service], and they'd stay all day, and they'd stay for the 7 p.m. [service]. I know from the black culture that it's perfectly normal to stay and worship and be in fellowship all day long at church. That is your community. That's how you get fed. And this is what these people were doing. Once a week they were able to get together and have this. This was their support system.

And this one person, Caucasian person, told them, "You have to leave at the end of the 11:00 service." And I tried to explain, going, "No, these people really need this. No one's being hurt, they're just sitting there laughing, doing whatever. Why can't they sit there and just enjoy what that space can give them?"

But I think by the time they tried to reverse it, it was too late, and I don't see them [asylum seekers] anymore.

Asylum seekers creatively responded to a set of structurally conditioned spatial and temporal constraints that effectively produced the space of MCCT itself as one more example of a literal waiting room of history: the geographical remoteness of affordable housing vis-à-vis a downtown church; the dearth of transportation options between city and suburbs on Sundays; the relative paucity of spaces that even provisionally center both queerness and blackness at once; experiences of atmospheric racism in church; and the gap between the 11 a.m. and 7 p.m. services. For these subjects, on those afternoons, church was an object worth repairing precisely in order to inhabit it on their own terms as black people and as precarious migrants. Resonant with what Katherine McKittrick (2011) theorizes as a "black sense of place," people in the refugee program recast this organization of space and time, conditioned by a cascade of structural forms of oppression and characterized, above all, by *waiting*. Asylum seekers informally generated a black place that was about more than a binary between resistance and oppression can capture—a space of fellowship, sociality, "enjoy[ment of] what the space can give."

What, then, are we to make of such a violent act of racist expulsion—of banishment from church space, from congregational and queer citizenships—that would seek to expunge such ordinary and radical black place making? How are we to make sense of such an act in a space that promises "a house of prayer for all people"? On affective terms, such expulsion ironically (and all the more violently) recalls and reiterates the very forms of repudiated desire and expulsion from home that prompt people to come to church seeking wholeness in the first place (Georgis 2006). Although Karen never explicitly mentioned dramas around refugee (in)authenticity as such, I contend that the subsequent efforts to foreclose this articulation of black queer space and citizenship point to the limits of normatively white identitarian framings of queer citizenship. Black queer sociality of the kind Karen described was understood by some white congregants as *outside,* beyond the scope of what a space for LGBTQ and allied Christian fellowship could accommodate. We have seen a litany of moments of racism that cleave "black" from "queer" throughout this book—through formal analogy or marginalization. But such an understanding of black and queer socialities as *discrete* also conditions the reticence to regard certain black performances of gender as "really" gay, as "really" having a place in church or in Canada, on precisely the terms Fernando and Craig described earlier. Antiracist and queer scholars have mapped some of the contradictory ways in which blackness and queerness simultaneously figure as constitutively opposed and discrete (Jakobsen 2003; Ferguson 2003) and as complexly bound, encountering each other in figurations of shame, debasement, and camp (Stockton 2006). For some within MCCT, black queerness figures as both an object of exceptional, urgent rescue from "over there" and an object of scrutiny, fear, and suspected inauthenticity "over here." Only some forms of black queerness, and only some black queer geographies, are intelligible or desirable to a white LGBTQ savior citizenship; more spontaneous or informal forms of sociality may quite literally be asked to leave the waiting room altogether.

Such atmospheric racism and xenophobia in church, including exceptional and everyday acts of banishment and expulsion, also point us to a different explanation for why asylum seekers tend not to remain at MCCT after they receive official refugee status from the IRB. If the "welcome home" guarantee that the church extends to asylum seekers is in fact an unfulfilled promise—a promise punctured and deflated by racist acts of banishment and more quotidian forms of scrutiny and suspicion—then what would predispose claimants to remain involved after receiving refugee status?[4] Rather than a space that simply emancipates, the church itself is a waiting room in a circuit of waiting rooms that comprise asylum seekers' everyday affective geographies; and waiting rooms, as we have seen, produce an affectively exhausting liminality, carrying the constant and harrowing threat of xenophobic banishment. An identitarian LGBTQ lens fetishizes asylum seekers' declining attendance after attaining refugee status as a straightforward index of claimants' inauthenticity. In this view, the role of the sovereign Canadian citizen or congregant is beneficent, innocent, generous but wary of being exploited. At stake here is not only "the world"—the refugee that needs saving—but the self, the nation-state, or the xenophobic church member whose anxiety about refugee inauthenticity could lead them to do grave harm. By contrast, improper queer citizenship—one that unsettles the antirelational sense of being "at home" that characterizes normatively white LGBTQ identity politics—recognizes that the church also deeply needs and places demands on asylum seekers and is capable of doing harm as well as extending support and solidarity.

Fortunately, identitarian, normatively white and Canadian framings of congregational and queer citizenship are subject to vigorous contestation within the congregation—a claim I will elaborate further in the following section on the theological rationale for the refugee program. For the moment, however, I want to turn more directly to a question that often surfaced as the target of anxiety surrounding refugee authenticity—claimants' "true" motivations for coming to church. As I have noted, when congregants who were not involved with the church refugee program asked me about the authenticity of claimants' reasons for being in church, my initial retort, drawing on the interviews I had conducted, was typically to insist that claimants' motivations were in fact genuine. I felt pressure to defend claimants from the charge of disingenuous, self-interested participation. I felt compelled to shed light on asylum seekers' "true" spiritual and social affinities for MCCT, in order to dispel politically vexing caricatures of claimants as in church only to advance their immigration cases. Often, I would respond by citing several interviewees who talked about growing up under a mix of Christian theological influences in the Caribbean—Baptist, Seventh-Day Adventist, Jehovah's Witness, Pentecostal, Catholic—and subsequently found comfort in the polyglot character of MCCT's liturgy. Or I would mention informants who described the church as a space of love and belonging, a rare antihomophobic beacon in a conservative religious landscape. Yet as my fieldwork progressed, I was increasingly struck by how fundamentally opaque people's motivations were—fieldwork, or perhaps the recursive exchange between encounter and written reflection, being the best teacher of critiques of epistemology. While this opacity initially frustrated my political impulse to refute what I understood as pernicious, xenophobic discourse, it ultimately helped me to understand with more precision the stakes and significance of the refugee program.

The need to answer back to the caricature of asylum seekers haunted many of my conversations with people in the refugee program. Just as the

206 · FROM IDENTITY TO PRECARITY

refugee claimants I spoke with were quick to condemn (and thus disavow) the figure of the fake refugee, they were equally likely to disavow the disingenuous religious participant. One asylum seeker, Elizabeth, told me she first heard about the church from her immigration lawyer but had no idea MCCT even had a refugee program. Elizabeth described a particularly strong attachment to Rev. Hawkes's sermons. Although she noted that she would like to hear "a little more of the Bible and a little less politics" from the pulpit, she told me that Hawkes's spiritual teachings and not the refugee program were the primary factor in her attendance. In fact, Elizabeth said, if she arrived at church too late for a sermon, she would turn around and go home without signing the blue connection card that would register her attendance and help her amass the proper dossier for her refugee claim.

At the time of my conversation with Elizabeth, I responded eagerly, as her comments provided more fodder for my budding case that refugee-program participants were in fact much more genuine congregational citizens than racist and xenophobic stereotypes would allow for. But as I reflected on the conversation in my field notes, it occurred to me that Elizabeth's account of her preoccupation with Rev. Hawkes's sermons may have other important but less transparent implications. After she described her daunting, nearly two-hour commute to church from the amalgamated city's northeast side, she concluded with an acknowledgment that attending worship services simply wasn't possible every Sunday. Moments like this acknowledgment, and the claim about returning home if she had missed the sermon, made me wonder all the more whether asylum seekers regarded me as officially attached to the church, despite my insistence that I was a university-based researcher independent of MCCT. Thus, the imperative to attest to one's authenticity—as an LGBTQ asylum seeker *or* as a researcher with good intentions—imposed a vexing epistemological limit on my fieldwork.

Such repudiations—not only of the sexually "fake" asylum seeker but of the disingenuous or disinterested churchgoer—prove particularly thorny, because they come into conflict with the church's promise of a capacious environment for heterogeneous *beliefs* as well as identities. Church leadership prides itself on a liberal pluralist Christian theology that posits the teachings of Jesus as one path among many to spiritual enlightenment, an affirmation of the many names by which God is known, and a Communion ritual that does not require membership in MCCT or in any Christian church to participate (MCC Toronto 2016). Such a rendition of religious heterogeneity—many paths to a singular God—risks privileging Abraha-mic monotheism over other systems and practices of belief. Even so, call-ing into question the authenticity of asylum seekers' or *anyone's* spiritual or religious connection to MCCT cuts against what many at the church might consider a foundational commitment to religious pluralism—a commit-ment that materializes, to a certain extent, in the bodies in the room. Over the course of my fieldwork, I encountered churchgoers (citizens and asy-lum seekers) who identified as atheist, agnostic, Sufi, Jewish, or Muslim, or relayed itineraries and histories with roots in those experiences of faith or of no faith. A 2011 congregational snapshot survey of nearly four hundred churchgoers on a particular summer day (Eastman 2011) indicated that 8 percent of those present claimed a non-Christian religious background or affiliation, nearly 18 percent claimed no religious background at all, and 18 percent of worshippers also participate in the activities of some other religious organization alongside MCCT. Finally, as we will see shortly, the dominance of Christianity as Canada's "shadow establishment" religion (Martin 2000) coupled with the MCCT refugee peer-support program's comparative open-endedness on questions of identity and belief have made the church, in some respects, the default, if not the only, option for LGBTQ asylum seekers in the greater Toronto area.

Elizabeth was far from the only person to describe the centrality of spirituality in her engagement with the church or to position the religious character of MCCT's refugee program as unique within the continuum of social supports for LGBTQ asylum seekers and other migrants. But sociality—in excess of distinctions between the religious and the secular—figured equally prominently. Several of the men involved in the refugee program with whom I spoke cited friendship, romance, sex, and other forms of connection—the prospect of meeting men, following a romantic prospect or partner—as key factors in coming to church. Fernando giggled as he told me he wasn't even aware of the refugee program when he first came to MCCT—he just "liked a boy who went there." Daniel, my clos-est friend in the refugee program, explained elaborate fantasies about gay male sociality in the United States and Canada that he had nurtured when he was a young man in Jamaica—fantasies that hinged in part on having a gay male weekend brunch group. While the church music resonated with his childhood, the avowedly secular Daniel said it was a gay male social world populated not only with lovers but with friends that prompted him to come to church and kept him in the pews each Sunday.

Yet intimacy, and particularly the genre of romantic love, occupied a more ambivalent position in other people's accounts of their move to Canada and engagement with the church and refugee program. Early in my fieldwork, I paid a guest visit to a meeting of the refugee peer-support program to advertise my study and invite people interested in an interview to contact me. When I first arrived in the sanctuary (the only space at the church big enough to accommodate such a large program), I was under the impression that I would make a quick announcement at the beginning and then leave, thus respecting the peer-led, refugee-only character of the group. In fact, I learned that announcements took place at the end of the meeting, and I was invited (in effect, required) to stay for the duration of the meeting. This particular gathering featured a presentation from a settlement coordinator from a Toronto ethnospecific AIDS service organization, who mapped the range of social services available to asylum seekers as they awaited their hearings. In a passing comment early in the talk, the presenter speculatively summarized the place his listeners occupied in a trajectory of immigration, and the fantasy of the good life that he presumed organized their attachments to life (Berlant 2011a): "You come to Canada, now you're looking for a job or going to school, and maybe looking for someone to love." This unremarkable gesture to the normative trappings of "happiness" elicited a few titters in the hundred or so people gathered in the pews, and one half-whispered retort that has left an imprint on me ever since: "Love's got nothing to do with it," a woman a row or two behind me intoned.

"Love's got nothing to do with it."

I continue to be productively puzzled by this comment. Because I didn't see who voiced it, and because it was intended not for my ears so much as for the people sitting with the speaker in her pew, I never had the opportunity to follow up with the speaker or ask her what she meant or to whom the statement was addressed. Instead, the insight hovers, then diffuses out into multiple permutations—cutting, yet cryptic. Love's got nothing to do with what? Migration? Canada? The church? Other waiting rooms? The speaker's day-to-day life? Queerness? Refugeeness? How might we understand the disarticulation of the figuration of romantic love as a cornerstone of fantasies of the good life, on the one hand, from "it," the project of life at hand, on the other?

While I remain generatively confused about the speaker's meaning, her comment reverberated in a conversation about asylum and romance I had a few months later with Elizabeth. Elizabeth spoke to me pointedly and at length about her frustration with the strict constraints that her categorization as an asylum seeker, a subject-in-waiting, imposed on her. With the date of her refugee hearing still up in the air and strict limitations on her employment in the meantime, she got a job cleaning homes and offices. Because of strict caps on social assistance for refugees, most of Elizabeth's income went to rent and food, which she told me left her "working for crumbs to stay in this country." Continuing, she showed me photographs on her tablet of the broken door of her Scarborough (East End Toronto) basement apartment, which faced a boiler room. But most strikingly, Elizabeth told me, the liminality and precariousness of her status—in employment, housing, immigration, sociality—meant that romantic love was, chaotically and frustratingly, both the first and the last thing on her mind. Alongside showing me the photographs, Elizabeth checked e-mail intermittently during our conversation. She flagged my attention to her inbox, which contained nearly a hundred unanswered messages from women on online dating sites:

> Elizabeth: When people say you landed, you arrived in Canada, or you're a refugee claimant, refugee claimant—it's not a happy place to be, 'cause it's a limbo stage. And limbo stage does not help you. It helps in a way when you pass that limbo stage, but limbo stage, I mean, to be in limbo—[you] can't make long-term plans. Why would you want to make long-term plans when you haven't had a hearing, you don't have your papers saying, "Welcome to Canada"? You have no welcome. You made a claim. You made an application. You're waiting for your answer. And if it wasn't for those groups to help and constantly just sit down and talk about your stress. . . . There's no answer to it, but talking about it helps.
>
> I go online, Zoosk, trying to meet a girl. It doesn't work. I meet someone from the church, when we start talking, they e-mailed me, "Oh, you go to MCC?" And I say, "Yes, I do!" We decide to meet. . . . [She makes a face of disdain.]
> *No chemistry?*
> Elizabeth: Not only no chemistry, but that person should not be going to church! I don't want to be a judge, but you know what I mean. It's not spiritual. . . . [Elizabeth goes on to describe the

woman, whom she met for only two dates. According to Elizabeth, the woman had an expectation of casual sex that Elizabeth
did not share and exhibited an exploitive and crass pattern of
behavior, leading Elizabeth to stop seeing her.]
So, looking for a partner, into the groups, into that same
LGBT group—I'm the type of person, I'm not looking for that,
I'm looking for a long-term relationship, and picking up with
someone that's filing for refugee claimant, it has a lot of set-
backs. First of all, you don't know if the person really likes you,
or if they really just want to get involved with you so as to get
more evidence that they're gay, 'cause you do need the evidence.
I'm not getting involved with it.
I just want someone—I'm old, I'm picky, I'm choosy. I'm not
a young chick. [She laughs.] The relationship I want to get into
for life, or start it saying it's for life. And people under stress like
me, it's not good for me. So, finding partners within the group,
I don't know how they do it unless they come with the partner.
But to get a partner within these groups that you're exposed
to . . .
Because everyone's in that limbo status, like you said.
Elizabeth: And I don't want limbo life. You're looked at suspi-
ciously when you give people who have their papers here, you
tell them of your status, your immigration status, then you're
looked at. There's a period, during that time, when you wait, I
wouldn't advise anyone to get into a relationship. I would not
get into a relationship. I tried it online with one who was still
in the closet. I liked her. That one, I liked. But she was in the
closet. In denial . . .
So, you don't want to get in that. I'm not coming from my
country, declaring my sexuality or my orientation, and being
put in the same situation that I ran away from. So, I said,
"Thank you, but . . ." That one broke my heart. So, the country
is big. They have lots of gays as well. I thought everybody was
open! [She laughs.] And so, I give up on the dating sites. Hon-
estly, I give up on the dating sites for now. I get ninety-nine
people wanting to meet on Zoosk, I just don't respond. After
two experiences, not my scene.

Both Elizabeth's experiences of frustrated desire and the haunting side comment about the irrelevance of love shed further light on the contradictory character of "sexual migration," and on the queerness of the asylum seeker. Leading scholarship on sexual migration has argued the ambivalent position of love as a motivating factor in movement, and challenged a neat distinction between "good" and "bad," "authentic" and "inauthentic" feelings (Manalansan 2008; Parreñas 2011; see also Brennan 2004). Such work has played an important role in de-dramatizing sexual migration by contesting pernicious and dominant tropes, such as that of the migrant sex worker "faking it" to secure an affluent partner and a path to the good life. Insights from my fieldwork further contribute to the de-dramatization of sexual migration, suggesting that sometimes sexual migration might not involve much sex at all. On the one side, life in Canada is understood to offer not only the promise of freedom from homophobic persecution but the opportunity to cultivate a good (normatively conceived) life of work and love. On the other side, the liminal character of life in Canada as an in-land refugee claimant defers and places significant material and affective constraints on those very opportunities. "Precaritization" (Puar et al. 2012)—in this case, increasingly austere and draconian organization of refugeeness in Canada—is producing nonnormative temporal and spatial orientations toward sex, love, and desire that are not LGBTQ—or "not" LGBTQ—so much as queer.

Elizabeth's reflection on "limbo life," the liminal and infantilizing character of asylum-seeker status, also speaks back to debates in subjectless queer critique about temporality, futurity, and politics. Asylum-seeker status marks subjects as only potentially eligible for a future, incorporation within the sociosymbolic order, and forward movement. The refugee-claims process dangles out the promise of becoming a subject with futurity, teleology, a path to citizenship and the good life, but it requires that one archive and performatively attest to one's authentic LGBTQ identity, and even then there are no guarantees. Asylum seekers are subjects who *want* futurity, both in the sense that they pursue it and in the sense that the juridical and material conditions under which they organize their lives threaten to foreclose it. As is well known, queer theoretical conversations about temporality have long debated the *normative* stakes of an orientation toward futurity (Edelman 2004; Muñoz 2009; Caserio et al. 2006). Here, however, I am less preoccupied with negating or championing the desire for futurity than with how that repudiated desire—a desire shaped in waiting rooms by nation-state violence and ordinary congregational xenophobia—*figurally* positions asylum seekers as queer. As figures whose precarious everyday geographies comprise literal waiting rooms of history, asylum seekers lie on the edges of sociosymbolic legibility and its push toward forward movement—whether they are "truly" LGBTQ or not.

"So What?": Answering the Authenticity Imperative Queerly

In the preceding section, I sketched at length people's wide range of overlapping, variegated motivations for participating in MCCT and in the refugee program—spirituality, sociality, sex, friendship, love, or anything but—in order to highlight the layered, complex, contradictory, and ultimately opaque character of people's attachments to refugeeness, LGBTQness, church, and Canada. By engaging asylum seekers' everyday geographies in the context of state-led precaritization, I developed an argument for asylum seekers as queer subjects, consigned to the literal waiting rooms of history. I also noted that the circuit of waiting rooms that comprise asylum seekers' everyday itineraries includes the church itself, where atmospheric racism and xenophobia reverberate with nation-state discourses on the "fake" refugee and precipitate acts of exclusion. Initially during my fieldwork, I attempted to directly confront and contest the imperative that asylum seekers face to attest to their authenticity as congregational and queer citizens. However, my conversations with asylum seekers and program leaders taught me to embrace an improper approach to queer citizenship—to acknowledge and affirm the opacity of people's "true" motivations, and to attend first and foremost to the grave reality of people's experiences of precarity generated by paranoid, austere immigration policy.

An interview I conducted with Hugh, a prominent Toronto immigration lawyer whom we first encountered in chapter 3, further suggested to me that discourses on the much-worried-about authenticity of asylum seekers obscured more complex and insidious architectures of power shaping the lives of such migrants. Hugh pointed to the significance of ironic structural conditions impelling asylum seekers' involvement at MCCT.

Hugh: The MCC Peer Support Program also provides letters of reference or support for refugees going through the refugee hearing process, which is very, very important in refugee claims—almost too important these days. So, if somebody doesn't show up at a hearing with a letter from the MCC, the decision maker's like, "Oh, where's your MCC letter?" Like they almost expect it to be there, otherwise there's a big question about why it's not there. That expectation is just part of the bureaucratic decision-making process, the bureaucratic mentality of wanting to check all the boxes and cross all the *t*'s, dot the *i*'s. *It is fascinating, though, that that's become an expectation. Surprising to me.*

Hugh: It is, because you think if somebody doesn't connect with MCC for whatever reason, then are they somehow prejudiced by that?

Yeah, like they could be Muslim, or whatever . . .

Hugh: Right, and they probably feel obligated to do so because there's a sense that the letter holds a great deal of credibility, which is fortunate and unfortunate.

Haltingly, Hugh describes an inadvertent consequence of the growth and success of MCCT's refugee program: the enshrinement of a letter of support from the church as part of a de facto "checklist" for Toronto-based in-land refugee claimants. Hugh attributed this incorporation not to any particular practice at MCCT so much as to a tendency endemic to bureaucracy to regularize and routinize the forms of admissible evidence. Given that refugee advocacy and support necessarily trades in the juridical grammars of the nation-state, the circuit of complicity between MCCT and the nation-state immigration apparatus should not prove particularly surprising here. Indeed, Canadian LGBTQ immigration-law scholar Nicole LaViolette (2009) points to the ordinary complicity of NGOs with the state in determining the legibility and viability of asylum claims as a basis for more concerted, more effective action on the part of those civil-society organizations.

Yet MCCT, of course, is not simply a garden-variety NGO, with unmarked investments in practices of belief. "Secular" NGOs are themselves animated by beliefs in sacred objects of their own (e.g., "social justice"). But, as a large, mainline Protestant Christian church, MCCT makes a particular set of promises ("a house of prayer for all people") and occupies a position of Christian privilege that both abets and hinders in materializing that universality. Here, we see the ironic consequences of Christian hegemony play out with particular acuity. In part because mainline Christianity in "multicultural" Canada is accompanied by a "sense of rightness" (Berlant and Warner 1998, 554), MCCT, with its charismatic leadership, strong music ministry, and liberal, universalist message, has been well positioned to magnetize and in some cases monopolize public attention, as Hawkes and the church have done successfully for decades. The congregation also inherits a long and normalized tradition of faith communities welcoming the stranger or providing sanctuary. That tradition is invoked to a chaotic and contradictory range of political ends, including both practices of faith-based resistance to nation-state violence in the name of higher forms of sovereignty (Hondagneu-Sotelo 2008; Yukich 2013), and the neoliberal devolution of social provisioning for refugees to nongovernmental organizations, including faith communities (Kenney 2010). Many progressive and mainline communities of faith—as well as community groups citing no faith at all—support refugees, including some LGBTQ refugees. Yet MCCT's reputation, combined with its liberal Christian universalist mandate not to screen on the basis of gender identity, sexual orientation, or religious affiliation, has made its refugee peer-support program a tremendously popular vehicle for people trying to expedite their own survival. The church's emphasis on vulnerability over identity as grounds for support has also brought it out of step with some secular programs that do employ identity as a shibboleth. Thus, a combination of factors—Christian hegemony, celebrity, liberal universalist theology, and one queer Christian church's aspiration to be "Canada's leading progressive diverse community of faith"—have rendered MCCT not quite the only game in town but certainly a key conveyor of recognition and legitimacy for LGBTQ asylum seekers in the greater Toronto area and a source of support that asylum seekers, regardless of their own beliefs, cannot afford to miss (MCC Toronto 2016).

This "fortunate and unfortunate" consequence of the church's purchase on legibility raises a vital normative question: If people in the greater Toronto area making refugee claims on the basis of sexual orientation or gender identity in effect have little or no choice but to come to MCCT as a kind of ephemeral queer commons, what is the appropriate ethical and political response on the part of nonrefugees attached to the church who support the refugee program? As we will see, church leaders respond not by dissimulating about claimants' identities so much as by shifting the emphasis:

turning scrutiny away from asylum seekers' authenticity and back toward the importance of solidarity with all asylum seekers as precarious subjects. It is to the question of queer ethical and political responsibility on the part of non–asylum seekers, and the articulation of affinities on a more capacious basis than mere identity politics, that I now turn.

If the hope of improper queer citizenship is to nurture the formation of coalitions among people with incommensurable histories of trauma and pleasure, alienation, affinity, and loss, then where is the queer potential in the scene of the church refugee program? As has become painfully clear, dramas over (in)authentic LGBTQ-ness and refugeeness play a central role in relegating asylum seekers to history's literal waiting room, and the dramas of race and authentic queer citizenship most certainly extend to congregational space. At the same time, however, by critically de-dramatizing the question of refugee authenticity, the refugee program responds to the precarity, the queer nonsovereignty, of asylum seekers. In the church's more critical permutations, such as the church refugee program, MCCT provides support and solidarity to asylum seekers not on the basis of their LGBTQ identity but on the basis of the vulnerability engendered by changing federal refugee policy.

As I noted earlier, while the MCCT refugee program's intake and documentation processes are rigorous, it is a policy of the program not to scrutinize or even ask after participants' claims on LGBTQ identity. This refusal may seem unremarkable or intuitive—after all, despite liberal discourse's claims to the contrary, sexuality is notoriously opaque. Yet the church and secular social service organizations supporting LGBTQ refugees have faced pressure from Citizenship and Immigration Canada to strongly emphasize the LGBTQ character of their programming—to make clear that the services are intended for "true" queers. On this front, the church has declined to comply—a refusal that positions the refugee program as quietly subversive. In a coffee shop near the church, I asked Keith, a volunteer involved in the refugee program who later became a minister in the UFMCC, about the program's refusal to scrutinize the authenticity of participants' sexual orientation or gender identity–related claims:

It's really important to keep in mind what that program's all about, and it's a support program, it's to exchange information so that people know how their experience measures against somebody else's and get some direction from someone else as well. So, you can't go, you can't watch people in their bedroom, you can't see what they're telling.

So really, it's about faith, isn't it? It's about meeting people where they are, and accepting them as they present themselves and accepting that. And that's something that in this world that's very fulfilling in and of itself. How many times in life are we just accepted, as opposed to being questioned and judged?

Another thing he [Rev. Hawkes] had said to me [about the program] which made a whole lot of sense as well is, "Okay, so let's say that they're not gay or lesbian." The reason people who are coming from communities where if they ended up going back to their community and word got out that they had claimed to be gay or lesbian, the likelihood of them being killed or experiencing severe harm is really big. So, coming to this support group takes a whole lot of courage on a number of different levels.

And the other aspect is the whole "What about bi people"? You know, you look at that whole spectrum of sexuality, and are you set on one specific point or not? So, it takes a whole lot of different concepts and raises questions around them. Who are we to say? So, as a result, there isn't room for judgment. There isn't room to say, "Well, you must do this, you must do that, you must believe," because if we were to do any of that, that's totally the antithesis of who MCC is, and that's what I love about MCC: this and this, not or.

Keith ties a refusal to police the sexual identities and practices of refugee-program participants to *faith*—a faith that asks believers to accept others "as they present themselves." This faith-based conception of a trusting relation to strangers critically addresses incitements to police and to authenticate claimants' identities both from the nation-state and from within the ordinary of congregation itself. On the one hand, faith calls for a progressive ethicopolitical orientation toward others that exceeds and flouts the austere and scrutinizing gaze of the nation-state. Faith, for Keith, models a more capacious, less paranoid vision of citizenship than that practiced by the putatively secular federal government at the time or by racist practices of suspicion and expulsion by some within the church. On the other hand, Keith's invocation of faith, of what MCCT is (and isn't) "all about," serves as a challenge within MCCT for congregants who are not asylum seekers to live up to that alternative ethicopolitical vision. Keith argues for citizenship within MCCT and LGBTQ community as variable, idiosyncratic, and heterogeneous, refusing to posit a preferred idiom for participation, contribution, or spiritual connection. If MCCT indeed does make good on its claim to proffer a "vibrant, inclusive, and progressive" alternative vision, both to conservative and mainline Christianities and to the secular state, then the onus is on (nonrefugee) congregants *not* to scrutinize, patronize, or police the authenticity of asylum seekers—and to welcome them as fellow queers.[5]

Further, Keith claims, for some migrants, even those who are not LGBTQ-identified, formally claiming LGBTQ identity—requesting documentation and testimony from bureaucracies and loved ones back home— can implicitly comprise an irrevocably endangering act. Keith's account of the harms faced even by "fake" asylum seekers in homophobic environments is highly speculative and risks consolidating dominant geographical imaginaries about diaspora, sexuality, and home—but I would suggest that it's also doing far more than letting Keith fashion himself as yet another Canadian white knight (Razack 2004). Keith suggests that Toronto and the many other places Torontonians call or have called home are hardly discrete spaces but are often tightly linked by family and friend connections, travel, remittances, social networks, religious polities, international capital, coordinated actions among state actors, and, above all, gossip. Cultural studies scholar Jenny Burman's (2011) powerful transnational mapping of the material, affective, and (bio)political ties between Jamaica and Toronto corroborates such an allusion, elucidating that both migration and emotional investments between the Caribbean and Canada's largest city need to be understood as tautly networked, sustained, and circular rather than unidirectional or assimilative. Indeed, one of the most recurrent tropes in my interviews with asylum seekers was a feeling of diasporic claustrophobia—a sense that one's ethnic community in Toronto was discomfitingly small and altogether too close to "back home."

It is precisely such a dense clustering of linkages that can make claiming LGBTQ identity in Canada a practice that risks exile—a door through which, as Dionne Brand (2002) and Dina Georgis (2006) might put it, there is no return. I invoke the metaphor of the "door of no return" here not to analogize between transatlantic slavery and queerness, nor to overlook the heterogeneity and hierarchy of mobilities among queer diasporic subjects, but simply to extend Georgis's contention about the psychic affinity between queerness and diaspora, an affinity rooted in the groundless ground of expulsion from and loss of home. For diasporic subjects claiming LGBTQ identity as a path to status in Canada, Keith suggests, queerness lies in the geographical and psychic vulnerability brought about by the claim itself, not its "truth" or "falsity." Whether claimants are "truly" LGBTQ or not, it is the waiting room itself—a space of nation-state austerity and paranoia, of everyday racism and xenophobia, of diasporic claustrophobia—that produces asylum seekers as queers demanding solidarity. Recognizing the queerness, vulnerability, and nonsovereignty of others, Keith notes, is a matter of faith that is "fulfilling" for everyone in the scene—pointing to the ways in which nonrefugees might take responsibility for the sense of enjoyment they take in supporting asylum seekers, rather than disavow it in adhesion to salvific ego ideals.

Keith provided me with a powerful meditation on the refugee program's refusal to police or ask after identity. Yet his start as an official program volunteer was, at the time of our interview, relatively recent, leaving me curious about the program's provenance and initial formation. This curiosity led me to ask senior pastor Hawkes about the theological, ethical, and political rationale for the refusal to police identity. Over brunch one Sunday afternoon at his preferred spot in Toronto's gay village, I asked Rev. Hawkes and his husband, John Sproule, about how theology informed the refugee program. The two articulated a similar understanding of the more-than-identitarian imperative to support asylum seekers, based not on LGBTQ identity but on precarity much more broadly conceived—especially economic precarity:

> One thing that strikes me as especially progressive and exciting about the refugee program is the fact that people's sexual orientations aren't policed. Especially because of the [at the time Conservative] government we're under, where there's so much scrutiny on refugees to prove that they're "really gay." I was wondering where that decision or policy or practice came from. Why was it important to not screen people?

Brent: I know that there were other organizations in the GLBT community doing refugee work, and some of them had really wrestled with the idea that they knew some people were pretending to be gay, or that they knew of some lawyers who were telling clients, "Pretend that you're gay and your refugee status may be approved." And I know that in one organization, the endorsement letters that were being given were even being photocopied and altered and sold for three hundred dollars. So, people would take the letter on the letterhead and then they would take out the name and key details, change it, photocopy it, and they were selling those letters.

And so, some organizations' response to that was to try to be more rigid around "Are you really gay or not?" And I remember our conversations around that. And I remember that I said, "I don't want people to be abusing our letter system and our support system. I think we should not be giving letters to people that we don't have some experience with." Yes, we can give a generic letter: "We understand so-and-so is from Kenya, and we know that in Kenya it's an awful situation." Those kinds of letters are easy to give. But if we're going to give letters saying, "We support this individual because they have shown that they're really committed to the community, or they've been really involved in the gay community," we have to have evidence to support that, experience to support that.

But I said, "Frankly, does it make any difference if they're gay or not, if they're escaping Kenya? If they could have a better life here? If they're economic refugees, as opposed to refugees based on sexual orientation, they're still refugees." And, it sounds trite on my part, but if you go out on a space station and look back at Earth, you see no boundaries, you see no national boundaries. We are our brothers' and sisters' keeper. We are responsible. And so, some people will come through and abuse the system, and so what? Let's spend our energy helping people and not waste our energy worrying about it. . . .

John: I can think of one heterosexual refugee. He's very comfortable with the gay community. But his parents and family had been murdered in his country. I mean, no question, if he had stayed there, he'd be dead.

Brent: I think I know him, he was in church this morning.

John: Oh, was he?

Brent: Yeah, he was back.

John: Cool.

Brent: Disappeared for a while.

John: Yes. So, a lot of the people who are coming to us in refugee situations come from intensely deplorable situations of persecution. One would expect things like post-traumatic stress syndrome and things happening. So, anything that we can be doing—

Brent: And even if it's not escaping persecution, even if it's just escaping poverty. The thing that concerns me more is not that someone's sexual orientation should limit their ability to get help. What concerns me more, and I addressed this this morning, is the attitude in our congregation that somehow "The refugees are using us." Or, "They come, they volunteer for a little while, we do the training, they get their letter, they get approved, and we never see them again."

So that's why I addressed that head-on this morning, and I've done it on other occasions, too: If they come, if they get help, we're still doing our job. If they don't stay, that's okay. They cross the bridge, they've moved on. That's okay. So, we have to see ourselves as that place where there are gonna be lots of people come through, and it could be helpful for them to just accept themselves for being gay. It's the same thing if someone accepts themselves as being gay and then goes back to their United Church [of Canada], back to their church of origin, because they feel better about themselves. We've still done our job.

Although gestures to a borderless planet and the trope of African poverty invite a critical appraisal of Hawkes's account as feel-good liberal internationalism or a "one world" universalism that he acknowledges risks triteness, such an analysis would not exhaust the depths of Hawkes's response to my query about the refugee program. Powerfully, Hawkes unsettles the trope at the heart of austere nation-state immigration politics—the racialized fake refugee—with a simple "So what?" Unimpeded by the prospect that some small number of people will inexorably "cheat the system," he still insists on a more ample understanding of the congregation's and the nation's capacities and responsibilities. The pastor directly confronts the recirculation of austere, xenophobic, nationalist, and racist discourses about the racialized fake refugee within the congregation. Destabilizing LGBTQ or Canadian identity as a solid or primary foundation for providing refugee support, he insists on a congregational social justice praxis that recognizes a *multiplicity* of forms of vulnerability, including economic precarity. By suggesting that a congregational "we" does its job "if people get help," Hawkes gestures to a "we" concerned as much with solidarity across differences as with the important but more identitarian premise of reconciling homosexuality and Christianity. Turning attention away from the identitarian preoccupation of "authentic" queer citizenship that circulates in both immigration offices and scenes of gossip and scrutiny in church, Hawkes calls upon the congregation to strive toward a more capacious, improper queer citizenship. Far from shying away from the nation-state, then, improper queer citizenship confronts the nation-state *through* Hawkes's query, challenging the exploitation of sovereign, transparent LGBTQ identity by nation-state immigration officials with an impish "So what?" This "So what?" is both antisocial and profoundly social, negating normative framings of LGBTQ identity as it avows more capacious forms of solidarity and citizenship in excess of the nation-state.

Revising Paranoid Judgment

For a few months after Paige's asylum hearing, a pivotal event in her life that had the more humdrum effect of introducing me to the gray space of one of history's (and Canada's) literal waiting rooms, I didn't see or hear much from Paige or Edie, in or out of church. I sent Paige a few text messages asking how things had gone and hoping she was well. Grimly, I wondered whether Paige had been deported. I imagined Paige on a one-way ticket with a destination of SVD, the E. T. Joshua Airport near Kingstown, likely headed back to the threats and beatings and familial expulsion and gossip she had described to me, to (un)cannily familiar sensations, atmospheres, faces. I imagined my strange, well-meaning texts ignored by her phone's anonymous new owner, or bouncing off some satellite and dissipating after reaching a disconnected number. Then, on the other hand, Paige might have had a successful hearing, and she and Edie might have decided to move on with their lives, like many people in the program whose asylum claims eventuate in success. Then, just over four months after Paige's hearing, I got an e-mail from Edie. The decision on Paige's hearing was a positive one. I am elated and relieved!

I wrote the preceding reflection in my field notes in January 2014, when I received word from Edie about Paige's successful request for permanent residence in Canada. Edie's message, like many facets of my engagement with the church refugee program, continues to surprise me. I had been surprised by the alacrity with which I'd written a letter of support for Paige—that I had jumped right in, sidelining my ambivalence and tactically playing the white gay savior-citizen in the modest hope of contributing to the survival of someone I liked but didn't ultimately know that well. I was pleasantly surprised by the news that Paige had received refugee status—due to a suspicion not of Paige but of an immigration system for which, as Craig taught me, there can never be "enough proof." It surprised me to hear from Edie at all, and given what I had learned about the scrutiny and racial microaggressions that asylum seekers could face at MCCT, it wouldn't have bothered me if Paige had simply moved on from the church, and with her life.

There is nothing necessarily redemptive or radical about surprise. But, as Eve Kosofsky Sedgwick ([1997] 2003) suggests, it is our affective relationship to surprises that enables and constrains our capacity for reparative insight—a capacity that I argue is crucial for improper queer citizenship. Surprises can invite us to reconsider whether objects—like church or citizenship—might be worthy of repair, and to inaugurate practices of integration and working out "good-enough" relations to objects in ways that contribute to radical world building. This fieldwork was marked as much by bad surprises as by good ones, particularly Karen's haunting story about the expulsion of asylum seekers between the morning and evening worship services. It is my hope that facing such a bad surprise—an act of racial exclusion that, for many in the congregation, would prove unsurprising—can provide an occasion not for paranoia but for learning within the church. By way of conclusion, I want to highlight a final pairing—a bad surprise and a good surprise—that have helped me understand possibilities and limitations at church as a space of improper queer citizenship.

First, I was surprised—disappointed, really—by my initial attempts to righteously answer to the trope of the inauthentic refugee with evidence of my interviewees' genuine spiritual, social, and political attachments to queerness and to the church. I am embarrassed by my tactical and provisional *optimism* during fieldwork, by my sense that good social science could make transparent people's true motivations—student of ethnography and psychoanalysis that I purport to be! Not only did asylum seekers' motivations prove complex and contradictory (when they were not altogether opaque), but answering charges of "fake" refugeeness, even and perhaps especially in the "authoritative" position of the empirical researcher, simply reiterated the drama of (in)authenticity articulated officially by the state but circulated through the everyday and played out at the affective, atmospheric level. However, realizing my own distressing fidelity to the fantasy of empirically verifiable queerness, and the utter inadequacy of such a tactic, was also an occasion for learning, and for rethinking the groundless grounds of queer citizenship: what makes asylum seekers *queer* subjects demanding solidarity isn't their authenticity or their inauthenticity, the legibility or illegibility of their desire or sexuality, or even the "validity" of their fears of persecution, but the affective and material vulnerability that the Canadian waiting room imposes on their ordinary lives. This revelation about the queerness of asylum seekers *as such* sits to the side of important but established debates about the limits of Western epistemologies of sexuality and the violent consequences of their uptake by the state, and puts queer subjectless critique to work as a basis for understanding the effects of state violence and alternative forms of citizenship that contest such violence. Coming up with better ways to apprehend the slipperiness of gender and sexual diversity, whether ethnographic or juridical, is surely a worthwhile project; but so is recognizing the queerness, beyond identity, of precarious lives that demand an answer, regardless of sameness or difference, distance or proximity, or linguistic classification, on the basis of a shared vulnerability, and thus an improper queer citizenship (Butler 2012).

Second, hearing MCCT's nonidentitarian basis for its refugee program shocked me, this time in a good way. It surprised me that the better alternative to engaging the drama of the (in)authentic refugee was not to answer it but to flout it altogether, with a capacious, queer "So what?" Moreover, that such an impish retort to the authenticity imperative had come from an institution largely, and often rightly, theorized as a paragon of essentialist identity politics (Warner 2005) points to the potential value of remaining unsure about the identity-based social movements and political projects through which we move and with which we critically engage as scholars and activists. There's a lot that happens at MCCT that gives me pause and that makes me upset ethically and politically, but those feelings do not exhaust my capacity to learn about a complex, unfinished scene to which I am also attached.

This second surprise—MCCT's resistance to the authenticity imperative—proves generative for much broader debates about citizenship. In her recent writing on precarity and ethics, Judith Butler (2012) reads Hannah Arendt to argue against the premise of choice in matters of cohabitation and citizenship in an irrevocably plural world. In her writing on the Nazi war criminal Adolf Eichmann, Arendt ([1963] 2006) insisted—against other interpretations—that Eichmann's only crime was that "he thought he could choose with whom to inhabit the earth" (Butler 2012, 143). Revisiting Arendt for the present, Butler argues that "we must devise institutions and policies that actively preserve and affirm the *nonchosen* character of open-ended and plural cohabitation" (144 [emphasis added]). In this sense, MCCT joins other faith communities in challenging the conceit that state power can and should meddle so violently with the nonchosen character of sharing the earth (Hondagneu-Sotelo 2008; Yukich 2013). Identitarian queer citizenship, mobilized by the Canadian nation-state and echoed within some grumbly corners of the congregation, violently deigns to choose among refugees, electing to share space only with "authentic" claimants—those whose fears of persecution are "well founded" because their LGBTQ-ness is transparently "real" and their countries of nationality are self-evidently "unsafe." By refusing to police the "true" sexual orientation and gender identity of participants, and by providing support on the basis of participation and vulnerability rather than identity, the MCCT refugee peer-support program steps back from that dangerous, arrogant biopolitical premise.[6] Hawkes reconceptualizes the "job" of a citizen, a church, a nation-state as one of solidarity with people on the basis of their vulnerability alone. In this way, the program challenges both the secular nation-state and xenophobia within the congregation, instantiating an alternative, subjectless, improper queer citizenship. As such, this one program at one queer church proffers an instructive, if modest, alternative to a secular nation-state that has arrogated the lethal right to determine with whom its citizens will share the earth (Butler 2012; Arendt [1963] 2006).

Conclusion

Loving an Unfinished World

The human capacities to imagine and play are not always the products of a good holding environment. Sometimes they are the resources whereby those deprived of a world enact alternatives by way of their own insistent creativity.

—Bonnie Honig, "The Politics of Public Things: Neoliberalism and the Routine of Privatization"

We live in a moment when the very real threats posed by white supremacist, misogynist, and homophobic cultural nationalism in much of the global North, combined with the (both grounded and groundless) persecutory anxieties of the left, have led to a panicked fortification of neoliberal identitarian politics (feminist, multicultural, queer) as "the most we can hope for," with liberal agents of the state vociferously, almost coercively, greeted not as lesser evils but as liberators (Brown 2004). Fetishized identitarian firsts and milestones—in 2016, for instance, Justin Trudeau became the first Canadian prime minister to march in the Toronto Pride parade—simultaneously reflect, foreclose, and offer rich departure points for the more substantive collective labor of political discernment and critique. Indeed, a similar and closely related shame structure—whereby the religious right becomes the horizon and thus the limiting foil for theological imagination—has haunted me in my work on this book. During my writing process, a religious college at my own institution, the University of Toronto, surreptitiously and unjustifiably terminated beloved antihomophobic staff, while a campus faith center invited notoriously misogynist, transphobic, and homophobic faith leaders as guest speakers. So, given the important and often life-saving contrast that movements like MCC provide to conservative Christians in Canada, as well as elsewhere, it might be asked, Who am I to look such a miraculous gift horse in the mouth? (In times such as these, it is enlightening to [re]turn to an apposite send-up of jingoistic Cold War nationalism in Jim Henson's *The Great Muppet Caper* [1981], particularly a scene in which Fozzie Bear's most effective rhetorical incitement to his colleagues, who are somewhat skittish about engaging in conflict with the film's antagonists, have legitimate questions about strategy and feasibility, and have assembled few weapons beyond a whoopee cushion, is simply "We don't want the *bad guys* to win!")

Yet rather than accommodate such a neat splitting between good and bad political or theological part objects, here, I would argue that the contradictions of liberal polities, including liberal religious polities, are worth apprehending with great care, because they provide insight into the affective conditions that precede more obvious moments when theological and political liberalisms *fail* to magnetize people. Why indeed, for instance, do so few people of color, particularly asylum seekers, remain at MCCT? And what does it mean that MCCT's refugee program has proven far more radical and bold in its vision of contemporary citizenship vis-à-vis asylum seekers than has the congregation at large in hearing the long-standing claims of racialized people already in its midst? What are we to make of this apparent impasse between the "international" and the "domestic"? How might this schism replicate the worrisome caesura between "saving the world" and "saving the self" that the Reverend Darlene Garner diagnoses as lying at the core of bad colonial Christian missiology, an orientation with echoes in contemporary homonationalism (Puar 2007; Dryden and Lenon 2015)? And, finally, how might things be otherwise?

Though all of us who live and participate in liberal polities live intimately with the contradictions of liberalism, whether we realize it or not, it is often those who live with the most acute, painful, and indeed deadly awareness of the contradictions of liberalism who have produced the most capacious alternative maps of the world as it might be, as it should be (see Walcott 2003). In engaging the limits of liberal forms of queer religious polity, I have sought not simply to *expose* contradiction—a goal already accomplished quite effectively by existing literature on the MCC movement (see, e.g., McQueeney 2009)—but also to demonstrate the ethical and political richness of the alternative constellations of belonging imagined and practiced by those who live most acutely with the pain of contradiction. The reparative calculi of racialized people in church—not only sobriety about the limits of the object but a simultaneous impulse to compose ameliorative possibility in the midst and in excess of a limited environment—attest to the salience of Klein's (1975) depressive position for contemporary genealogies of repair, and to the vitality of affect in apprehending how people live (with) contradiction (Berlant 2011a). Though the inquiry has rarely been framed on terms as explicit as in the brilliant intervention of Bernice Johnson Reagon ([1981] 2000), I would argue that much queer, feminist, and antiracist scholarship on affect implicitly addresses a political and historical question: What are the *affective* conditions under which differently marginalized people might engage in meaningful solidarity and reciprocal intimacy with one another? In considering the centrality of psychic and spiritual life to nonidentitarian and coalitional forms of queer politics, *A House of Prayer for All People* has proffered one partial, provisional set of answers: that meaningful solidarity, in the fleeting moments when it does take form, requires a suspension of identitarian referents, a muddling of the boundaries of "LGBTQ" or "queer," of "me" and "not-me," an empathy with the vulnerability of the Other (including one's own alterity) as such; that reciprocal intimacy would require the relinquishment of fantasies of safe space or identitarian "home" that tend to privilege those most closely approximating "ideal-typical" citizenship; that anti-identitarian critique can in fact advance the interests of marginalized people, opening up alternative profusions and constellations of belonging.

Yet, if it has succeeded, this book has also enriched broader efforts to contest the axiomatic status of religion and citizenship as bad objects for queers, efforts that refuse to cede the monopoly on either term to the most conservative faith voices or most obvious forms of nation-state power, respectively. If identitarian queer citizenship proves haunted by its complicity in nation-state violence, then what I have called improper queer citizenship impishly challenges the nation-state, imaginatively cooking up and extending more capacious ways of organizing sympathy, solidarity, belonging, and rights. The difficult affects that exclusion from normative nation-state citizenship—or exclusion in and from faith community—can produce may understandably (and unfortunately) lead to strident insistence on sovereignty, respectability, and identitarian queer citizenship. But attending to loss, to nonsovereignty, to queer damage can also stimulate the reinvigoration of political desire on more capacious, imaginative terms. As a religious space and an urban queer commons, MCCT is an important place where people both shy away from and beautifully turn toward that nonsovereignty, with a range of effects that I have sought to map. In repairing a potentially bad religious object, the improper queer citizens whose narratives I've sought to curate here simultaneously recast citizenship in ways that, at their best moments, creatively flout identitarian strictures and the boundaries of "me" and "not-me."

As I have come to interview and befriend people within MCCT and the MCC movement, I have had occasion to learn from the critical hesitations and praxes of others, and to reflect on my own habits of thinking and, especially, feeling. Asylum seekers, radical congregants, and church leaders of color—particularly women of color—taught me a great deal not only about the affective, ethical, and political challenges of attaching to a predominantly white and cis male church but about the political visions and senses of potentiality that motivated them to do so. Such potentiality does not redeem "mainstream" LGBTQ institutions like MCCT or naturalize the racism, xenophobia, and sexism that infuse them, but it does invite us to take inspiration from the affective sophistication of queer citizens who inhabit such institutions with a critical difference. Improper queer citizens take up the mantle of citizenship in the church, the city, the nation, and the globe, not as spaces of settled "welcome home" but on terms that are tactical and proleptic, that savvily and somberly aim to make good on the never-completed promise of "a house of prayer for all people." By conducting sustained ethnographic research, I have come to appreciate how people's attachments and engagements—with church, LGBTQ community, God, various forms of state authority, diasporic community—can reflect enormous of levels of affective and political nuance, generosity, and creativity. Becoming aware of my own propensity for harsh judgments—of people's seemingly "bad" attachments and institutional object-choices—has enabled me, on intermittent and fortuitous occasion, not to suspend but to revise judgment. Revising judgment tends to lead not toward optimism—cruel or otherwise—but toward what Klein calls a "depressive" engagement with the world, an orientation to the world that remains well aware of the hypocrisies of many forms of both religion and citizenship but also responsive to good surprises when they grace us.

This project does not end, then, in a particularly satisfying or emotionally comfortable place, because that is not what improper queer citizenship demands of any of us, however differently formed we are as subjects. Queer citizenship without identitarian or national referent means relinquishing the comfortable but profoundly violent premise that one can choose with whom to cohabit the earth (Butler 2012; Arendt [1963] 2006; Hanhardt 2013). It negates the premise of "safe space"—be it radical queer or cultural nationalist—echoing Bernice Reagon's ([1981] 2000) insistence on the impossibility of identitarian "barred rooms," and Klein's ([1935] 1988, 305) insight that "no really ideal part" of the self or its objects exists. Fundamentally coalitional, spaces of improper queer citizenship are not homey, canny, or womblike; they are irrevocably and at times distressingly plural, messy, and shared. These subjectless premises, articulated in the MCCT refugee program and the critical citizenship claims of racialized and feminized congregants, unsettle more identitarian and nationally framed forms of queer belonging and solidarity.

Just as crucially, critical inhabitations of citizenship in church engage in transformative, downwardly redistributive material and affective work. When Hawkes calls out xenophobic fears of "fake" refugee claimants "using" the church, he also invokes more expansive queer and faith-based geographies of identification and solidarity, pushing queer citizenship beyond the fetishes of identity and nationhood. When minoritized people challenge the racism and sexism they experience in church—or by police on the streets of Toronto—they are not simply asking for their pain to be heard but also engaging in a capacious alternative world-building project, challenging and inviting everyone to inhabit the church, and inhabit the world, "as a minority among [fellow] minorities" (Asad 2003, 180). When Darlene Garner calls on the MCC movement and "international turns" in global-North queer activism more broadly to ponder "Why are you doing this?," she helps inaugurate the possibility (there are no guarantees) that becoming articulate about desire might lead to more ethical and relational forms of global church and transnational politics. When Hawkes asks after the prime minister's wife, he isn't simply celebrating liberal progress but cheekily proffering a bold alternative vision of the national body politic and intimate citizenship, and challenging the nation-state to attend to the ghosts that still haunt progress. Improper queer citizens inflect liberal and representational projects—from Sunday Christian worship services, to national memorials, to global LGBTQ community building, to refugee support work—with critical differences, "minor" desires, and alternative agendas.

Crucially, such creative acts do not stem from practitioners' "good politics" alone. Indeed, as Deborah Gould (2009) observes, "any investigation of political behavior needs to acknowledge the fact that people are simultaneously cognitively and affectively driven" (102). People's capacity for expansive, improper, or subjectless geographies of citizenship depends not only on conscious, righteous analysis—on politics that says all the right things—but on complex itineraries of spiritual and *affective* integration, itineraries that are nurtured in shared and intimate spaces of citizenship like church. And it is in the domain of affect that queer approaches to citizenship can learn the most from critical practitioners and worshippers at MCCT and in the MCC movement. In a poignant, formidable interview titled "Learning to Love Again," Wendy Brown turns to the affective register to confront the contemporary left's archive of defeat, grappling with the question "What do we [the left, broadly conceived] need to give now in order that there may be democratic futures?" Brown responds, "'What we might need to give now' would be something like a giving up of certain investments, not only in what we imagine the left must be *for*, but also *what we imagine we must keep separate or oppositional*" (Colegate et al. 2006, 41 [emphasis added]).

What would it mean for queer theory or politics to give up investments in citizenship and religion as always already "bad objects" (West 2014)? And what, on affective and not only conceptual terms, would it take to precipitate such a shift in queer investments? I have traced the insights and praxes of improper queer citizens who relate to citizenship and religion at scales from the church to the globe, not as bad objects but as messy, incomplete objects, riven with good and bad fragments. Oscillating between attachment, desire, contestation, and solidarity, these improper queer citizens routinely consider "refus[ing] citizenship altogether" (Brandzel 2005, 198) but ultimately revise paranoid judgment in order "*to assemble and confer plenitude* to an object that will then have resources to offer to an inchoate self" (Sedgwick [1997] 2003, 149 [emphasis added]). As the nation-state haunts queer politics, improper queer citizenship defiantly trolls the nation-state right back, inhabiting citizenship at multiple scales and beholden to no single locus of belonging or fixed referent for what counts as "religious" or "queer." To catch up with the praxes of faith activists and communities, and to engage in mutually enlivening idea generation, queer theoretical approaches to citizenship and to religion should follow suit. Prolifically multiscalar, neither cruel-optimistic nor simply paranoid, the promise of improper queer citizenship invites our humility and our playfulness as we ask what it might mean to love (in) a violent, contradictory, and altogether unfinished world (Isin 2007; Berlant 2011a; Stewart 2008).

Acknowledgments

First and foremost, my deepest thanks go to my interview subjects at the Metropolitan Community Church of Toronto, in the MCC movement, and in broader Toronto queer and trans communities. I hope my work supports efforts to realize a church that moves meaningfully closer toward the vision of love, justice, and substantive equality held out in promises of "a house of prayer for all people." The Reverend Dr. Brent Hawkes and his husband, John Sproule, encouraged and welcomed me with open arms to do this work, as did Brent's skillful executive assistant, Annabelle Menezes. When I began this project, I told Brent that he should prepare for me to be critical of the church, even as I am also attached to it. Gently and playfully, he responded by citing Ephesians 4:15: "Speak the truth with love." I hope he and others find in these pages an articulation of difficult truth that is also deeply loving.

This book was enabled by visits to and communication with a number of archives, including the Canadian Lesbian and Gay Archives in Toronto, the Manitoba Gay and Lesbian Archives in Winnipeg, the Montreal Gay Archives, the Toronto Reference Library, Library and Archives Canada in Ottawa, the City of Toronto Archives, the CTV Archives in Scarborough, and the One National Archives in Los Angeles. Consultations with Don McLeod at the University of Toronto Libraries were crucial. Special thanks to Julie Podmore, Alan Miller, and Helen Lenskyj for support in archives. Thanks also to Andrea Houston, Gerald Hannon, Ken Popert, Andrea Gordon, John Gordon, Black Lives Matter Toronto, and the intrepid Jordan Hale for help with images.

Working with the University of Minnesota Press has proven an occasion for intellectual growth and for gratitude. Jason Weidemann has been extremely generous and available with his time and formidable expertise. Erin Warholm-Wohlenhaus, Molly Fuller, Laura Westlund, and Tammy Zambo provided indispensable guidance and attention. Muhammad Velji made quick work with the book's index. I am grateful to David Churchill and to an anonymous Press reader whose rather different but ultimately complementary critiques of the project have (I hope) resulted in a text that is as inviting to readers as it is unapologetically engaged with spatial, queer, critical race, and psychoanalytic theory. All limitations, of course, remain my own.

People read acknowledgments to academic books for multifarious reasons, but among the most common are the rather salacious hopes of finding out who funded the author and whom the author was dating. For better or worse, the conditions that enabled me to do this work are not quite congruent with the axiomatic vision of a good life presumed by such curiosity. As a U.S. citizen who was neither a citizen nor a permanent resident of Canada as I wrote and revised this project, I was ineligible for most federal grants and received no funding outside the University of Toronto, where the School of Graduate Studies, Department of Geography and Program in Planning, Women and Gender Studies Institute, Asian Institute, and Mark S. Bonham Centre for Sexual Diversity Studies munificently made it possible for me to keep the lights on, and helped with many book-related costs. (It must be noted that research funds from my new institutional home, Harvey Mudd College, generously covered the cost of indexing.) I was also single for most of that time. I note these conditions not to cast myself as some kind of scrappy, monastic, enterprising academic individual toiling in solitude, but for precisely the opposite reason: to underscore that I could not have done this work without a rich constellation of intimate and intellectual relationships, relationships proffering the dialogue and fun that I needed in order to write. Indeed, the life and thought that inform this book have been graced with a community of friends and interlocutors who kept me alive and made my life more worth living, my work more worth doing. Since the identity politics of the 1990s are back, anyway, perhaps it's apt here to recall the concluding message of Sandra Bernhard's one-woman show and film: "Without you, I'm nothing" (Boskovich 1990).

At the University of Toronto, Deb Cowen was a superlative and magnanimous graduate cosupervisor; she first directed me toward the refugee ministry at the Metropolitan Community Church of Toronto and has pushed my thinking on citizenship the most. Dina Georgis, my other cosupervisor, provided remarkably incisive, intuitive, and empathetic guidance on writing and life. Emily Gilbert was an outstanding committee member, providing careful, sustained, and profoundly thoughtful attention to my work. Ju Hui Judy Han, Rachel Silvey, Mari Ruti, and Katharine Rankin all brought great insight and humor to my committee. David Eng's trenchant, generous questions about faith and about object relations, which presaged many of the questions from Press reviewers, had an indelible impact on my work. The University of Toronto was an ideal milieu in which to grow as a scholar and colleague. There are far too many colleagues for me to adequately thank each of them here, but those whose thinking has productively informed this book include Alissa Trotz, Rinaldo Walcott, Brenda Cossman, Debby Leslie, Naisargi Dave, Natalie Kouri-Towe, Hannah Dyer, OmiSoore Dryden, Fan Wu, J. P. Catungal, Marcus McCann, Matt Farish, and Sherene Razack. Conversations with Judith Butler and especially Lauren Berlant during their visits to Toronto reminded me to approach my writing with rigor and levity in equal measure. Brilliant students such as Jandell-Jamala Nicholas, Ronja Sørensen, Skye Collishaw, Alisha Stranges, Jasmine Hodgson-Bautista, and Franklin Adamson helped make me a better teacher and writer, and I am grateful to them for it.

Interlocution at several conferences pushed my work in directions I am excited to continue to develop. In relation to this book, I am especially grateful to have crossed paths with Kent Brintnall, Joe Fischel, Heather White, J. Brendan Shaw, Yui Hashimoto, Larry Knopp, Gavin Brown, Lynne Gerber, R. Stephen Warner, Tamar Shirinian, Sharon Groves, Rachel Buff, Natalie Oswin, Krista Benson, Catherine Jean Nash, Farhang Rouhani, Derek Ruez, and Steve Pile.

Finally, I am most grateful to my families, both chosen and unchosen, for their unfailing support. In Toronto, both within and beyond the university, my life has been enriched and in a very important sense reproduced and regenerated by the companionship of Lia Frederiksen, Eli Erickson, Emily Reid-Musson, Adam Perry, Jordan Hale, Madelaine Cahuas, Beyhan Farhadi, Mai Nguyen, Rebecca Osolen, Sonia Grant, Nicole Latulippe, Elsie Lewison, Alex Gatien, Heather McLean, Abbey Jackson, Victoria Keller, Mecha Cavallo, Wesley Brunson, Jonathan Valelly, Marc Tremblay, Jess Wilczak, Caitlin Henry, Carmen Teeple Hopkins, Savitri Persaud, Vince Chan, Mylène Gamache, Tyler Carson, Bronwyn Bragg, Ricky Varghese, Umair Abdul Qadir, Mic Carter, Stephanie Rutherford, Jen Roberton, Emily Milton, Taj Nabhani, Eugene Ting, Michael Connors Jackman, Tim McCaskell, Richard Fung, Abby Jackman, Jenna Lee Forde Caprani, Alia Scanlon, John Paul Ricco, Jeff Reinhart, Shannon Black, Glenn Betteridge, Matthew Simpson, Ralph Carl Wushke, and Veronica Zaretski. I thank Pat DeYoung and Julia Wawrzyniak-Beyer for their wisdom, patience, and counsel.

Outside Toronto, Steve and Caren Knox made London, Ontario, a home away from home away from home for various holidays over the past seven years. Caitlin Hawley kept me giggling from Stockholm. Karin Aguilar–San Juan and Sharon Haire in St. Paul have been the best "lesbian surrogate moms" I could ask for. Karin, Scott Morgensen, Adrienne Christiansen, David Blaney, Susanna Drake, Paul Dosh, Patrick Schmidt, and Dan Trudeau provided important models for my intellectual and professional itinerary over the past decade. Staying in touch with Hannah Emple, Aaron Brown, Megumi Kanada, Eric Goldfischer, Aaron Brosier, Emma Gallegos, Véronique Bergeron, Emily Gastineau, Nicole Kligerman, Brian Stephenson, Jason Rodney, and Bobbi Gass has been enlivening for my mind and my heart. My Chicago family—Samuel Galloway, Hannah Johnson Truskoski, Anna Joranger, Blake Wilkinson, Meredith McBride, Matthew Meltzer, Molly Walker, Chris Clowers, and Caroline Rendon—has shared rich moments of reflection with me on long jaunts by Lake Michigan, followed by pizza and, of course, ample glasses of wine. In Wisconsin, conversations with Mary Jo and Jeff Randall, Julia Collins, Ron Zdroik, Suzi Moore, Karen Engelking, Susan Endes, Lucky Tomaszek, Darthe Jennings, Joyce Cable, Dennis McBride, Amy Silverman, Emily Widen, Jim Voss, Mike and Julie Walker, and Ann and Mike Joranger made visits home full of moments of renewal, ever-salacious political gossip, and care.

Deepest gratitude extends to my biological family, which is, of course, in adulthood also chosen, in its own way. My sister Kadie's preoccupations with time and the archive both complement and challenge mine with space and dialogue, and our intellectual and political debates have proven as fruitful as they have flippant and loving. My father Dan's general irreverence is tempered by a seriousness about religion that has enriched my treatment of faith in this book, as has his unfailing and generous encouragement and that of my stepmother, Barb. As many historical differences separate us, my mother, Kristie Kroening, has in so many ways provided *the* example for how I approach research, teaching, and life (to say nothing of our uncanny physical resemblance). Conversations with her and my stepfather, Al Nichols, have gifted me not only with moral support but also with important opportunities to elucidate this book's ethical and political stakes.

Finally, I dedicate this book to my late grandmother, Elfrieda Mehlhorn, who passed away just three months before I began attending MCCT. Frankly, I'm not sure what my grandma—a pro-choice, Republican, German American farmer's wife who responded to my desire to go to graduate school with the characteristically terse, wry observation, "Well, you always could talk"—would make of this book. But I suspect and hope that, given her own experiences of religious expulsion, patriarchal violence, and educational disenfranchisement, and her appreciation for impish humor, she would, in her own way, be proud—or at least, and better, amused.

Notes

Introduction

Throughout this book, full names refer to notable public figures whose identities would be difficult to conceal and who agreed to have their names shared. When an informant is described on a first-name basis, it indicates I have used a pseudonym to protect confidentiality.

1. Scholarly work inspired by subjectless queer critique, and by Foucault's ([1976] 1978) earlier account of sexuality as a discourse of power rather than an identity, is vast, and it is not within the scope of my project to review it here. For one important review on geographical sexuality scholarship without "proper objects," see Oswin 2008.

2. Indeed, resonances across black feminist and psychoanalytic, particularly Kleinian, thinking—on the political and psychic impossibility of a "safe" womblike home space, on the necessity of coalition as an impure object, and on living with the anxiety such impurity inexorably entails—have not gone unnoticed. See, e.g., the work of Cynthia Burack (2004 59, 75) and Judith Butler (2015, 151–52).

3. I take a cue here from David Valentine (2007), whose excellent ethnographic work in New York uses his bike rides across the city to open up the multisited and patchy character of transgender community formation and category imputation. Recounting my walk also echoes the long-standing figure of the flaneur, the spectatorial urban wanderer (Benjamin 2002)—a figure that has been criticized for its disembodied, tacitly masculinist, and normatively white gaze but has also been approached as an idiom that can be queerly inhabited (Munt 1995).

4. My social location not only afforded me coveted access to a modest solo domestic space; it inflected my capacity to move through the city. While I have experienced more verbal homophobic harassment living in the city's gay village than anywhere else in my life—something I attribute in part to the visible demarcation of the neighborhood to antagonists as gay—as a middle-class white man, I have also had to contend with precious little in the way of street harassment, which is far from a universal experience in that neighborhood; see Roberton (2016).

1. Too Diverse?

1. This is, of course, a project that socially engaged psychoanalytic theory shares; see Eng (2010), especially chap. 5.

2. When I spoke with Rev. Hawkes about the worrisome Goldilocks schema in November 2015, he told me that he had no interest in watering down or "diluting" representations of racial diversity at the church but that he also feared the equally tokenizing practice of relegating people of color to leading worship one or two weeks a month. Hawkes averred that recruiting additional deacons of color remains a challenging but vital goal.

3. Here it might be interesting to read King David against the Greek mythological figure of Orestes; see Klein ([1935] 1998).

2. Pastor–Diva–Citizen

1. Indeed, that very spring, BLMTO had successfully demanded a coroner's inquest into the death of Andrew Loku, a father of five from South Sudan with a history of mental illness who was killed by police in July 2015 (Ballingall 2016).

2. While Hawkes did not expressly "forgive" Toronto Police Services ("the hurt remains"), his attempt to use the gesture of accepting apology to posit or affirm norms defined by putatively nonhomophobic police ("the healing can begin") ought to give us pause, and invites us to heed the philosopher Jacques Derrida's (2001) famous critique of politically instrumental forms of forgiveness. For Derrida, "Each time forgiveness is at the service of a finality, be it noble and spiritual (atonement and redemption, reconciliation, salvation), each time it aims to reestablish a normality . . . by a work of mourning, by some therapy or ecology of memory, then the 'forgiveness' is not pure—nor is its concept. Forgiveness is not, it *should not be,* normal, normative, normalizing. It *should* remain exceptional and extraordinary, in the face of the impossible: as if it interrupted the ordinary course of historical temporality" (31–32 [emphasis original]).

3. The visceral appeal of such an attachment may not immediately register for some feminist and queer scholars on the secular left. Yet, as Ann Pellegrini (2009) suggests, understanding religious affect is a vital project for feminist and queer politics and scholarship, both in order to develop a more careful map of public feelings in general and particularly to center genealogies of feminist and queer movements that are not white.

4. There is no scholarly or political consensus as to whether "bathhouse raids" or "bathhouse riots" is a more apt term. While "Toronto bathhouse raids" yields several times as many Google search results as "Toronto bathhouse riots," the latter phrase seems to have captured the imagination of some gay publications in the United States and Canada, perhaps because it foregrounds queer resistance.

NOTES · 239

Although I am cognizant of the political value of recuperating and understanding queer anger and dissent, I am particularly compelled by "bathhouse raids" because of its focus on the losses and vulnerability engendered and laid bare by state violence, and on the possibility of coalitional response around shared vulnerability.

5. Thanks to Syrus Marcus Ware and Catherine Jean Nash for each making this point.

6. Even more compelling but omitted from the film was Hawkes's hunger strike, a protest that led the conservative *Toronto Sun* to opine, "It is perhaps too much to hope that [Ontario attorney general Roy McMurtry] . . . will let Mr. Hawkes continue not eating" ("Homomartyrdom?" 1981; Downing 1981).

7. Historically regarded as a third party at the federal scale, and usually holding policy positions to the ideological left of both the Liberals and the Conservatives, the New Democratic Party has played a significant role in coalition governments with Liberal leadership but has never been at the helm of the federal government. In 2011, the NDP gained a landmark 67 seats in Parliament, winning 103 seats to the Conservatives' 166 and the Liberals' 34 (Elections Canada 2011).

8. While Saunders was celebrated by some as the first black police chief in Toronto, his policy record within Toronto Police Services positions him as no friend to BLM or other groups organizing against racial profiling or police brutality in the city. See Gillis (2015).

3. "Why Are You Doing This?"

1. This sense of obligation to depart from Christianity's colonial past in building a global church resonated in my conversation with the denomination's most recent permanent moderator, the Reverend Dr. Nancy Wilson, when she came to Toronto for World Pride in 2014. Wilson described a sophisticated praxis sensitive to power relations not only between North and South but also within global South churches, and an awareness of how the global denomination could be mobilized to contest or consolidate power differentials in global South communities.

2. Thanks to R. Stephen Warner for making this point.

3. For a fabulous exposition on the potential valences of "minor" theory in human geography, see Cindi Katz's provocative essay "Towards Minor Theory" (1996).

4. In its contemporary form, the UFMCC Council of Elders (members of which are now appointed by a democratically elected moderator) provides ecclesial and spiritual leadership; a separate, democratically elected Governing Board sets the budget and authorizes commissions to study issues and make policy recommendations (Universal Fellowship of Metropolitan Community Churches 2014).

4. From Identity to Precarity

1. Rinaldo Walcott merits special thanks for his guidance on the ethics of solidarity in writing refugee-support letters and on marshaling one's academic expertise and credentials on the side not of salvation but of people's survival.

2. The indictment in this chapter of the violences inflicted by Conservative immigration policies should in no way be taken as unique to the Conservatives. Indeed, how the Liberal government, which has derived rather positive optics from admitting twenty-five thousand Syrian refugees and in May 2017 announced changes to best practices surrounding LGBTQ refugees, ultimately performs remains to be seen.

3. For Eng (2010), queer liberalism's teleological, developmental rendition of sexual identity formation occludes the chaotic, contradictory, and thoroughly modern character of heterogeneous nonnormative sexual identities and practices that exist in far more complex relation to Western discourses of sexuality. Yet at stake in this chapter is less a critique of queer liberalism, or an ethnographic uncovering of the complexity of the lives and practices it renders illegible (see Shuman and Bohmer 2014), but an exploration of how differently positioned people negotiate its effects.

4. One also wonders: How do those white people in church who actively scrutinize people of color know which asylum seekers remain part of a congregation and which do not—particularly if some of those same whites also cannot tell even longtime black congregants apart, as we saw in chapter 1?

5. First, although the adjectival trio of "vibrant, inclusive, and progressive" is not formally part of the church's mission or vision statements, it is quite commonly used at MCCT to describe the church. Second, while it is beyond the scope of this project, a related, and potentially illuminating, line of inquiry here might be to examine the ways in which gestures of "hospitality"—beneficent welcome to asylum seekers—and their LGBTQ permutations might shore up and/or render tremulous Canadian colonial claims on indigenous land (see Roache 2015; Morgensen 2012).

6. Engin Isin (2012) raises critical questions about an attachment to the state, and about what he sees as the secular Pauline valorization of choice in responding to the unchosenness of plurality in Arendt's account of citizenship. Isin's reading could probably challenge Butler and MCCT as well. Yet Isin's gloss on Arendt emphasizes haunting by much longer Jewish and Christian genealogies, whereas Butler expressly reads Arendt against herself, raising important questions about whether reading thinkers against themselves can provide a way out of those thinkers' complicit genealogies, or at least can make it possible to take up what's most salient or emancipatory about their oeuvres on critical, synthetic, and integrative terms (see Seitz 2017).

Bibliography

Abu-Lughod, Lila. 2002. "Do Muslim Women Really Need Saving?" *American Anthropologist* 104 (3): 783–90.

Agamben, Giorgio. 2005. *State of Exception.* Translated by Kevin Attell. Chicago: University of Chicago Press.

Aguirre-Livingston, Paul. 2011. "Dawn of a New Gay." *The Grid TO,* 9 June. http://www.thegridto.com/city/sexuality/dawn-of-a-new-gay/.

Ahmed, Sara. 2009. "Problematic Proximities; or, Why Critiques of 'Gay Imperialism' Matter." *Alanalentin.net,* 9 November. http://www.alanalentin.net/2009/11/09/problematic-proximities-or-why-critiques-of-gay-imperialism-matter/.

Alexander, M. Jacqui. 2006. *Pedagogies of Crossing: Meditations on Feminism, Sexual Politics, Memory, and the Sacred.* Durham: Duke University Press.

Alford, C. Fred. 2001. *Melanie Klein and Critical Social Theory: An Account of Politics, Art, and Reason Based on Her Psychoanalytic Theory.* New Haven: Yale University Press.

Allen, Jafari Sinclaire. 2009. "For 'the Children' Dancing the Beloved Community." *Souls: A Critical Journal of Black Politics, Culture, and Society* 11 (3): 311–26.

Altman, Dennis. 1997. "Global Gaze / Global Gays." *GLQ: A Journal of Lesbian and Gay Studies* 3 (4): 417–36.

Anderson, Ben. 2006. "Becoming and Being Hopeful: Towards a Theory of Affect." *Environment and Planning D: Society and Space* 24 (5): 733–52.

Anderson, Bridget, Nandita Sharma, and Cynthia Wright, eds. 2009. "No Borders as a Practical Political Project." *Refuge: Canada's Journal on Refugees* 26 (2): 5–18.

Arendt, Hannah. (1963) 2006. *Eichmann in Jerusalem: A Report on the Banality of Evil.* New York: Penguin.

Asad, Talal. 2003. *Formation of the Secular: Christianity, Islam, Modernity.* Palo Alto: Stanford University Press.

August, Martine. 2008. "Social Mix and Canadian Public Housing Redevelopment: Experiences in Toronto." *Canadian Journal of Urban Research* 17 (1): 82–100.

Badiou, Alain. (1988) 2013. *Being and Event.* Translated by Oliver Feltham. London: Bloomsbury Academic.

Ball, Jason. 2015. "Once upon a City: Allan Gardens' Rich History of Revolution."

Toronto Star, 3 December. https://www.thestar.com/yourtoronto/once-upon
-a-city-archives/2015/12/03/once-upon-a-city-allan-gardens-rich-history-of
-revolution.html.

Ballingall, Alex. 2016. "Coroner Says Black Lives Matter Helped Prompt Loku Inquest." *Toronto Star,* 15 April. https://www.thestar.com/news/gta/2016/04/15/
coroner-says-black-lives-matter-helped-prompt-loku-inquest.html.

Bannerji, Himani. 2000. *Dark Side of the Nation: Essays on Multiculturalism, Nationalism, and Racism.* Toronto: Canadian Scholars Press.

Beauvais, Mike. 2011. "Controversial Group Did the Right Thing to Bow Out
of Pride, Rev. Brent Hawkes Says." *Toronto Observer,* 15 April. http://toronto
observer.ca/2011/04/15/controversial-group-did-the-right-thing-to-bow-out
-of-pride-rev-brent-hawkes-says/.

Benedicto, Bobby. 2014. *Under Bright Lights: Gay Manila and the Global Scene.*
Minneapolis: University of Minnesota Press.

Benjamin, Walter. 1986. "Critique of Violence." In *Reflections: Essays, Aphorisms,
Autobiographical Writings,* edited by Peter Demetz, 277–300. New York:
Schocken.

———. 2002. *The Arcades Project.* Translated by Kevin McLaughlin. Cambridge:
Harvard University Press.

Berlant, Lauren. 1994. "'68, or Something." *Critical Inquiry* 21 (1): 124–55.

———. 1997. *The Queen of America Goes to Washington City: Essays on Sex and
Citizenship.* Durham: Duke University Press.

———. 2000. "The Subject of True Feeling: Pain, Privacy, and Politics." In *Transformations: Thinking through Feminism,* edited by Sara Ahmed, Jane Kilby,
Celia Lury, Maureen McNeil, and Beverley Skeggs, 33–47. London: Routledge.

———. 2007. "Citizenship." In *Keywords in American Cultural Studies,* edited by
Bruce Burgett and Glenn Hendler, 37–42. New York: New York University
Press.

———. 2011a. *Cruel Optimism.* Durham: Duke University Press.

———. 2011b. "Starved." In *After Sex? On Writing since Queer Theory,* edited by
Janet Halley and Andrew Parker, 79–90. Durham: Duke University Press.

Berlant, Lauren, and Lee Edelman. 2013. *Sex; or, The Unbearable.* Durham: Duke
University Press.

Berlant, Lauren, and Michael Warner. 1998. "Sex in Public." *Critical Inquiry* 24 (2):
547–66.

Bérubé, Allan. 2001. "How Gay Stays White and What Kind of White It Stays." In
The Making and Unmaking of Whiteness, edited by Birgit Brander Rasmussen,
Eric Klinenberg, Irene J. Nexica, and Matt Wray, 234–65. Durham: Duke Uni-
versity Press.

Bialystok, Franklin. 2000. *Delayed Impact: The Holocaust and the Canadian Jewish
Community.* Montreal: McGill-Queen's University Press.

Biles, John, and Humera Ibrahim. 2009. "Religion and Public Policy: Immigration, Citizenship, and Multiculturalism—Guess Who's Coming to Dinner?" In *Religion and Ethnicity in Canada*, edited by Paul Bramadat and David Seljak, 154–77. Toronto: University of Toronto Press.

Black, Debra, and Nicholas Keung. 2012. "Immigration and Refugee System: Canada Made Controversial Changes in 2012." *Toronto Star*, 29 December. http://www.thestar.com/news/investigations/2012/12/29/immigration_and_refugee_system_canada_made_controversial_changes_in_2012.html.

Blatchford, Christie. 2011. "Layton's Death Turns into a Thoroughly Public Spectacle." *National Post*, 22 August. http://fullcomment.nationalpost.com/2011/08/22/christie-blatchford-laytons-death-turns-into-a-thoroughly-public-spectacle/.

Bochove, Peter. 2011. "A Deliberate Campaign against Gay Sexuality." *Toronto Xtra!*, 7 February. http://dailyxtra.com/deliberate-campaign-gay-sexuality.

Body Politic Collective, The. 1974. "Contradictions." *The Body Politic*, April, 2.

———. 1981. "Brent Hawkes: Hungry for Rights." *The Body Politic*, April, 11.

Boellstorff, Tom. 2005. *The Gay Archipelago: Sexuality and Nation in Indonesia*. Princeton: Princeton University Press.

Bondi, Liz. 2008. "On the Relational Dynamics of Caring: A Psychotherapeutic Approach to Emotional and Power Dimensions of Women's Care Work." *Gender, Place, and Culture* 15 (3): 249–65.

Boudreau, Julie-Anne, Roger Keil, and Douglas Young. 2009. *Changing Toronto: Governing Urban Neoliberalism*. Toronto: University of Toronto Press.

Bradshaw, James. 2011. "A Month in the Works, Layton's Funeral Meant to Inspire." *Globe and Mail*, 24 August. http://www.theglobeandmail.com/news/politics/a-month-in-the-works-laytons-funeral-meant-to-inspire/article591925/.

Brah, Avtar. 1996. *Cartographies of Diaspora: Contesting Identities*. London: Routledge.

Bramadat, Paul, and David Seljak, eds. 2009. *Religion and Ethnicity in Canada*. Toronto: University of Toronto Press.

Brand, Dionne. 2002. *A Map to the Door of No Return: Notes to Belonging*. Toronto: Random House Canada.

———. 2005. *What We All Long For*. Toronto: Knopf Canada.

Brandzel, Amy L. 2005. "Queering Citizenship? Same-Sex Marriage and the State." *GLQ: A Journal of Lesbian and Gay Studies* 11 (2): 171–204.

Brennan, Denise. 2004. *What's Love Got to Do with It? Transnational Desires and Sex Tourism in the Dominican Republic*. Durham: Duke University Press.

Brintnall, Kent L. 2011. *Ecce Homo: The Male-Body-in-Pain as Redemptive Figure*. Chicago: University of Chicago Press.

Britzman, Deborah P. 2000. "If the Story Cannot End: Deferred Action, Ambivalence, and Difficult Knowledge." In *Between Hope and Despair: Pedagogy and the Remembrance of Historical Trauma*, edited by Roger I. Simon, Sharon Rosenberg, and Claudia Eppert, 27–57. Lanham, Md.: Rowman & Littlefield.

Brock, Rita Nakashima, and Rebecca Ann Parker. 2008. *Saving Paradise: How Christianity Traded Love of This World for Crucifixion and Empire*. Boston: Beacon.

Brown, Gavin. 2009. "Thinking beyond Homonormativity: Performative Explorations of Diverse Gay Economies." *Environment and Planning A* 41 (6): 1496–1510.

Brown, Michael P. 2000. *Closet Space: Geographies of Metaphor from the Body to the Globe*. London: Routledge.

Brown, Wendy. 1995. *States of Injury: Power and Freedom in Late Modernity*. Princeton: Princeton University Press.

———. 1999. "Resisting Left Melancholy." *boundary 2* 26 (3): 19–27.

———. 2002. "Suffering the Paradoxes of Rights." In *Left Legalism / Left Critique*, edited by Wendy Brown and Janet Halley, 420–34. Durham: Duke University Press.

———. 2003. "Neo-liberalism and the End of Liberal Democracy." *Theory and Event* 7 (1).

———. 2004. "'The Most We Can Hope For . . .': Human Rights and the Politics of Fatalism." *South Atlantic Quarterly* 103 (2–3): 451–63.

———. 2015. "Religious Freedom's Oxymoronic Edge." In *Politics of Religious Freedom*, edited by Winnifred Fallers Sullivan, Elizabeth Shakman Hurd, Saba Mahmood, and Peter G. Danchin, 324–34. Chicago: University of Chicago Press.

Buff, Rachel, ed. 2008. *Immigrant Rights in the Shadows of Citizenship*. New York: New York University Press.

Burack, Cynthia. 2004. *Healing Identities: Black Feminist Thought and the Politics of Groups*. Ithaca: Cornell University Press.

Burman, Jenny. 2011. *Transnational Yearnings: Tourism, Migration, and the Diasporic City*. Vancouver: University of British Columbia Press.

Burton, Antoinette. 1994. *Burdens of History: British Feminists, Indian Women, and Imperial Culture, 1865–1915*. Chapel Hill: University of North Carolina Press.

Bush, George W. 2006. State of the Union Address. American Presidency Project, 31 January. University of California Santa Barbara. http://www.presidency.ucsb.edu/ws/index.php?pid=65090.

Butler, Judith. 1990. *Gender Trouble: Feminism and the Subversion of Identity*. London: Routledge.

———. 1994. "Against Proper Objects: Introduction." *differences: A Journal of Feminist Cultural Studies* 6 (2–3): 1–26.

———. 1997. *The Psychic Life of Power*. Palo Alto: Stanford University Press.

———. 1998. "Merely Cultural." *New Left Review* 227: 33–44.

———. 1999. Preface to *Gender Trouble: Feminism and the Subversion of Identity* (1999 ed.), by Judith Butler, vii–xxvi. London: Routledge.

———. 2004. *Precarious Life: The Powers of Mourning and Violence.* London: Verso.

———. 2012. "Precarious Life, Vulnerability, and the Ethics of Cohabitation." *Journal of Speculative Philosophy* 26 (2): 134–51.

———. 2015. *Notes toward a Performative Theory of Assembly.* Cambridge: Harvard University Press.

Butler, Judith, and Gayatri Chakravorty Spivak. 2007. *Who Sings the Nation-State?* Chicago: Seagull Press.

Caldwell, John. 2003. "When the Rainbow Isn't Enuf." *The Advocate,* 30 September.

Canadian Council for Refugees. 2013. "CCR Decries Dramatic Drop in Refugees Resettled to Canada." Press release, 7 March. http://ccrweb.ca/en/bulletin/13 /03/07.

Canadian Press. 2016. "Toronto Reverend Brent Hawkes Pleads Not Guilty to Sex-Assault Charge." *Toronto Star,* 11 April. https://www.thestar.com/news/ canada/2016/04/11/reverend-brent-hawkes-pleads-not-guilty-to-sex-crime-allegations.html.

Caserio, Robert L., Lee Edelman, Judith Halberstam, José Esteban Muñoz, and Tim Dean. 2006. "The Antisocial Thesis in Queer Theory." *PMLA* 121 (3): 819–28.

Catungal, John Paul. 2013. "Ethno-specific Safe Houses in the Liberal Contact Zone: Race Politics, Place-Making, and the Genealogies of the AIDS Sector in Global-Multicultural Toronto." *ACME: An International E-Journal for Critical Geographies* 12 (2): 250–78.

CBC News. 2014. "Rev. Brent Hawkes, Pride Parade Grand Marshal, on Metro Morning." CBC News, 27 June. http://www.cbc.ca/news/canada/toronto/ rev-brent-hawkes-pride-parade-grand-marshal-on-metro-morning-1.2689524.

———. 2016a. "Black Lives Matter Toronto Stalls Pride Parade." CBC News Toronto, 3 July. http://www.cbc.ca/news/canada/toronto/pride-parade-toronto -1.3662823.

———. 2016b. "Point of View: Pride 'Firmly Rooted in a Tradition of Protest': Black LGBT Community Leaders on Parade Controversy." CBC News Toronto, 6 July. http://www.cbc.ca/news/canada/toronto/black-lives-matter -toronto-pride-community-1.3665886.

———. 2016c. "Toronto Police Chief Mark Saunders Apologizes for 1981 Gay Bathhouse Raids." CBC News Toronto, 23 June. http://www.cbc.ca/news/canada/ toronto/police-apology-raids-1.3647668.

Celikates, Robin, and Yolande Jansen. 2013. "Reclaiming Democracy: An Interview with Wendy Brown on Occupy, Sovereignty, and Secularism." *Critical Legal Thinking: Law and the Political,* 30 January. http://criticallegalthinking .com/2013/01/30/reclaiming-democracy-an-interview-with-wendy-brown-on -occupy-sovereignty-and-secularism.

Cervantes, Vincent. 2016. "Sacred Geography: A Queer Latino Theological Response to Orlando." *Religion Dispatches*, 23 June. http://religiondispatches.org/sacred-geography-a-queer-latino-theological-response-to-orlando/.

Chakrabarty, Dipesh. 2000. *Provincializing Europe: Postcolonial Thought and Historical Difference*. Princeton: Princeton University Press.

Chambers-Letson, Joshua. 2006. "Introduction: Reparative Feminisms, Repairing Feminism: Reparation, Postcolonial Violence, and Feminism." *Women and Performance: A Journal of Feminist Theory* 16 (2): 169–89.

Cho, Margaret. 2006. *I Have Chosen to Stay and Fight*. New York: Penguin.

Churchill, David S. 2003. "Personal Ad Politics: Race, Sexuality, and Power at *The Body Politic*." *Left History* 8 (2): 114–34.

City of Toronto. 2014. "Toronto Facts: Diversity." City of Toronto website. http://www1.toronto.ca/wps/portal/contentonly?vgnextoid=dbe867b42d853410Vgn VCM10000071d60f89RCRD&vgnextchannel=57a12cc817453410VgnVCM1000 0071d60f89RCRD.

Cobb, Michael. 2006. *God Hates Fags: The Rhetorics of Religious Violence*. New York: New York University Press.

Cohen, Cathy J. 1997. "Punks, Bulldaggers, and Welfare Queens: The Radical Potential of Queer Politics?" *GLQ: A Journal of Lesbian and Gay Studies* 3 (4): 437–65.

Cohen, Tobi. 2013. "Ex-Chairman Raises Bias Concerns as Refugee Board Seeks New Leader." Canada.com, 1 March. Accessed at: http://o.canada.com/news /national/ex-chairman-raises-bias-concerns-as-refugee-board-seeks-new -leader/comment-page-1.

Colegate, Christina, John Dalton, Timothy Rayner, and Cate Hill. 2006. "Learning to Love Again: An Interview with Wendy Brown." *Contretemps* 6 (1): 25–42.

Coloma, Roland Sintos, Bonnie McElhinny, Ethel Tungohan, John Paul C. Catungal, and Lisa M. Davidson, eds. 2012. *Filipinos in Canada: Disturbing Invisibility*. Toronto: University of Toronto Press.

Connolly, William E. 1991. *Identity/Difference: Democratic Negotiations of Political Paradox*. Minneapolis: University of Minnesota Press.

———. 2008. *Capitalism and Christianity, American Style*. Durham: Duke University Press.

Cossman, Brenda. 2007. *Sexual Citizens: The Legal and Cultural Regulation of Sex and Belonging*. Palo Alto: Stanford University Press.

Costa, Daniela. 2013. "The Changing Face of Toronto's Village." *Toronto Xtra!*, 3 April. http://www.dailyxtra.com/toronto/news-and-ideas/news/the-changing -face-toronto%E2%80%99s-village-53862.

Cotroneo, Christian. 2005. "'Canada's Official Homosexual' George Hislop Dies at Age 78." *Toronto Star*, 10 October.

Cowen, Deborah. 2010. Review of *Terrorist Assemblages: Homonationalism in Queer Times*, by Jasbir K. Puar. *Social and Cultural Geography* 11 (4): 399–401.

Creelman, Brent. 2010. "Pride Toronto Reverses Ban on 'Israeli Apartheid.'" *Toronto Xtra!*, 23 June. http://dailyxtra.com/ideas/blogs/latest-news-roundup/pride-toronto-reverses-ban-israeli-apartheid-49256.

Crenshaw, Kimberlé Williams. 1991. "Mapping the Margins: Intersectionality, Identity Politics, and Violence against Women of Color." *Stanford Law Review* 43 (6): 1241–99.

Cresswell, Tim. 1996. *In Place / Out of Place: Geography, Ideology, and Transgression*. Minneapolis: University of Minnesota Press.

Cromwell, Craig. 2015. "Augustas Dennie Home Project." GoFundMe website. https://www.gofundme.com/ugzb3k4.

Dave, Naisargi N. 2012. *Queer Activism in India: A Story in the Anthropology of Ethics*. Durham: Duke University Press.

Dean, Tim. 2009. *Unlimited Intimacy: Reflections on the Subculture of Barebacking*. Chicago: University of Chicago Press.

Deleuze, Gilles, and Félix Guattari. (1975) 1986. *Kafka: Toward a Minor Literature*. Translated by Dana Polan. Minneapolis: University of Minnesota Press.

———. (1980) 1987. *A Thousand Plateaus: Capitalism and Schizophrenia*. Translated by Brian Massumi. Minneapolis: University of Minnesota Press.

Derrida, Jacques. 2001. *On Cosmopolitanism and Forgiveness*. London: Routledge.

Dick, Joel, on behalf of the Social Justice Network of MCC Toronto. 2014. "Letter to the Toronto Police Service regarding Recent Incidents." Tumblr, 23 February. http://mcctoronto.tumblr.com/post/77595945893/letter-to-the-toronto-police-service-regarding-recent.

Dinshaw, Carolyn. 1999. *Getting Medieval: Sexualities and Communities, Pre- and Postmodern*. Durham: Duke University Press.

Dinshaw, Carolyn, Lee Edelman, Roderick A. Ferguson, Carla Freccero, Elizabeth Freeman, Judith Halberstam, Annamarie Jagose, Christopher Nealon, and Nguyen Tan Hoang. 2007. "Theorizing Queer Temporalities: A Roundtable Discussion." *GLQ: A Journal of Lesbian and Gay Studies* 13 (2–3): 177–95.

Doucet, Michael J. 1999. *Toronto in Transition: Demographic Change in the Late Twentieth Century*. CERIS Working Paper 6. Toronto: Joint Centre of Excellence for Research on Immigration and Settlement. http://www.ceris.metropolis.net/wp-content/uploads/pdf/research_publication/working_papers/wp6.pdf.

Downing, John. 1981. "Modern Martyrdom." *Toronto Sun*, 17 February.

Dryden, OmiSoore H., and Suzanne Lenon. 2015. *Disturbing Queer Inclusion: Canadian Homonationalisms and the Politics of Belonging*. Vancouver: University of British Columbia Press.

Duggan, Lisa. 2003. *The Twilight of Equality? Neoliberalism, Cultural Politics, and the Attack on Democracy.* Boston: Beacon.

———. 2012. "Beyond Marriage: Democracy, Equality, and Kinship for a New Century." *Scholar and Feminist Online* 10 (1–2). http://sfonline.barnard .edu/a-new-queer-agenda/beyond-marriage-democracy-equality-and-kinship -for-a-new-century/.

Eames, David. 1982. "Harry Sutherland's *Track Two.*" *Cinema Canada* 87: 34.

Eastman, Don. 2011. "The 2020 Vision Project: Metropolitan Community Church of Toronto Snapshot Survey of Congregational Demographics." E-mail message to author, 25 February 2013.

Easton, Rob. 2015. "Canada Must Do More to Protect LGBT People Abroad." *Daily Xtra!,* 1 October. http://www.dailyxtra.com/canada/news-and-ideas/news/ canada-must-protect-lgbt-people-abroad-161867/.

Edelman, Lee. 2004. *No Future: Queer Theory and the Death Drive.* Durham: Duke University Press.

Elections Canada. 2011. "General Election—May 2, 2011." Elections Canada website. http://www.elections.ca/content.aspx?section=ele&document=index&dir =pas/41ge&lang=e.

Eng, David L. 2010. *The Feeling of Kinship: Queer Liberalism and the Racialization of Intimacy.* Durham: Duke University Press.

Eng, David L., Judith Halberstam, and José Esteban Muñoz. 2005. "Introduction: What's Queer about Queer Studies Now?" *Social Text* 23 (3–4): 1–17.

Fanon, Frantz. (1952) 2008. *Black Skin, White Masks.* Translated by Richard Philcox. New York: Grove.

Fedio, Chloé. 2011. "Transcript of Eulogies by Rev. Sarah and Michael Layton." *Toronto Star,* 27 August. http://www.thestar.com/news/canada/2011/08/27/transcript _of_eulogies_by_rev_brent_hawkes_and_sarah_and_michael_layton.html.

Ferguson, Roderick A. 2003. *Aberrations in Black: Toward a Queer of Color Critique.* Minneapolis: University of Minnesota Press.

Fortier, Craig. 2013. "No One Is Illegal Movements in Canada and the Negotiation of Counter-national and Anti-colonial Struggles from Within the Nation-State." In *Producing and Negotiating Non-citizenship: Precarious Legal Status in Canada,* edited by Luin Goldring and Patricia Landolt, 274–90. Toronto: University of Toronto Press.

Foucault, Michel. (1976) 1978. *The History of Sexuality.* Vol. 1, *An Introduction.* Translated by Robert Hurley. New York: Vintage.

———. (1984) 1990. *The History of Sexuality.* Vol. 2, *The Use of Pleasure.* Translated by Robert Hurley. New York: Vintage.

Fraser, Nancy. 1996. *Justice Interruptus: Critical Reflections on the "Postsocialist" Condition.* London: Routledge.

Freud, Sigmund. (1914) 1957. "On Narcissism." In *The Standard Edition of the Com-*

plete Psychological Works of Sigmund Freud, vol. 14. Edited and translated by James Strachey, 73–102. London: Hogarth Press.

———. (1917) 1953. "Mourning and Melancholia." In *The Standard Edition of the Complete Psychological Works of Sigmund Freud*, vol. 14. Edited and translated by James Strachey, 237–58. London: Hogarth Press.

———. (1927) 1989. *The Future of an Illusion*. In *The Standard Edition of the Complete Psychological Works of Sigmund Freud*, vol. 21. Edited and translated by James Strachey. London: Hogarth Press.

Fuss, Diana. 1995. *Identification Papers: Readings on Psychoanalysis, Sexuality, and Culture*. London: Routledge.

Gentile, Patrizia, and Gary Kinsman. 2015. "National Security and Homonationalism: The QuAIA Wars and the Making of the Neoliberal Queer." In *Disturbing Queer Inclusion: Canadian Homonationalisms and the Politics of Belonging*, edited by OmiSoore H. Dryden and Suzanne Lenon, 133–49. Vancouver: University of British Columbia Press.

Georgis, Dina S. 2006. "Cultures of Expulsion: Memory, Longing, and the Queer Space of Diaspora." *New Dawn: The Journal of Black Canadian Studies* 1 (1): 4–27.

———. 2013. *The Better Story: Queer Affects from the Middle East*. Albany: State University of New York Press.

———. 2014. "Discarded Histories and Queer Affects in Anne Carson's *Autobiography of Red*." *Studies in Gender and Sexuality* 15 (2): 154–66.

Gerber, Lynne. Forthcoming. "A Church Alive: HIV/AIDS in a Queer San Francisco Church."

Giametta, Calogero. 2014. "'Rescued' Subjects: The Question of Religiosity for Non-heteronormative Asylum Seekers in the UK." *Sexualities* 17 (5–6): 583–99.

Gibson-Graham, J. K. 2006. *A Postcapitalist Politics*. Minneapolis: University of Minnesota Press.

Gill, Nick. 2010. "New State-Theoretic Approaches to Asylum and Refugee Geographies." *Progress in Human Geography* 34 (5): 626–45.

Gillis, Wendy. 2015. "Why Mark Saunders is a 'Bittersweet' Appointment for Toronto's Black Community." *Toronto Star*, 24 April. https://www.thestar.com/news/gta/2015/04/24/why-mark-saunders-is-a-bittersweet-appointment-for-torontos-black-community.html/.

Goddard, John. 2011. "McCains Donate $1 Million to Gay-Friendly Church." *Toronto Star*, 17 January. http://www.thestar.com/news/gta/2011/01/17/mccains_donate_1_million_to_gayfriendly_church.html.

Gordon, Avery. 1997. *Ghostly Matters: Haunting and the Sociological Imagination*. Minneapolis: University of Minnesota Press.

Gould, Deborah B. 2009. *Moving Politics: Emotion and ACT UP's Fight against AIDS*. Chicago: University of Chicago Press.

Grewal, Inderpal, and Caren Kaplan. 2001. "Global Identities: Theorizing Transnational Studies of Sexuality." *GLQ: A Journal of Lesbian and Gay Studies* 7 (4): 663–79.

Grundy, John, and Miriam Smith. 2005. "The Politics of Multiscalar Citizenship: The Case of Lesbian and Gay Organizing in Canada." *Citizenship Studies* 9 (4): 389–404.

Guidotto, Nadia. 2006. "Homo(sexual) Sacer: Biopolitics and the Bathhouse Raids in Toronto, 1981." LLM thesis, Osgoode Hall Law School, York University.

Hage, Ghassan. 1998. *White Nation: Fantasies of White Supremacy in a Multicultural Society*. Sydney, Australia: Pluto Press.

Halberstam, Judith. 2005. *In a Queer Time and Place: Transgender Bodies, Subcultural Lives*. New York: New York University Press.

Hall, Edward T. 1963. "A System for the Notation of Proxemic Behavior." *American Anthropologist* 65 (5): 1003–26.

Halley, Janet E. 2000. "'Like Race' Arguments." In *What's Left of Theory? New Work on the Politics of Literary Theory*, edited by Judith Butler, John Guillory, and Kendall Thomas, 40–74. London: Routledge.

Han, Ju Hui Judy. 2010. "Reaching the Unreached in the 10/40 Window: The Missionary Geoscience of Race, Difference, and Distance." In *Mapping the End Times: American Evangelical Geopolitics and Apocalyptic Visions*, edited by Jason Dittmer and Tristan Sturm, 183–207. London: Ashgate.

Hancock, Ange-Marie. 2011. *Solidarity Politics for Millennials: A Guide to Ending the Oppression Olympics*. New York: Palgrave Macmillan.

Hanhardt, Christina B. 2013. *Safe Space: Gay Neighborhood History and the Politics of Violence*. Durham: Duke University Press.

Hannon, Gerald. 1982. "Raids, Rage, and Bawdyhouses." In *Flaunting It! A Decade of Gay Journalism from "The Body Politic"; An Anthology*, edited by Ed Jackson and Stan Persky, 273–94. Vancouver: New Star Books; Toronto: Pink Triangle Press.

Haraway, Donna. 1988. "Situated Knowledges: The Science Question in Feminism and the Privilege of Partial Perspective." *Feminist Studies* 14 (3): 575–99.

———. 1997. *Modest_Witness@Second_Millennium.FemaleMan_Meets_OncoMouse: Feminism and Technoscience*. London: Routledge.

Harvey, David. 2007. *The Limits to Capital*. New ed. London: Verso.

Henry, Frances. 1994. *The Caribbean Diaspora in Toronto: Learning to Live with Racism*. Toronto: University of Toronto Press.

Holston, James, and Arjun Appadurai. 1996. "Cities and Citizenship." *Public Culture* 8 (2): 187–204.

"Homomartyrdom?" 1981. *Toronto Sun*, 18 February.

Hondagneu-Sotelo, Pierrette. 2008. *God's Heart Has No Borders: Religious Activism for Immigrant Rights*. Oakland: University of California Press.

Honig, Bonnie. 2013. "The Politics of Public Things: Neoliberalism and the Routine of Privatization." *No Foundations: An Interdisciplinary Journal of Law and Justice* 10: 59–76.

Horner, Thomas M. 1978. *Jonathan Loved David: Homosexuality in Biblical Times.* Louisville: Westminster John Knox Press.

Houston, Andrea. 2016a. Twitter post, 24 June, 1:38 p.m. https://twitter.com/dreahouston/status/746442487305207808.

———. 2016b. Twitter post, 24 June, 1:39 p.m. https://twitter.com/dreahouston/status/746442713948631040

———. 2016c. Twitter post, 24 June, 1:59 p.m. https://twitter.com/dreahouston/status/746447616590876672

Hulchanski, J. David. 2010. *The Three Cities within Toronto: Income Polarization among Toronto's Neighbourhoods, 1970–2005.* University of Toronto, Centre for Urban and Community Studies. http://www.urbancentre.utoronto.ca/pdfs/curp/tnrn/Three-Cities-Within-Toronto-2010-Final.pdf.

Humphreys, Laud. 1972. *Out of the Closets: The Sociology of Homosexual Liberation.* New York: Prentice-Hall.

Isin, Engin F. 2002. *Being Political: Genealogies of Citizenship.* Minneapolis: University of Minnesota Press.

———. 2007. "City.State: Critique of Scalar Thought." *Citizenship Studies* 11 (2): 211–28.

———. 2012. "Citizens without Nations." *Environment and Planning D: Society and Space* 30 (3): 450–67.

Isin, Engin F., and Greg M. Nielsen, eds. 2008. *Acts of Citizenship.* Chicago: University of Chicago Press.

"Jack Layton: 1950–2011." 2011. *Toronto Xtra!*, 21 August. http://dailyxtra.com/canada/news/jack-layton-1950-2011.

Jackman, Michael Connors. 2015. "Media Legacies: Community, Memory, and Territory." In *Reclaiming Canadian Bodies: Visual Media and Representation*, edited by Lynda Mannik and Karen McGarry, 201–27. Waterloo, Ont.: Wilfrid Laurier University Press.

Jakobsen, Janet R. 2002. "Can Homosexuals End Western Civilization as We Know It? Family Values in a Global Economy." In *Queer Globalizations: Citizenship and the Afterlife of Colonialism*, edited by Arnaldo Cruz-Malavé and Martin F. Manalansan IV, 49–70. New York: New York University Press.

———. 2003. "Queers Are Like Jews, Aren't They? Analogy and Alliance Politics." In *Queer Theory and the Jewish Question*, edited by Daniel Boyarin, Daniel Itzkovitz, and Ann Pellegrini, 64–89. New York: Columbia University Press.

Jakobsen, Janet R., and Ann Pellegrini. 2003. *Love the Sin: Sexual Regulation and the Limits of Religious Tolerance.* New York: New York University Press.

Johnson, E. Patrick. 2001. "'Quare' Studies; or, (Almost) Everything I Know about

Queer Studies I Learned from My Grandmother." *Text and Performance Quarterly* 21 (1): 1–25.

Joseph, Miranda. 2002. *Against the Romance of Community.* Minneapolis: University of Minnesota Press.

Kane, Laura. 2014. "Toronto Police Inquest Rules Deaths as Homicides; Recommends Training Changes." *Toronto Star,* 12 February. http://www.thestar.com/news/crime/2014/02/12/police_shootings_inquest_rules_deaths_as_homicides.html.

Kapoor, Ilan. 2005. "Participatory Development, Complicity, and Desire." *Third World Quarterly* 26 (8): 1202–20.

Katz, Cindi. 1996. "Towards Minor Theory." *Environment and Planning D: Society and Space* 14 (4): 487–99.

Kenney. Jason. 2010. "Speaking Notes for the Honourable Jason Kenney, P.C., M.P. Minister of Citizenship, Immigration, and Multiculturalism." Citizenship and Immigration Canada, 29 June. http://www.cic.gc.ca/english/department/media/speeches/2010/2010-06-29.asp.

Kern, Leslie. 2010. *Sex and the Revitalized City: Gender, Condominium Development, and Urban Citizenship.* Vancouver: University of British Columbia Press.

Keung, Nicholas. 2012. "Biometrics Data Collection: Canadian Visa Applicants from 29 Countries Will Be Fingerprinted." *Toronto Star,* 7 December. http://www.thestar.com/news/canada/2012/12/07/biometrics_data_collection_canadian_visa_applicants_from_29_countries_will_be_fingerprinted.html.

———. 2013. "Asylum Claims Plummet—But Is Canada Sacrificing Refugees for Efficiency?" *Toronto Star,* 15 December. http://www.thestar.com/news/canada/2013/12/15/asylum_claims_plummet_but_is_canada_sacrificing_refugees_for_efficiency.html.

Khoo, Tseen-Ling. 2003. *Banana Bending: Asian-Australian and Asian-Canadian Literatures.* Montreal: McGill-Queen's University Press.

King, Tiffany Lethabo. 2015. "Post-identitarian and Post-intersectional Anxiety in the Neoliberal Corporate University." *Feminist Formations* 27 (3): 114–38.

Kinsman, Gary. 1987. *The Regulation of Desire: Homo and Hetero Sexualities.* Montreal: Black Rose Books.

Klein, Melanie. (1935) 1998. "A Contribution to the Psychogenesis of Manic-Depressive States." In *Melanie Klein: Love, Guilt, and Reparation and Other Works, 1921–1945.* London: Vintage.

———. 1975. *Envy and Gratitude and Other Works, 1946–1963.* New York: Free Press.

Kouri-Towe, Natalie. 2011. "Sanitizing Pride." *Briarpatch,* 6 May. http://briarpatchmagazine.com/articles/view/sanitizing-pride.

Kristeva, Julia. 1991. *Strangers to Ourselves.* Translated by Leon S. Roudiez. New York: Columbia University Press.

Lalani, Azzura. 2017. "Toronto Pastor Brent Hawkes Acquitted of Sex Charges." *Toronto Star,* 31 January. https://www.thestar.com/news/gta/2017/01/31/verdict -expected-today-in-toronto-pastor-brent-hawkes-trial.html.

LaViolette, Nicole. 2009. "Independent Human Rights Documentation and Sexual Minorities: An Ongoing Challenge for the Canadian Refugee Determination Process." *International Journal of Human Rights* 13 (2–3): 437–76.

———. 2013. "Sexual Orientation, Gender Identity, and the Refugee Determination Process in Canada." Paper prepared for the Refugee Protection Division of the Immigration and Refugee Board of Canada. http://papers.ssrn.com/sol3 /papers.cfm?abstract_id=2276049.

Lee, Edward Ou Jin, and Shari Brotman. 2011. "Identity, Refugeeness, Belonging: Experiences of Sexual Minority Refugees in Canada." *Canadian Review of Sociology* 48 (3): 241–74.

Lenon, Suzanne. 2005. "Marrying Citizens! Raced Subjects? Re-thinking the Terrain of Equal Marriage." *Canadian Journal of Women and the Law* 17 (2): 405–21.

———. 2011. "Why Is Our Love an Issue? Same-Sex Marriage and the Racial Politics of the Ordinary." *Social Identities: Journal for the Study of Race, Nation, and Culture* 17 (3): 351–72.

Levinas, Emmanuel. 1969. *Totality and Infinity: An Essay on Exteriority.* Translated by Alphonso Lingis. Pittsburgh: Duquesne University Press.

Lewis, Rachel A. 2014. "'Gay? Prove It': The Politics of Queer Anti-deportation Activism." *Sexualities* 17 (8): 958–75.

Lidstone, Robert S. L. 2006. "Refugee Queerings: Sexuality, Identity, and Place in Canadian Refugee Determination." Master's thesis, Simon Fraser University.

Lim, Jason. 2009. "Queer Critique and the Politics of Affect." In *Geographies of Sexualities: Theory, Practices, and Politics,* edited by Jason Lim, Gavin Brown, and Kath Brown, 53–67. London: Ashgate.

Ling, Justin. 2012. "Government Releases Refugee 'Safe' Countries List." *Daily Xtra!,* 14 December. http://dailyxtra.com/canada/news/government-releases -refugee-safe-country-list-51068.

Lorinc, John, Michael McClelland, Ellen Scheinberg, and Tatum Taylor. 2015. *The Ward: The Life and Loss of Toronto's First Immigrant Neighbourhood.* Toronto: Coach House Books.

Love, Heather. 2007. *Feeling Backward: Loss and the Politics of Queer History.* Cambridge: Harvard University Press.

Luibhéid, Eithne, and Lionel Cantú Jr., eds. 2005. *Queer Migrations: Sexuality, U.S. Citizenship, and Border Crossings.* Minneapolis: University of Minnesota Press.

Mackey, Eva. 2002. *The House of Difference: Cultural Politics and National Identity in Canada.* Toronto: University of Toronto Press.

Mahmood, Saba. 2004. *The Politics of Piety: Islamic Revival and the Feminist Subject.* Princeton: Princeton University Press.

Makin, Kirk. 2012. "Despite Legal About-Face, Harper Has 'No Intention' of Re-opening Same-Sex Marriage." *Globe and Mail*, 12 January. http://www.theglobe andmail.com/news/politics/despite-legal-about-face-harper-has-no-intention -of-reopening-same-sex-marriage/article1358276/.

Malleson, Tom, and David Wachsmuth, eds. 2011. *Whose Streets? The Toronto G20 and the Challenges of Summit Protest.* Toronto: Between the Lines.

Mamdani, Mahmood. 2005. *Good Muslim, Bad Muslim.* New York: Random House.

Manalansan, Martin F, IV. 2003. *Global Divas: Filipino Gay Men in the Diaspora.* Durham: Duke University Press.

———. 2008. "Queering the Chain of Care Paradigm." *Scholar and Feminist Online* 6 (3). http://sfonline.barnard.edu/immigration/manalansan_01.htm.

Marshall, Lee. 2014. "Refugee Claimants Struggling to Find Health Care after Cuts." *Globe and Mail*, 17 August. http://www.theglobeandmail.com/life/health-and -fitness/health/refugee-claimants-struggling-to-find-health-care-after-cuts/ article20090315/.

Martin, David. 2000. "Canada in Comparative Perspective." In *Rethinking Church, State, and Modernity: Canada between Europe and America*, edited by David Lyon and Marguerite van Die, 23–33. Toronto: University of Toronto Press.

Martínez, Shane. 2011. "OCAP Rallies in Solidarity with Moss Park Residents." Basics Community News Service, 1 December. http://basicsnews.ca/ocap -rallies-in-solidarity-with-moss-park-residents/.

Marz, Alex. 2011. "Jack Layton State Funeral." YouTube, 8 September. https://www .youtube.com/watch?v=RmsLDn-uIV4.

Massad, Joseph. 2007. *Desiring Arabs.* Chicago: University of Chicago Press.

Massey, Doreen. 2005. *For Space.* London: Sage.

Massumi, Brian. 2002. *Parables for the Virtual: Movement, Affect, Sensation.* Durham: Duke University Press.

McAlister, Melani. 2008. "What Is Your Heart For? Affect and Internationalism in the Public Sphere." *American Literary History* 20 (4): 870–95.

McCaskell, Tim. 2016. *Queer Progress: Homophobia to Homonationalism.* Toronto: Between the Lines.

McClintock, Anne. 1995. *Imperial Leather: Race, Gender, and Sexuality in the Colonial Contest.* London: Routledge.

MCC Toronto. 2014. "Our History—A Timeline." Metropolitan Community Church of Toronto website. http://www.mcctoronto.com/history.

———. 2016. "What We Believe." Metropolitan Community Church of Toronto website. http://www.mcctoronto.com/who-we-are/what-we-believe.

———. 2017. "MCC Toronto—Videos." Metropolitan Community Church of Toronto Facebook page. https://www.facebook.com/pg/MCCToronto/videos.

McDirmid, Jessica. 2014. "Rev. Brent Hawkes Honoured to Lead WorldPride

Parade." *Toronto Star,* 22 June. http://www.thestar.com/news/pridetoronto/2014/06/22/rev_brent_hawkes_honoured_to_lead_worldpride_parade.html.

McDonald, Marci. 2010. *The Armageddon Factor: The Rise of Christian Nationalism in Canada.* Toronto: Vintage Canada.

McGowan, Mark G. 2008. "Roman Catholics (Anglophone and Allophone)." In *Christianity and Ethnicity in Canada,* edited by Paul Bramadat and David Seljak, 49–100. Toronto: University of Toronto Press.

McKittrick, Katherine. 2011. "On Plantations, Prisons, and a Black Sense of Place." *Social and Cultural Geography* 12 (8): 947–63.

McLeod, Donald W. 1996. *Lesbian and Gay Liberation in Canada: A Selected Annotated Chronology, 1964–1975.* Toronto: ECW Press / Homewood Books.

———. 2014. *Lesbian and Gay Liberation in Canada: A Selected Annotated Chronology, 1976–1981.* Toronto: Homewood Books.

McQueeney, Krista. 2009. "'We Are God's Children, Y'all': Race, Gender, and Sexuality in Lesbian- and Gay-Affirming Congregations." *Social Problems* 56 (1): 151–73.

Mills, Matt. 2011a. "Orozco Detention Hearing Scheduled for May 17." *Toronto Xtra!,* 16 May. http://dailyxtra.com/canada/news/orozco-detention-hearing-scheduled-may-17.

———. 2011b. "Track Two." *Toronto Xtra!,* 7 February. http://dailyxtra.com/track-two.

Minh-ha, Trinh T. 1989. *Woman, Native, Other: Writing Postcoloniality and Feminism.* Bloomington: Indiana University Press.

Mongia, Radhika Viyas. 1999. "Race, Nationality, Mobility: A History of the Passport." *Public Culture* 11 (3): 527–55.

Moreton, Bethany. 2010. *To Serve God and Wal-Mart: The Making of Christian Free Enterprise.* Cambridge, Mass.: Harvard University Press.

Morgensen, Scott L. 2011. *Spaces between Us: Queer Settler Colonialism and Indigenous Decolonization.* Minneapolis: University of Minnesota Press.

———. 2012. "Queer Settler Colonialism in Canada and Israel: Articulating Two-Spirit and Palestinian Queer Critiques." *Settler Colonial Studies* 2 (2): 167–90.

Mountz, Alison. 2010. *Seeking Asylum: Human Smuggling and Bureaucracy at the Border.* Minneapolis: University of Minnesota Press.

———. 2011. "Where Asylum-Seekers Wait: Feminist Counter-topographies of Sites between States." *Gender, Place, and Culture* 18 (3): 381–99.

Muñoz, José Esteban. 2009. *Cruising Utopia: The Then and There of Queer Futurity.* New York: New York University Press.

Munt, Sally R. 1995. "The Lesbian Flâneur." In *Mapping Desire: Geographies of Sexualities,* edited by David Bell and Gill Valentine, 104–14. London: Routledge.

Murphy, Kevin P. 2010. "Gay Was Good: Progress, Homonormativity, and Oral History." In *Queer Twin Cities: Twin Cities GLBT Oral History Project,* edited by Michael David Franklin, Larry Knopp, Kevin P. Murphy, Ryan P. Murphy, Jennifer L. Pierce, Jason Ruiz, and Alex T. Urquhart, 305–18. Minneapolis: University of Minnesota Press.

Murray, David A. B. 2014. "The Challenge of Home for Sexual Orientation and Gendered Identity Refugees in Toronto." *Journal of Canadian Studies / Revue d'Études Canadiennes* 48 (1): 132–52.

Nash, Catherine Jean. 2005. "Contesting Identity: Politics of Gays and Lesbians in Toronto in the 1970s." *Gender, Place, and Culture* 12 (1): 113–35.

———. 2006. "Toronto's Gay Village (1969–1982): Plotting the Politics of Gay Identity." *Canadian Geographer / Le Géographe Canadien* 50 (1): 1–16.

———. 2014. "Consuming Sexual Liberation: Gay Business, Politics, and Toronto's Barracks Bathhouse Raids." *Journal of Canadian Studies* 48 (1): 82–105.

Nash, Jennifer C. 2013. "Practicing Love: Black Feminism, Love-Politics, and Post-intersectionality." *Meridians: Feminism, Race, Transnationalism* 11 (2): 1–24.

Nguyen, Mimi Thi. 2012. *The Gift of Freedom: War, Debt, and Other Refugee Passages.* Durham: Duke University Press.

No One Is Illegal Toronto. 2010. "Harper Repeats Past Immigration Blunders, Targets Migrants." No One Is Illegal–Toronto website, 21 October. http://toronto.nooneisillegal.org/node/491.

Oliver, Kelly. 2004. *The Colonization of Psychic Space: A Psychoanalytic Social Theory of Oppression.* Minneapolis: University of Minnesota Press.

O'Neill, Kevin. 2009. "'But Our Citizenship Is in Heaven': A Proposal for the Study of Christian Citizenship in the Global South." *Citizenship Studies* 13 (4): 333–47.

Ong, Aihwa. 2006. *Neoliberalism as Exception: Mutations in Citizenship and Sovereignty.* Durham: Duke University Press.

Oswin, Natalie. 2008. "Critical Geographies and the Uses of Sexuality." *Progress in Human Geography* 32 (1): 89–103.

———. 2010. "The Modern Model Family at Home in Singapore: A Queer Geography." *Transactions of the Institute of British Geographers* 35 (2): 256–68.

Painter, Joe. 2006. "Prosaic Geographies of Stateness." *Political Geography* 25 (7): 752–74.

Painter, Joe, and Chris Philo. 1995. "Spaces of Citizenship: An Introduction." *Political Geography* 14 (2): 107–20.

Parker, Rebecca Ann. 2006. *Blessing the World: What Can Save Us Now.* Boston: Skinner House Books.

Parker, Stephen E. 2012. *Winnicott and Religion.* New York: Jason Aronson.

Parreñas, Rhacel Salazar. 2011. *Illicit Flirtations: Labor, Migration, and Sex Trafficking in Tokyo.* Palo Alto: Stanford University Press.

Peat, Don. 2011. "Hawkes Prepares for Layton's Funeral." *Toronto Sun,* 26 August. http://www.torontosun.com/2011/08/26/hawkes-prepares-for-laytons-funeral.

Pellegrini, Ann. 2009. "Feeling Secular." *Women and Performance: A Journal of Feminist Theory* 19 (2): 205–18.

Penney, James. 2012. *The Structures of Love: Art and Politics beyond the Transference.* Albany: State University of New York Press.

Perry, Troy D., as told to Charles L. Lucas. 1972. *The Lord Is My Shepherd and He Knows I'm Gay.* Los Angeles: Nash.

Perry, Troy D., with Thomas L. P. Swicegood. 1990. *Don't Be Afraid Anymore: The Story of Reverend Troy Perry and the Metropolitan Community Churches.* New York: St. Martin's Press.

Petro, Anthony. 2015. *After the Wrath of God: AIDS, Sexuality, and American Religion.* Oxford: Oxford University Press.

Pitman, Teresa. 2011. "Post-doc Relays History of Toronto's Don River." *University of Guelph Campus News,* 14 November. http://news.uoguelph.ca/2011/11/14/post-doc-relays-history-of-torontos-don-river/.

Popert, Ken. 1979. "Vestments and Investments." *The Body Politic,* July 17.

Porter, Catherine. 2012. "Rev. Brent Hawkes Reflects on Sermon for Jack Layton." *Toronto Star,* 3 August. http://www.thestar.com/news/gta/2012/08/03/porter_rev_brent_hawkes_reflects_on_sermon_for_jack_layton.html.

Prashad, Vijay. 2002. *Everybody Was Kung Fu Fighting: Afro-Asian Connections and the Myth of Cultural Purity.* Boston: Beacon.

Pratt, Minnie Bruce. 1984. "Identity: Skin Blood Heart." In *Yours in Struggle: Three Feminist Perspectives on Anti-Semitism and Racism,* edited by Ellen Bulkin, Minnie Bruce Pratt, and Barbara Smith, 11–63. New York: Long Haul Press.

Probyn, Elspeth. 2005. *Blush: Faces of Shame.* Minneapolis: University of Minnesota Press.

Puar, Jasbir K. 2002. "Circuits of Queer Mobility: Tourism, Travel, and Globalization." *GLQ: A Journal of Lesbian and Gay Studies* 8 (1–2): 101–37.

———. 2007. *Terrorist Assemblages: Homonationalism in Queer Times.* Durham: Duke University Press.

Puar, Jasbir K., Lauren Berlant, Judith Butler, Bojana Cvejic, Isabelle Lorey, and Ana Vujanovic. 2012. "Precarity Talk: A Virtual Roundtable." *Drama Review* 56 (4): 163–77.

Puar, Jasbir K., Ben Pitcher, and Henriette Gunkel. 2008. "Q&A with Jasbir Puar." *darkmatter: In the Ruins of Imperial Culture,* 2 May. http://www.darkmatter101.org/site/2008/05/02/qa-with-jasbir-puar/.

Rankin, Jim, Patty Winsa, Andrew Bailey, and Hidy Ng. 2014. "Carding Drops but Proportion of Blacks Stopped by Toronto Police Rises." *Toronto Star,* 26 July. http://www.thestar.com/news/insight/2014/07/26/carding_drops_but_proportion_of_blacks_stopped_by_toronto_police_rises.html.

Raphael, Kate. 2010. "Open Letter to Democracy Now!—Stop Promoting Queer

Militarism." *Democracy Sometimes*, 3 February. http://democracy-sometime
.blogspot.ca/2010/02/03/open-letter-to-democracy-now-stop.html.

Rayter, Scott. 2012. "Introduction: Thinking Queerly about Canada." In *Queerly Canadian: An Introductory Reader in Sexuality Studies*, edited by Maureen FitzGerald and Scott Rayter, i–xxvi. Toronto: Canadian Scholars' Press.

Razack, Sherene. 2004. *Dark Threats and White Knights: The Somalia Affair, Peacekeeping, and the New Imperialism.* Toronto: University of Toronto Press.

———. 2008. *Casting Out: The Eviction of Muslims from Western Law and Politics.* Toronto: University of Toronto Press.

Reagon, Bernice Johnson. (1981) 2000. "Coalition Politics: Turning the Century." In *Home Girls: A Black Feminist Anthology*, edited by Barbara Smith. 2nd ed. New Brunswick: Rutgers University Press.

Rehaag, Sean. 2008. "Troubling Patterns in Canadian Refugee Adjudication." *Ottawa Law Review* 39 (2): 335–65.

Reid, Graeme. 2010. *Above the Skyline: Reverend Tsietsi Thandekiso and the Founding of an African Gay Church.* Pretoria, South Africa: Unisa Press.

Reid, Tiana. 2014. "The Toronto Police's Long History of Racial Profiling." *VICE Canada*, 12 February. http://www.vice.com/en_ca/read/the-toronto-polices
-carding-practices.

Rennie, Steve. 2012. "Tories Target Alleged Fake Refugee Bids." *Canadian Press*, 21 February. http://thechronicleherald.ca/canada/63981-tories-target
-alleged-fake-refugee-bids.

Ridgley, Jennifer. 2008. "Cities of Refuge: Immigration Enforcement, Police, and the Insurgent Genealogies of Citizenship in U.S. Sanctuary Cities." *Urban Geography* 28 (1): 53–77.

Roache, Trina. 2015. "Mi'kmaw Professor Calling on Indigenous Leaders to Push Canada to Accept More Syrian Refugees." Aboriginal Peoples Television Network, National News, 17 September. http://aptn.ca/news/2015/09/17/mikmaw
-professor-calling-on-indigenous-leaders-to-push-canada-to-accept-more
-syrian-refugees/.

Roberton, Jen. 2016. "LGBTQ2+ Experiences of Public Safety in the Urban Form: Bringing Queer and Trans Voices into Creating Safe Inclusive Communities." Master's thesis, University of British Columbia.

Rodriguez, Eric M., and Suzanne C. Oullette. 2000. "Gay and Lesbian Christians: Homosexual and Religious Identity Integration in the Members and Participants of a Gay-Positive Church." *Journal for the Scientific Study of Religion* 39 (3): 333–47.

Rofel, Lisa. 2007. *Desiring China: Experiments in Neoliberalism, Sexuality, and Public Culture.* Durham: Duke University Press.

Rose, Jacqueline. 2007. *The Last Resistance.* London: Verso.

Rubin, Gayle. 1984. "Thinking Sex." In *Pleasure and Danger: Exploring Female Sexuality*, edited by Carole Vance, 267–319. London: Routledge.

Said, Edward W. 1978. *Orientalism*. New York: Vintage.

Saldanha, Arun. 2006. *Psychedelic White: Goa Trance and the Viscosity of Race.* Minneapolis: University of Minnesota Press.

Sandoval, Chela. 2000. *Methodology of the Oppressed.* Minneapolis: University of Minnesota Press.

Sankaran, Priya. 2012. "Toronto Transgender People Say They're Targets of Police." CBC News, 28 June. http://www.cbc.ca/news/canada/toronto/toronto -transgender-people-say-they-re-targets-of-police-1.1255002.

Santner, Eric L. 2001. *On the Psychotheology of Everyday Life.* Chicago: University of Chicago Press.

———. 2011. *The Royal Remains: The People's Two Bodies and the Endgames of Sovereignty.* Chicago: University of Chicago Press.

Sartre, Jean-Paul. (1946) 1995. *Anti-Semite and Jew: An Exploration of the Etiology of Hate.* Translated by George J. Becker. New York: Schocken.

Scott, Joan Wallach. 2011. *The Fantasy of Feminist History.* Durham: Duke University Press.

Secor, Anna. 2004. "'There Is an Istanbul That Belongs to Me': Citizenship, Space, and Identity in the City." *Annals of the Association of American Geographers* 94 (2): 352–68.

Sedgwick, Eve Kosofsky. 1990. *Epistemology of the Closet.* Oakland: University of California Press.

———. (1997) 2003. "Paranoid Reading and Reparative Reading; or, You're So Paranoid, You Probably Think This Introduction Is about You." In *Touching Feeling: Affect, Pedagogy, Performativity*, 123–51. Durham: Duke University Press.

Seitz, David K. 2013. "Interview with Lauren Berlant." *Society and Space Open Site,* 22 March. http://societyandspace.com/material/interviews/interview-with -lauren-berlant/.

———. 2017. "'Second Skin,' White Masks: Postcolonial Reparation in *Star Trek: Deep Space Nine*." *Psychoanalysis, Culture, and Society*, 21 March.

Sewell, John. 1985. *Police: Urban Policing in Canada.* Toronto: John Lorimer.

Shakhsari, Sima. 2014. "The Queer Time of Death: Temporality, Geopolitics, and Refugee Rights." *Sexualities* 17 (8): 998–1015.

Sharma, Nandita. 2005. *Home Economics: Nationalism and the Making of "Migrant Workers" in Canada.* Toronto: University of Toronto Press.

Shohat, Ella. 2006. "Post-Fanon and the Colonial: A Situational Diagnosis." In *Taboo Memories, Diasporic Voices*, 201–32. Durham: Duke University Press.

Shore-Goss, Robert E. 2010. "Gay and Lesbian Theologies." In *Liberation Theologies in the United States: An Introduction,* edited by Stacey M. Floyd-Thomas and Anthony B. Pinn, 181–208. New York: New York University Press.

Shore-Goss, Robert E., Thomas Bohache, Patrick S. Cheng, and Mona West, eds. 2013. *Queering Christianity: Finding a Place at the Table for LGBTQI Christians.* Santa Barbara: Praeger.

Shuman, Amy, and Carol Bohmer. 2014. "Gender and Cultural Silences in the Political Asylum Process." *Sexualities* 17 (8): 939–57.

Sibley, David. 2003. "Geography and Psychoanalysis: Tensions and Possibilities." *Social and Cultural Geography* 4 (3): 391–99.

Siggins, Maggie. 1981. "Roots of Tragedy: Albert and Lemona Johnson: The Sweet Beginnings and Painful End of a Love Story." *Toronto Life,* February, 33–37, 56–65.

Simpson, Leanne. 2013. *Islands of Decolonial Love.* Winnipeg: ARP Books.

Smith, Miriam. 2007. "Framing Same-Sex Marriage in Canada and the United States: Goodridge, Halpern, and the National Boundaries of Political Discourse." *Social and Legal Studies* 16 (1): 5–26.

———. 2014. "Interview with Chris Bearchell, Lasqueti Island, 1996." *Journal of Canadian Studies* 48 (1): 252–75.

Smith, Neil. (1984) 2008. *Uneven Development: Nature, Capital, and the Production of Space.* Athens: University of Georgia Press.

Spade, Dean. 2011. *Normal Life: Administrative Violence, Critical Trans Politics, and the Limits of Law.* Boston: South End Press.

Spade, Dean, and Craig Willse. 2013. "Marriage Will Never Set Us Free." *Organizing Upgrade,* 6 September. http://www.organizingupgrade.com/index.php /modules-menu/beyond-capitalism/item/1002-marriage-will-never-set-us -free.

Spivak, Gayatri Chakravorty. 1988. "Can the Subaltern Speak?" In *Marxism and the Interpretation of Culture,* edited by Cary Nelson and Lawrence Grossberg, 66–111. Urbana: University of Illinois Press.

———. 1990. *The Post-colonial Critic: Interviews, Strategies, Dialogues.* London: Routledge.

Spurr, Ben. 2015. "The Downtown East Side's Balancing Act." *Toronto Now,* 25 March. https://nowtoronto.com/news/downtown-east-sides-balancing-act/.

Stewart, Kathleen. 2008. "Weak Theory in an Unfinished World." *Journal of Folklore Research* 45 (1): 71–82.

Stockton, Kathryn Bond. 2006. *Beautiful Bottom, Beautiful Shame: Where "Black" Meets "Queer."* Durham: Duke University Press.

Sumerau, J. Edward. 2012. "'This Is What a Man Is Supposed to Do': Compensatory Manhood Acts in an LGBTQ Christian Church." *Gender and Society* 26 (3): 461–87.

Support Brent. 2016. http://www.supportbrent.ca/.

Tapper, Josh. 2012. "United Church Members Vote for Boycott of Products from Israeli Settlements." *Toronto Star,* 16 August. http://www.thestar.com/news/canada/2012/08/16/united_church_members_vote_for_boycott_of_products_from_israeli_settlements.html.

Thrift, Nigel. 2007. *Non-representational Theory: Space, Politics, Affect.* London: Taylor & Francis.

Traub, Valerie. 2002. *The Renaissance of Lesbianism in Early Modern England.* Cambridge: Cambridge University Press.

Trudeau, Justin. 2016. "Prime Minister Justin Trudeau's Address to the 71st Session of the United Nations General Assembly." Justin Trudeau, Prime Minister of Canada website, 20 September. http://pm.gc.ca/eng/news/2016/09/20/prime-minister-justin-trudeaus-address-71st-session-united-nations-general-assembly/.

U.N. High Commissioner for Refugees. (1951) 2011. *Convention and Protocol Relating to the Status of Refugees.* http://www.unhcr.org/3b66c2aa10.html.

Universal Fellowship of Metropolitan Community Churches. 2014. "Overview." http://mccchurch.org/overview/.

———. 2016. "Global Presence." http://mccchurch.org/overview/global-presence/.

Valentine, David. 2007. *Imagining Transgender: An Ethnography of a Category.* Durham: Duke University Press.

Varsanyi, Monica. 2006. "Interrogating 'Urban Citizenship' vis-à-vis Undocumented Migration." *Citizenship Studies* 10 (2): 229–49.

Vendeville, Geoffrey. 2016. "Black Lives Matter Protesters Interrupt Pride Mural Unveiling by Toronto Pride." *Toronto Star,* 24 June. https://www.thestar.com/news/gta/2016/06/24/black-lives-matter-protesters-interrupt-pride-mural-unveiling-by-toronto-police.html.

Wade, Michael. 1982. "*Track Two*: The Film on the Toronto Bath Raids." *The Body Politic,* August, 27.

Walcott, Rinaldo. 2003. *Black Like Who? Writing Black Canada.* 2nd ed. Toronto: Insomniac Press.

———. 2009. "Multicultural and Creole Contemporaries: Postcolonial Artists and Postcolonial Cities." In *Postcolonial Challenges in Education,* edited by Roland Sintos Coloma, 161–77. New York: Peter Lang.

———. 2014. "Ferguson: Not So Far Away." *The Broadbent Blog,* 26 August. https://www.broadbentinstitute.ca/en/blog/ferguson-not-so-far-away.

Warner, R. Stephen. 2005. *A Church of Our Own: Disestablishment and Diversity in American Religion.* New Brunswick: Rutgers University Press.

Warner, Tom. 2002. *Never Going Back: A History of Queer Activism in Canada.* Toronto: University of Toronto Press.

Wekker, Gloria. 2006. *The Politics of Passion: Women's Sexual Culture in the Afro-Surinamese Diaspora.* New York: Columbia University Press.

West, Isaac. 2014. *Transforming Citizenships: Transgender Articulations of the Law.* New York: New York University Press.

White, Heather R. 2015. *Reforming Sodom: Protestants and the Rise of Gay Rights.* Chapel Hill: University of North Carolina Press.

Wiegman, Robyn. 2012. *Object Lessons.* Durham: Duke University Press.

Wilcox, Melissa M. 2003. *Coming Out in Christianity.* Bloomington: Indiana University Press.

Williams, Raymond. 1978. *Marxism and Literature.* Oxford: Oxford University Press.

Wilson, Nancy. 2013. *Our Church: Forty Years in the Queer Christian Movement.* Indianapolis: LifeJourney Press.

Winnicott, Donald W. 1953. "Transitional Objects and Transitional Phenomena." *International Journal of Psychoanalysis* 34: 89–97.

Yeğenoğlu, Meyda. 1999. *Colonial Fantasies: Towards a Feminist Reading of "Orientalism."* Cambridge: Cambridge University Press.

Yukich, Grace. 2013. *One Family under God: Immigration Politics and Progressive Religion in America.* Oxford: Oxford University Press.

Zoll, Rachel. 2013. "Metropolitan Community Churches: Do Gays Need a Church of Their Own Anymore?" *U.S. News and World Report,* 1 January. http://www.usnews.com/news/us/articles/2013/01/01/do-gays-need-a-church-of-their-own-anymore.

Filmography

Boskovich, John. 1990. *Without You, I'm Nothing.* Fox Video. DVD.

d'Entremont, Paul Émile. 2012. *Last Chance.* National Film Board of Canada. Video streaming. https://www.nfb.ca/film/last-chance/.

Falardeau, Philippe. 2012. *Monsieur Lazhar.* eOne Films. DVD.

Fung, Richard. 1986. *Orientations: Lesbian and Gay Asians.* Vtape. DVD.

Henson, Jim. 1981. *The Great Muppet Caper.* Walt Disney Home Entertainment. DVD.

Nicol, Nancy. 2002. *Stand Together.* Vtape. DVD.

———. 2006. *The End of Second Class.* Vtape. DVD.

———. 2007. *Proud Lives: Chris Bearchell.* Vtape. DVD.

Sutherland, Harry. 1982. *Track Two: Enough Is Enough.* Pink Triangle Press. YouTube. https://www.youtube.com/watch?v=iN4_8eurids.

Index

ability, 50. *See also* ableism; disability
abjection, 24, 199
ableism, 19, 66, 172. *See also* ability
abuse, 20, 30, 79, 113, 176, 219; police, 94, 98–99; sexual, 30, 101
accountability, 21, 72, 92, 106, 128, 165–66, 170, 175, 178, 189; police, 103, 112, 114
activism, 12, 16–17, 21, 27, 41, 47, 51, 94, 96, 113, 118, 120, 123, 158, 160, 163–66, 169, 175, 184, 191, 195, 223, 230; LGBTQ, 3, 29, 38, 87, 90, 92, 95, 98–99, 102–4, 115–16, 136–38, 146, 153, 155, 159, 168, 229; pastor, 19, 73, 79, 84, 91–93, 101, 117, 129; against police brutality, 18, 80, 86, 112
affect: contradictory, 12, 33, 81; and religion, 153, 171, 238n3. *See also* Thrift, Nigel
affective: attachment, 10, 24; charge, 116–17; complexity, 18, 27, 71, 78; conditions, 8, 12, 74, 226–27; difficulty, 12, 17–18, 27, 51, 69, 83, 86, 90, 111; encounter, 48, 61–66, 82, 109; pedagogy, 21, 88; repair, 4–5, 13, 33, 67, 91, 117, 130, 158, 230; representation, 44, 48–49, 59, 62–63; resonance, 146, 190; sophistication, 8, 11–12, 25, 82, 228; vulnerability, 177, 186, 203–4, 211, 223; work, 5, 26, 41, 60, 72, 82, 111, 130, 140,

158, 179, 229. *See also* Connolly, William E.
Africa, 60–62, 65, 96, 147, 159–60, 173, 185, 193, 195, 202, 220; Democratic Republic of Congo, 193; Kenya, 157, 219; Nigeria, 148, 159; South Africa, 173–74; Tanzania, 52; Uganda, 157, 159, 167–68
agency, 47–48, 56, 61, 140, 158, 161, 200; externalization of, 88, 129; of marginal people, 64–65, 76, 134–35, 186, 188; of the state, 11, 98, 190, 193, 195, 198, 225
agonism, 42, 74, 93, 115, 123, 132, 171, 226, 237n4
AIDS, 18, 29, 113, 115, 126, 183, 208
alienation, 35, 55–56, 58, 64, 65, 70, 96, 106, 215
ambivalence, 4, 22, 27, 33, 38, 45, 98, 101, 106, 114, 198, 208, 211, 222; of attachment, 23, 49, 62; critical, 31, 164, 170–71, 179, 186; of "global" queer community, 137–39, 159, 161, 163–64, 166, 168, 171, 179; of "subjectless" critique, 7. *See also* Johnson, E. Patrick
amelioration, 15, 36, 69, 72, 104, 139, 226
anger, 120, 127, 153, 239n4
antiblack racism, 22, 105, 114. *See also* racism

cisgender, 8, 17–18, 35, 66, 78–79, 172, 188. *See also* gender; nonnormative gender; transgender

citizenship, 2–3, 9, 13, 15–16, 19, 34, 38, 41, 54–56, 67, 80, 91, 105, 128, 132, 160, 174, 206–7, 216–17, 226; and affect, 4–5, 11, 15, 17–18, 21, 23, 26–28, 39, 45, 61, 71–72, 82, 107, 110, 129, 163, 179; global (queer), 66, 135–41, 143, 146, 154–55, 163–64, 168–69, 171–72, 175, 177–80; identitarian (queer), 10, 30, 49, 51, 72, 76, 109, 111, 168, 221, 224, 227; intimate, 125–27, 229–30; and MCCT, 20–23, 27, 33, 44, 49–50, 70, 78, 81–82, 140, 163, 169, 171, 186, 229; pastor-diva, 79, 92–93, 98, 118, 127; savior, 204, 222; sexual, 8; space of, 3–4, 20, 22, 26–27, 33, 50, 70, 82, 222, 229–30; transgender, 126–27; urban (queer), 23, 60, 79, 94, 107, 111, 117. *See also* improper queer citizenship

class, 3, 6, 32, 47–48, 83, 94–96, 103, 115, 127, 137, 174, 177; inequality, 36–37; middle, 8, 35–38, 66, 73–74, 76, 114, 165, 172, 237n4; working, 33, 36–37, 114, 164, 196

closet, the, 188, 210

coalition, 18, 38, 41, 47–48, 79, 88, 92, 98–99, 101, 104, 107–8, 110, 116–18, 120, 128, 215, 227, 229, 237n2, 239n4; across difference, 27, 103, 105, 109, 112–15, 221; futurity and, 129, 230; for Lesbian and Gay Rights in Ontario, 96; politics and, 26, 46, 74, 184; promise of, 105; queer, 6, 30, 74, 87; work, 17. *See also* Reagon, Bernice Johnson

Cohen, Cathy J., 6–7, 103. *See also* improper queer citizenship

coherence, 5, 10, 17, 44, 95, 127. *See also* incoherence

collectivity, 20, 43, 60, 70–71, 104, 106, 117, 187; desire for, 11, 47, 90, 107; space of, 4–5, 215

colonialism, 9, 51, 53, 65, 139, 146, 157, 160, 167, 172, 240n5; fantasy and, 154; missiology and, 30, 134–36, 226, 239n1; nation-state and, 8, 31, 168–70; neocolonialism, 20, 90, 136, 168, 187; neoliberalism, 187–88; and power, 154, 168, 172, 187. *See also* postcolonialism

comfort, 17, 23, 42, 49, 72, 81, 87, 170, 198, 205, 219, 228. *See also* uncomfortable

communion, 29, 33, 61, 81, 155, 206; open, 25, 41, 55, 145

complicity, 12, 30, 45, 104, 114, 136, 145, 160–61, 168, 170–71, 179, 187, 189, 213, 227, 240n6

Connolly, William E., 146. *See also* affective; resonance

consciousness, 15, 50, 77, 108, 117, 163, 230; false, 27; political, 9; self-consciousness, 58, 170; unconscious, 9, 86, 88

conservative, 42, 122, 124, 152, 185, 193, 239n6; neoconservative, 89; religious, 19, 29, 31–32, 46, 49, 84, 92, 98, 123, 132, 143, 145, 153, 159–61, 167, 205, 217, 225, 227

Conservative Party of Canada, 119, 124, 184, 194, 218, 239n7, 240n2

contestation, 6, 82, 100, 114, 187, 192, 212, 227, 230, 239n1; church as site of, 5, 18–19, 21, 24, 27, 54, 67, 72, 75, 138, 205; of injustice, 2, 11, 223; in LGBTQ organizing, 22, 89, 96, 114, 159, 211; political, 3, 104; space of, 4, 18, 27, 54

contingency, 16, 100, 116, 137, 152; geopolitical, 104, 173, 182, 188; historical, 45–46, 104, 115, 134

Edelman, Lee, 190
ego ideal, 139–40, 144, 161, 163, 170, 178, 218
emancipation, 11, 18, 47–48, 55, 62, 140, 144, 179, 204, 240n6; political, 31, 87
embodiment, 42–44, 60, 66, 81, 151, 237n3
Endicott, Fran, 108–11, 118
Eng, David L., 7, 9, 185, 189, 238n1, 240n3. *See also* global South; history
entrepreneurialism, 145–46, 149, 151, 153, 172, 193; evangelical, 139, 148, 152, 178–79
epistemology, 48, 91, 107, 188, 205–6, 223
erotic, 17, 56, 87, 126, 154, 156; homoerotic, 8, 80
evangelism, 32, 151, 161, 165, 167, 172; entrepreneurial, 139, 148, 152, 178–79; global, 131, 135–38, 143–46, 148, 152–53, 158, 160, 175, 177, 179–80, 183
exclusion, 6, 15, 43–44, 47, 82, 120, 127, 138, 140, 190–91, 202, 212, 227; in church, 65–67, 70–71, 187; constitutive, 32, 88, 95; gender/race, 58, 81, 222
experimentation, 9, 25, 32, 141, 144, 147, 175
exploitation, 9, 15, 26, 46, 48, 64, 93, 119, 124, 135, 145, 174, 177, 205, 210, 221

failure, 12, 14, 34, 39, 78, 90, 93, 98, 111, 124, 175, 189, 195, 197, 199, 226
faith, 16, 20, 33–34, 80, 82, 100, 134, 145, 152–53, 171, 175, 181, 186, 189, 207, 216, 218, 225; based activism, 51, 73, 81, 101, 118, 196, 230; bad, 15; community, 2–3, 23–24, 26, 30, 46,

52, 72, 77, 89, 138–39, 150, 158, 169, 214, 224, 227, 229; leader, 28, 84, 100, 129; space, 54, 65
Fanon, Frantz, 64–66. *See also* anti-Semitism; whiteness
fantasy, 32, 87, 126–27, 156, 161, 186, 200, 207–8, 223, 227; colonial, 154; of global queer solidarity, 4, 137–39, 144; of radical past, 90–91, 103, 117, 129–30; of sovereignty, 8, 72; of wholeness, 5, 137. *See also* Freud, Sigmund; Spivak, Gayatri Chakravorty
feminism, 36, 42, 87, 113, 154, 195, 225, 238n3; antiracism and, 43–44, 89, 91, 135, 227, 229; black, 6, 16–17, 47–49, 69, 81, 237n2; queerness and, 5, 103, 136; religion as "bad object" for, 4, 19, 27
fetish, 182; of identity, 3, 11, 46–47, 189, 204, 225, 229; racial fetishism in gay community, 96, 129
Filipina/o, 45, 57–59
First Nations, 30, 77
Foucault, Michel, 5, 7, 32, 137, 192, 200, 237n1. *See also* normalization; power; sexuality
freedom, 32, 101, 103, 126, 129–30, 135, 137, 141–42, 160, 162–63, 211; as a gift, 135, 154; practices of, 28; reproductive, 30; sexual, 4, 87
Freud, Sigmund, 88, 139, 163. *See also* fantasy; melancholia; narcissism
futurity, 2, 15, 68, 96, 151, 211; coalitional, 129, 230; comfortable, 198; democratic, 230; impure, 91; loss and, 14, 117, 190, 197; orientation to, 71, 211–12; possible, 49–51, 117–18, 120, 126, 172; queerness as, 80, 189. *See also* Brown, Wendy

Garner, Revered Elder Darlene, 90,
172–75, 177–79, 226
gender: binary, 43; bodies and, 42, 44,
81; citizenship and, 45, 63; equality and, 22, 56; exclusion, 58, 81;
identity, 18, 24, 30, 184, 186, 188–89,
191, 214–15, 224; inclusion, 132;
performance, 199, 204; representation, 49, 57, 61. *See also* cisgender;
nonnormative gender; transgender
genealogy, 9, 25, 138, 227, 238n3,
240n6; alternative, 12, 27–28, 74;
contestatory, 22, 89; Kleinian, 13
generosity, 46, 61, 74, 120, 129, 135, 151,
156, 188, 194, 205, 228
geography, 6, 22, 35, 55, 59, 120, 127,
135–36, 139, 145, 152, 156–57, 159,
163, 173, 187, 203, 218, 237n1; affective, 61, 109, 204; of citizenship, 3,
10, 19, 72, 179, 229; different scales
of, 5, 10–11, 72, 82, 179; everyday,
183, 185, 189–91, 212; history and, 9,
37, 45, 93, 104–5, 119, 122, 125, 131,
137; human, 9, 13, 239n3; imaginary, 160, 186, 217. *See also* scalar
thought; space
Georgis, Dina, 10, 106, 117, 126, 190,
217–18
global South, 134–35, 145, 175, 177, 185,
187, 239n1. *See also* Eng, David L.
God, vii, 2, 21, 26, 32, 52, 80, 100, 145,
147, 150, 157, 206–7, 228; "made me
gay," 23
"Goldilocks" diversity. *See* diversity
"good enough," 14, 17, 32, 50, 140, 156,
222; church as, 81–82, 91, 158, 178;
religion as, 4, 20, 51, 61, 72, 86
groundless grounds, 28, 191, 218, 223,
225
G20 Summit (2010), 94, 113, 162
Guattari, Félix. *See* Deleuze, Gilles

Halberstam, Judith (Jack), 7, 189–90.
See also queer space
Harper, Stephen, 119, 121, 123–24; government, 126
hate, 25, 64, 72, 109, 160
Hawkes, Reverend Dr. Brent, 19–21,
42, 68–70, 73, 92–93, 97, 106, 130,
152–53, 155, 158–60, 178, 196, 206,
216, 219–21, 224, 239n6; authority
of, 28, 171; charisma and, 18, 34, 91,
214; contradiction and, 86, 120, 124,
129; Israel and, 168–69; Jack Layton
funeral and, 119–27, 129, 157, 229;
Toronto Police and, 78–79, 84–86,
99–102, 105, 128–29, 218, 238n2;
Track Two and, 95, 98, 101, 103–4,
118, 121. *See also* pastor–diva–citizen
healing, 41, 55, 61, 67, 72, 84, 155,
238n2
hegemony, 48, 67, 139, 142, 148, 171,
178, 185; Christian, 23, 31, 52–54,
101, 120, 214
heterosexual, 8, 24, 73, 75, 78, 97, 109,
126, 148, 196, 199, 219; matrix, 5;
patriarchy, 44, 53
hierarchy, 9, 15, 56, 136, 144, 164, 175,
177, 217; racial, 87
history: ahistorical, 76; contingency
and, 45–46, 104, 115, 134; dust bin
of, 83, 132; geography and, 9, 37, 45,
93, 104–5, 119, 122, 125, 131, 137; of
the MCCT, 4, 23, 26, 39, 50, 55, 57,
89–92, 95, 116, 144–46, 148; oral, 87;
waiting room of, 185, 188, 191, 203,
212, 215. *See also* Eng, David L.
homogeneity, 9, 72, 81, 141, 191; of gay
white space, 18, 60
homonationalism, 4, 9, 17, 24, 167–69,
188, 192, 226. *See also* Puar, Jasbir K.
homophobia, 20, 29–30, 52, 78, 111, 124,
132, 183, 196, 211, 217, 225, 237n4;

26, 33, 100, 117, 130, 158, 179, 230; of
good and bad fragments, 4, 14, 16,
25, 67, 72, 80–81, 91, 129, 135, 140;
into nation, 12, 31. *See also* Klein,
Melanie
international, 22, 75, 132, 136, 153, 160–
62, 173, 217, 220, 226; human rights,
186; turn, 138, 155, 159, 229
intersectionality, 7, 24, 32, 39, 43, 45,
47–48, 64, 66, 69, 81, 102–4, 109–10,
128. *See also* Puar, Jasbir K.
intimacy, 4, 16, 22, 29, 31, 34, 52, 63,
71, 81, 88, 91, 93, 95, 97, 100, 106–7,
121, 124, 136, 142, 155, 164, 200, 208,
226–27; citizenship and, 125–27,
229–30
Isaiah 56:7, vii, 1–4, 17, 19, 23, 26–27,
44, 50, 55, 65, 72, 81, 89, 138, 203,
213, 227–28
Islam. *See* Muslim
Israel, vii, 168–69. *See also* Queers
against Israeli apartheid

Jamaica, 111–12, 167–68, 182, 199, 207,
217
Jewish people, 30, 63–64, 106–7, 207,
240n6
Johnson, E. Patrick, 7, 18
Johnson, Lemona "Monica," 111–12,
115, 118
Joseph, Miranda, 95, 136, 145
judgment, 16, 122, 216; critical, 1; paranoid, 15, 221–22, 230; revising one's,
158, 192, 228, 230. *See also* paranoia
justice, 39, 100, 195; ecological, 21, 73;
migrant, 195–97. *See also* social
justice

Kafka, Franz, 141–42
Khaki, El-Farouk, 52–53

King, Reverend Dr. Martin Luther, Jr.,
28, 103–4
King, Tiffany Lethabo, 48, 69, 81. *See
also* intersectionality
Klein, Melanie, 4, 12–16, 44, 46, 67,
71–72, 83, 86, 88, 91, 117, 129–30,
140, 144, 156, 170, 173, 226, 228–29,
237n2, 238n3. *See also* depressive
position; integration; love; object;
paranoia; phantasy; reparation;
splitting

law, 7, 18, 20, 75, 93, 100, 110, 116, 128,
132, 142, 158, 198; refugee, 11, 185–
86, 188, 193–94, 199, 213, 215
Layton, Jack, 19, 92, 118–23, 125–27,
129, 157
legibility, 24, 28–29, 38, 63, 103, 105,
188–89, 196–97, 201, 212–14, 223.
See also illegibility
Levinas, Emmanuel, 63–64. *See also*
Other
LGBTQ identity, 4, 8, 10, 23–25, 32,
45, 77–78, 80, 137, 184, 189, 191,
194–95, 205, 211, 221; authenticity
requirement, 183–84, 186, 188, 194,
196–201, 204–7, 211, 215–18, 221,
224; global, 179, 186
liberalism, 28, 44, 57, 60, 69, 78, 90,
118, 122, 126–27, 182, 194–95, 198,
215, 226; Christianity and, 21, 29–31,
44, 81, 92, 139, 145, 149, 153, 206,
214; Eurocentrism and, 185; humanitarianism and, 139, 144, 153–54,
163, 178; identity politics and, 3–4,
8, 25, 29, 74, 88, 116, 170–71, 191,
225, 229; liberationism and, 87, 94,
98; progress and, 89, 93, 120, 132,
229; queer, 9, 19, 21, 124, 185, 189,
192, 226, 240n3; secularism and, 2,

obligation, 58, 155, 159, 169, 192, 213, 239n1; ethical, 57, 63–64, 160, 170
Oedipus complex, 26, 130, 142
Ontario, 36, 77, 96, 102, 112, 147, 156; Court of Appeal, 123; Provincial Legislature, 99
ontology, 9–10, 153
open: communion, 25, 41, 55, 145; lines of flight, 49, 143–44; theology, 52, 145
open-endedness, 43, 54, 67, 207, 224
Operation Soap (Toronto's 1981 gay bathhouse raids), 79, 83, 85–86, 92–95, 97–100, 102, 106–7, 111–13, 115–16, 120, 238n4
oppression, 7, 20, 45, 48, 103–4, 113, 128, 143–44, 154, 169, 203
Orozco, Alvaro, 195–97
Oswin, Natalie, 189–90, 237n1. *See also* object
Other, 107, 117, 131, 145, 158, 175; Big, 121; colonial, 139–40, 154, 160–63; demand of, 80; external, 133, 178; vulnerability of, 64, 76, 227. *See also* Levinas, Emmanuel
overdetermination, 25, 64–65, 177

pain, 14, 17, 29, 53, 77, 81, 84, 86, 93, 103, 128–29, 181, 226, 229; gay, 110; and racialization, 105
paranoia, 13–14, 20, 25, 33, 39, 70, 91, 93, 135, 143, 170, 180, 192; austere refugee policy and, 184, 187, 189, 195, 198, 212, 216, 218; habits of reading and, 15; identity politics and, 46, 65, 72; judgment and, 15, 221–22, 230. *See also* Klein, Melanie
past, 68, 106, 133–34, 142, 148, 150, 166, 187, 239n1; preoccupation with, 65, 83, 92–93, 97; radical, 86–87, 89–91,

95, 103, 114–15, 117–18, 120, 129–30, 179. *See also* Love, Heather
pastoral, 20, 59, 79, 93; care, 41, 60–61, 158–59, 164; pedagogy, 120
pastor–diva–citizen, 79, 92–93, 98, 118, 127. *See also* Berlant, Lauren; Hawkes, Reverend Dr. Brent
Pellegrini, Ann, 27–28, 238n3. *See also* "bad object"
people of color: church leadership and, 50, 58, 72, 173, 228; queer, 7, 46, 48–50, 52, 60–61, 72, 83–84, 96, 109, 185; transgender, 114; women, 27, 49–50, 62, 81, 228; worship leaders as, 28, 44, 49–50, 61–62, 71, 81, 238n2
performance: of Christian authority, 100; of critical judgment, 1; of drag, 184; of identity, 28, 66; of futurity, 120; of gay normalcy, 122, 198, 204, 211; of masculinity, 199; of pastoral and church rituals, 19, 21, 55, 98, 119–20, 202; of state violence, 128
performativity, 4, 11, 50, 66, 93, 109, 117, 124, 127, 144, 155, 186, 194; of being a refugee, 199–200
Perry, Reverend Troy D., Jr., 19, 22, 103, 119, 145–46, 148–53, 178
persecution, 33, 156–57, 183–84, 188, 194–96, 198, 211, 220, 223–25
phantasy, 14, 88, 141. *See also* Klein, Melanie
Pink Triangle Press, 95, 97, 113
playfulness, 13, 15, 21, 26, 45, 122, 124, 172, 192, 225, 230; "come out and play," 58, 60–61
pleasure, 15, 47, 77, 125, 137, 153, 158, 166, 215; displeasure, 75
pluralism, 11, 21, 67, 72, 171, 206–7; of the world, 224, 229, 240n6. *See also* Arendt, Hannah

police. *See* Toronto police
policing authenticity, 198, 216–18, 224
political: authority, 100; consciousness,
9; danger, 8, 104, 174; desire, 24, 38,
77, 126, 227; economy, 61, 136, 138–
39, 141, 144; emancipation, 31, 87;
ethicopolitical, 30, 186
politics: of coalition, 26, 46, 74, 184; of
difference, 27, 49, 177; of identity,
5, 24, 45–47, 49, 58–60, 66, 72, 77,
81–82, 107, 111, 170–71, 192, 205, 215,
223; of recognition, 88; and sexuality, 7, 32, 39, 117, 160, 185; transformation in LGBTQ politics, 87, 93
postcolonialism, 38, 135, 154–55, 174,
185, 190. *See also* colonialism
potentiality: affective, 58, 61, 172;
church as site of, 28, 33, 49, 56,
60, 62, 66, 76, 78, 81, 91, 136, 156,
158–59, 164, 228; critical, 169; immanence and, 50, 61, 70–71, 88–89,
143; political, 17, 33, 55, 91, 93;
progressive, 51; queer, 50–51, 71, 95,
215. *See also* Muñoz, José Esteban
poverty, 165, 169, 220; antipoverty, 37
power, 5, 12, 18, 28, 31, 44, 52, 65, 68,
80, 93–94, 98, 101, 111, 123–24, 127,
129, 136, 159, 171, 179, 184, 194, 202,
212, 220, 237n1, 239n1; black, 87; colonial, 154, 168, 172, 187; difference
and, 7, 78, 133, 137, 164; divine, 100;
mapping of, 6, 10, 217; nation-state
and, 9, 24, 34, 74, 94, 106, 113, 192,
224, 227; police, 103; sites of, 7, 10;
topography of, 32; vectors of, 112; of
worship, 22, 61. *See also* Foucault,
Michel
practices, 8, 17, 57, 62, 126, 137, 191, 201;
of belief, 29, 207, 213; of colonialism, 160, 168, 187; ethicopolitical,
30, 186; everyday, 2, 16, 26, 151; of

freedom, 28; of improper queer
citizenship, 10–11, 18, 45, 61, 91,
98, 109, 170, 186, 218; liturgical,
42, 238n2; policing, 43, 114, 116;
reparative, 13, 15, 46, 67, 72, 82,
222; sexual, 154, 188, 216–17, 240n3;
spatial, 98; spiritual, 56, 67, 72, 214
praxis, 45, 72, 81–82, 169–71, 221, 228,
230, 239n1
prayer, 21, 32, 128, 151, 155; Lord's, 34,
52. *See also* Isaiah 56:7
precarity, 36, 64, 181, 192, 203, 223–24;
asylum seekers and, 55, 186–89, 191,
197–98, 209, 215, 218; precaritization, 187, 211–12. *See also* Butler,
Judith
present, 10, 14, 30, 68, 89, 92, 113–14,
134, 224; bad, 83, 88, 90–91, 115, 117,
129–30; stretched out, 197
Pride Parade. *See* Toronto Pride Parade
progress, 13, 51, 88, 127, 144, 183; liberal, 19, 89, 93, 120, 132, 229
progressive, 24, 26, 32, 49, 55, 73, 78,
125, 127, 129, 138, 152–53, 169, 179,
194, 216–18, 240n5; church, 31, 37,
88, 146, 172, 214; politics, 46, 77, 132,
134, 143–44, 165; potential, 51
prolepsis, 2, 11, 17, 30, 117–18, 120, 124–
26, 129, 228
promise, 46, 70–71, 127, 149, 211; of
belonging, 2, 5, 23, 26, 75, 206; of
coalition, 105; of critique, 191; of
improper queer citizenship, 4, 10,
12, 44, 50, 55, 73, 82, 138, 140, 230;
of "it gets better," 120, 211; spaces
of, 89, 106; unfulfilled, 3, 56, 74, 78,
204; of universality, 55; of welcome,
17, 19, 26, 54, 72, 81, 203, 213, 228
psychoanalysis, 5, 13, 19, 29, 44, 89–90,
109, 138–41, 143, 154, 178, 190, 223,
237n2, 238n1

Puar, Jasbir K., 8, 47–48, 69, 136, 168. *See also* assemblages; homonationalism; intersectionality

public thing, 45, 54, 225

purity, 120, 129–30, 190, 238n2. *See also* impurity

queer: affect, 29, 80, 87–88; attachment, 19, 222; church, 3–5, 13, 24, 26–27, 33, 39, 41, 66, 70, 81–82, 90, 120, 214, 222, 224; coalition, 6, 30, 74, 87; commons, 23, 214, 227; critique, 9–10, 12, 122, 186; damage, 5, 21, 25, 107, 129, 161, 164–65, 227; diaspora, 190, 217–18; genderqueer, 43, 56; imagination, 10, 185; interracial, 125, 127; liberal, 9, 19, 21, 124, 185, 189, 192, 226, 240n3; paranoia, 15; polity, 11, 28–29, 55, 226; potentiality, 71, 95, 215; repair, 25, 158, 192; solidarity, 4, 78, 191, 218, 223, 229; theory, 3, 5–7, 9–13, 16, 18, 27, 44, 54, 74, 82, 87, 103, 137, 230. *See also* asylum seekers; citizenship; Muñoz, José Esteban; subjectlessness

queer of color, 7, 46, 48–50, 52, 60–61, 72, 83–84, 96, 109, 185; black, 16, 44, 52, 63, 84, 86, 109, 129, 197, 202–4; Filipino, 57; Jewish, 107

queer radical, 44, 90, 165, 228; past, 86–87, 95

Queers against Israeli Apartheid (QuAIA), 22, 30, 77, 168. *See also* Israel

queer space, 23, 65, 84, 204; time, 184, 186, 189, 191, 197. *See also* Halberstam, Judith (Jack)

racialization, 6, 26–28, 32, 37–38, 45, 47, 50, 58, 60, 79, 81, 96, 102–5, 107, 112, 114, 117, 136, 174, 201, 226, 229;

alienation and, 55, 64; misrecognition and, 63, 65; pain and, 105; queerness and, 7–8, 42, 44, 49, 52, 61, 185; of refugees, 186, 220

racism, 6, 19–20, 24, 32, 36–37, 51, 53, 65, 67, 78, 87, 90, 93, 125, 128, 134, 139, 173, 186–87, 216, 218, 220, 229; atmospheric, 58, 84, 187, 201–4, 212; MCCT and, 46, 66, 75, 132–33, 167, 206, 222, 228; structural, 16, 96. *See also* antiblack racism

radical (politically), 2, 12, 21–22, 27, 45–46, 54, 59–60, 66, 71, 74, 84, 193, 203, 222, 226; past, 86–87, 89–91, 95, 103, 114–15, 117–18, 120, 129–30, 179; queer, 44, 90, 165, 228

Rainbow Railroad, 162, 169–70

Reagon, Bernice Johnson, 17–18, 41, 227, 229. *See also* coalition

recognition, 5, 44–45, 137, 144, 170, 175, 177, 186, 192; from church, 5, 49, 61–62, 81, 214; critical, 80, 177; misrecognition, 62–66, 71, 202; politics of, 88; self-recognition, 140; from state, 21, 123, 126–27

redemption, 24, 27, 30, 46, 91, 107, 120, 140, 143–44, 181, 222, 228, 238n2; and politically radical past, 89, 91, 115, 117, 120, 129–30, 179; unredemptive, 4, 118

redistribution, 2, 10, 54, 81, 122, 125, 192, 229

refugees, 66, 159–60, 165–67, 169–70, 177, 182–84, 189, 195, 202, 204, 209–11, 219, 221–22, 240n1; economic, 219; law and, 11, 186, 188, 199, 213; not-yet-refugee, 180; performativity of, 199–200; racialization of, 186, 220. *See also* asylum seekers; MCCT refugee program

refusal, 7, 9, 11, 18, 84, 107, 141, 174, 177–78, 227, 230; of proper objects,

DAVID K. SEITZ is assistant professor of cultural geography at Harvey Mudd College in Claremont, California.